The London Sunday Times says of th
book: "Much has been written about th
Borgias, but there still lacked a hand
volume, neither too heavy nor too luric
outlining their complete history; this boo
admirably supplies the want."

THE STORY O
THE BORGIA

BY

L. COLLISON-MORLE

Fully Illustrated with Twelve Plates

Here is the history of the Borgia
from the first Borgia Pope to St. Franc
Borgia, pictured against a backgroun
of social and political conditions of th
day. The truth is separated from th
many legends that have gathere
around that fated and famous famil
and the characteristics of its variou
members as individuals are striking
brought out. At the same time, t
leading men and women of the da
(particularly Machiavelli and Leonard
da Vinci) with whom the Borgias we
brought in contact, are grouped aroun
the central figures.

We have the stories of Pope Cali
tus III, the founder of the family,
Rodrigo Borgia as Cardinal, of his rel
tions with the mother of his childre
and the beautiful Giulia Farnese. W
read about his relations with Machia
velli and others, and his murder of th
condottieri. Full details are given
Lucrezia Borgia's marriages, her care
as Duchess of Ferrara and her flirt
tions there. Finally, there is a ma
nificent sketch of the career of S
Francis Borgia.

THE STORY OF
THE BORGIAS

MEDALS OF CESARE AND LUCREZIA BORGIA

THE STORY OF
THE BORGIAS

By

L. COLLISON-MORLEY

E. P. DUTTON AND COMPANY, INC.

PUBLISHERS   NEW YORK

FIRST EDITION

CONTENTS

CONTENTS

vi

LIST OF ILLUSTRATIONS

PREFACE

My object in this book has been to tell the story of the
Borgias with sufficient historical background to make
it intelligible and to endeavour above all to bring out
their characteristics as human beings. I have stuck
closely to facts throughout. In England Cesare has
hitherto monopolized the books upon the Borgias,
and of these Professor Woodward's *Cesare Borgia* is
one of the best and most valuable that has appeared.
There is, of course, a translation of Gregorovius'
standard *Lucrezia Borgia*, the importance of which can
hardly be exaggerated. The great historian rescued
Lucrezia once for all from the clutches of writers like
Dumas and Victor Hugo, and, in spite of Signor
Portigliotti's interesting and scholarly *I Borgia*, it is as
unlikely that the old coventional view of Alexander
VI and his children as a family of criminals without a
single redeeming virtue will hold the field again, as
that they will find many defenders of the type of
Leonetti.

The career of such a Pope, with its contrast between
his private life and his sacred office as Vicar of Christ,
can never lose its interest for humanity at large.
In him, as in his family and his contemporaries in
Rome, we see the corruption and the cruelty that
marked the Renaissance undraped by the curtain of
culture and beauty, of great literature and great art
that veils it in the attractive little courts of Northern
Italy, of Mantua or Urbino or Ferrara. Yet at
Ferrara the family tragedies among the d'Este rivalled
those of the Borgias themselves. The story of the
Borgias has something of the appeal of a detective

story. There is hardly one of the crimes that have been laid to their charge the evidence for which is conclusive. Hence the eagerness with which every scrap of evidence or information concerning them has been seized upon. Ultimately, of course, the interpretation of it must be a matter of temperament, but in making up our minds we have to take into consideration the moral standards and the habits of the times. Even now we cannot be sure that everything of value has been brought to light. The researches of Signor Luzio have revealed a quantity of new material, more especially about Lucrezia at Ferrara, which is of first-rate importance. Whenever possible I have drawn upon this in preference to older and better-known sources, as it has not yet been used in an English book.

L. C.-M.

CHAPTER I

THE solidly built house of the Borjas, to give them their Spanish name, dating from the fourteenth century and ornamented with the arms of the two Popes of the family, can still be seen in their native town of Xativa. Not far away is the more important Gandia, the little fishing-port with which their name was to become more closely associated. They are situated in the province of Valencia, in the south-east, facing the most fertile portion of the old Moorish kingdom. Gandia is in a plain, surrounded by plateaux, which owes its extraordinary fertility to the Moors. The castle, built by the Borgia dukes, looks out over gardens watered by the Alcoy, and most of their subjects were Moriscos.

Eight of the Borgias, each bearing the Borgia bull on a field of gold upon his shield, accompanied Don Jaime, King of Aragon, when he conquered Valencia in 1238. They were small land-owners. Esteban de Borja was entrusted with the task of distributing the lands round Xativa among the Christians. Naturally, he did not forget his own relatives and the Borgias became the most important family in the town. But there is no proof that they were descended from Count Pedro de Atarès, who was lord of Borja, near Taragona, in the twelfth century and was of royal birth, though Calixtus liked to think so when he mounted the throne of St Peter. The fortunes of the family began to rise with Rodrigo Gil de Borja. He

I

was popular with Don Pedro of Aragon and was able to marry Doña Sibilla de Oms, daughter of a distinguished family. The fourth son of this marriage, Jofrè de Borja y d'Oms, married a cousin, Isabella Borja. Her brother, Alonso de Borja, became Pope Calixtus III, while her son, Rodrigo, became Pope Alexander VI. Her daughter, Juana, married a Lançol–Romani, and her children and grandchildren, who rose to prominence under Alexander, called themselves Borgia–Lançol. The belief, long current, that Rodrigo was really a Lançol may be due, as Woodward suggests, to the fact that they were his only legitimate relatives in Rome during his Papacy. This is a brief summary of the Borgia genealogy, a subject upon which much has been written. The main facts are now beyond dispute.

The Borgias owed their rise to eminence to the great forward movement of the Catalans, which resulted in the conquest of Naples by Alfonso I in 1442. With him came Alonso de Borja, or Alfonso Borgia, as he was soon to be called. Born on the last day of 1378, the fateful year of the beginning of the great schism in the Papacy, which he was to help to heal, he went to the University of Lerida, where he studied canon law. Such was the ability he showed that he was made lecturer in the subject ; indeed, he came to be considered one of the best and most eloquent canonists of his day. But his abilities soon marked him out for a higher sphere. He had the gift for dealing with men, the tact and diplomatic skill, as well as the physical strength and the well-balanced vigour of the best of the Borgias. How he attracted the notice of the king we do not know, but Alfonso had an eye for a man and the genuine respect of the best of the Renaissance princes for scholarship and intellect. So well did he appreciate him that he made him his secretary and came to regard him as one of his most trusted counsellors. He gave him the important See of Valencia in 1429, when he was not yet a priest. In 1436 he was in charge of Don Ferrante, the heir-apparent, when he came to Naples. Nor were his services to the Papacy less notable. It was largely due to his influence that the Spanish anti-Pope was induced to resign and he was made a cardinal by Eugenius IV in 1444. As ambassador in Rome he did more than anyone else to persuade Eugenius to grant Alfonso the investiture of his new kingdom, and the Pope always regarded him as a friend.

His character and ability won universal respect, but his election to the Papacy was a surprise. The Conclave had virtually resolved itself into another incident in the age-long struggle between the Colonna and the Orsini. Delay was dangerous to the city owing to the threatening behaviour of these powerful and unruly barons, and the ambassadors, whose duty it was to watch over the safety of the Conclave, begged the cardinals to come to a speedy decision. As neither party could carry the day, a neutral candidate had to be found. The result was a postponement of a real election by the choice of an old man who could not live long. The nice balance of the Italian parties made the elevation of a foreigner almost a necessity and the venerable Bishop of Valencia, then in his seventy-seventh year, became Pope on April 8th, 1455. He chose the name of Calixtus.

Calixtus had the belief in his star of a true Borgia, and, indeed, of most successful men. Many years earlier, when a young priest, he had joined the crowd that thronged round St Vincent Ferrer, when the great preacher was at Valencia, and besought him to remember them in his prayers. The story goes that the holy man turned to him, as if inspired by a sudden impulse, with the words : " My son, I wish you joy. Remember that one day you will be called to become the glory of your country and your family. You will be invested with the highest dignity that can fall to the lot of man. I myself, after my death, shall be especially honoured by you. Strive to persevere in your virtuous way of life." Alfonso often told the story to his friends and it is not surprising that one of his first acts as Pope was to complete the prophecy by making his early well-wisher a saint.

Borgia's election created no enthusiasm among Italians. A foreign Pope was never popular, least of all a Catalan. Alfonso's conquest of Naples had made " l'avara povertà di Catalogna ", as Dante puts it, more hated than ever, and now the rising tide of their fortunes had carried one of them to the throne of St Peter. On the whole, however, the fears of an influx of Catalan adventurers, such as settled upon Naples like a flock of locusts, were not realized. Some there were and they were duly hated by the jealous Romans, who characteristically magnified their numbers.

The Pope was aged and infirm, spending most of his time in bed, but he showed no lack of energy. He had two ruling passions, the preaching of a great Crusade to drive back the Turk from Constantinople and the Borgia love of his family and the desire to push its interests. No one was better fitted to inspire a Crusade than the Borgia Pope, in spite of his age, for hatred of the Infidel was in his very blood. He brought to the task the energy, the dogged persistence and determination that were then raising Spain to the first place among the nations of Europe. He began with a solemn vow, duly signed and sealed, that he would devote his strength to the defeat of the Turk and the recovery of Constantinople. In spite of the army of priests and monks he sent out to preach the Crusade and raise funds, his efforts bore little fruit, owing to the indifference of the Christian princes. The day of the crusades was over. Alfonso of Naples won the Pope's lasting enmity by using the fleet he had been able to raise on the plea of the Crusade to attack Genoa. But at least he had the satisfaction of

4

the crushing defeat of the Turks at Belgrade by Hun-
yadi, little though the victory owed to Western Europe.

The meagreness of the contributions received compelled Calixtus to resort to every possible means of
raising money. He sold his jewels, saying that he
would be satisfied with a linen mitre to help the cause.
He left the great buildings of his predecessor unfinished
and dismissed the workmen. His economies were
naturally unpopular in the quarters affected. The
Humanists soon found that the palmy days of Nicholas
V with his ever-open purse were over and Calixtus's
reputation has suffered in consequence. Calixtus was
primarily a lawyer with little taste for literature. He
had no intention of spending the money of the
Church for the furtherance of learning while the Turk
was advancing, and naturally a body of men so vocal,
so venomous and once again so impecunious as the
Humanists did not let him off easily. He was accused
of dispersing the Vatican library and giving hundreds
of books to Cardinal Isidore and to his Catalan
satellites. The charge is proved false from the
catalogue compiled by order of Calixtus himself.
All he did was to give a couple of manuscripts of small
value to King Alfonso and one or two others to friends.
But it seems that he sold some of the gold and silver
clasps and the rich ornaments of their bindings to
raise money for the war. In spite of his crusading
enthusiasm Calixtus made little mark as Pope and the
information we possess about him is scanty. Indeed,
were it not for his nephew, Rodrigo, he would have
passed almost unnoticed.

Borgia had his share of the temperament of his race,
or perhaps we should say of the sensuality of his day.
It is virtually certain that he was the father of the Francisco Borgia whose portrait, by a pupil of Pinturicchio, in an attitude of prayer, is among the most
familiar of those in the Borgia apartments of the
Vatican. With his flat head, his drooping cheeks, his

heavy jaw and his unkempt hair, as Portigliotti points out, he recalls the plebeian and rather angular face of his father as it appears upon his tomb, now in the vaults of the Vatican. Such slips were then too common to be taken seriously or to weaken the high esteem in which the Pope's character was held. But at least he kept his son in the obscure position of a minor canon of St Peter's. It was left for the unblushing Alexander to make him a cardinal. Being Bishop of Cosenza, in Calabria, he was generally known as the Cardinal of Cosenza. Always at his cousin's side, he played a not unimportant part in the story of the family.

Calixtus reserved for his two nephews, Pedro Luis and Rodrigo, the sons of his sister Isabella, the passionate family affection which was so pronounced a trait of the Borgias. Doubtless they owed something to their d'Oms blood, something that was lacking in the coarser fibre of their uncle, the Pope. Rodrigo was his favourite. He attracted attention as a child in Valencia by his looks and even his enemies admit his charm and his brilliant gifts. His uncle, who would have scorned such preferment himself, conferred several Catalan benefices upon him when he was a mere boy. Another sister of the Pope had married Juan de Mila and her son, Luis Juan, also basked in the ecclesiastical favour of Calixtus. Immediately after his election he sent for these two lads from Spain and packed them off to Bologna to study canon law. A week later he made Rodrigo a Notary of the Apostolic See and bestowed more benefices upon him, but he kept him with Gaspare da Verona, a teacher of repute, as tutor. Luis de Mila, already Bishop of Segovia, was appointed Governor of Bologna and Vicar-General.

Before the end of 1455 the Pope was proposing to give his two nephews the red hat. Such violations of a coronation oath were then almost universal. But the

6

CARDINAL FRANCISCO BORGIA, BY PINTURICCHIO

step was not taken till February in the following year in a secret Consistory, with the consent of all the cardinals present. In the event of the Pope dying before the announcement, they bound themselves on pain of excommunication to treat the appointments as having been published and allow the pair to vote at the next Conclave.

Rodrigo spent sixteen months at the University, for which he always retained his affection. In his position it is not surprising that he enjoyed himself there, though he undoubtedly worked. Bologna, however, was not particularly proud of her distinguished son. The note on his diploma records his death in 1503, adding *et sepultus in inferno*—" and buried in Hell ". Perhaps the treatment the Bentivoglio experienced at his hands may help to explain such bitterness. He was granted the degree in canon law, for which the normal course was five years, in October, 1456. A month later these privileged cousins made their entry into Rome as cardinals. In September, when most of the Sacred College had left town to escape the heat and the prevalent sickness, the Pope had taken the opportunity of making the appointments public. On November 17th they received their red hats and a week later took place the ceremony of the opening of their mouths by their uncle. Luis de Mila was a complete nonentity, and we hear nothing more of him.

By the end of the year the lucky Rodrigo was made Legate of Ancona. Here he was able to show what was in him by his administrative ability and the vigour with which he put down rebels. He recovered Ascoli for the Church and brought back its tyrant to Rome. He was complimented by Æneas Sylvius, who said that he would be the glory of the House of Borgia ; and though the compliments of the courtly Piccolomini, Cardinal of Siena, need not be taken too literally, the mere fact that he troubled to pay them shows that the young Borgia was making his mark.

7

Even this was not enough for the doting uncle. In 1457 Rodrigo was given the highest office in the Church next to that of the Pope himself. He was made Vice-Chancellor when he was only twenty-seven.

Indeed, it was generally known that the aged and invalid Pope, a martyr to gout, was almost completely under the thumb of his relatives. He complained more than once of his sister Isabella, who insisted on enriching her daughters, all of whom received handsome dowries, from the purse of St Peter. His nephews not only used their power to traffic in benefices, as was then common, but also in other more questionable ways. A story, which sheds a lurid light on the times, is told in the *Commentarii* of Pius II. One day a Papal Secretary told a group of friends that, if they had any shady business on hand, now was their time, as the Pope was granting everything. One of them took him aside and asked him whether marriage within the forbidden degree was included. It was a delicate matter, but the Secretary said that he would speak to Cardinal Rodrigo, adding that the difficulty could be got over only by a large sum of money. A bull was duly granted to Count Jean d'Armagnac, signed by Calixtus, in which a dispensation for the fourth degree of relationship had been altered to the first, as the Count wished to marry his own sister. The price was 24,000 gold ducats, one-third of which went to Rodrigo. The facts came out only when the Count, on being asked for another 24,000 ducats, protested to Pope Pius II. It is, however, pretty certain that Rodrigo knew nothing of the forgery.

Don Pedro Luis, or Pierluigi Borgia, the Pope's soldier nephew, was hardly less dear to him than Rodrigo : indeed, according to a letter of the time, he looked upon him as little less than a second Cæsar. Handsome and dashing, he had neither the tact, nor the diplomatic skill, still less the ability and power of work of his more subtle churchman brother. Moreover, he had a double dose of Spanish pride, and the position to which his infatuated uncle raised him increased the bitter hatred this young Catalan upstart inspired among the Romans, whom he treated with overbearing insolence. In 1455 he was made Captain-General of the Church and Castellan of S. Angelo, and then Governor of Terni, Narni, Orvieto, Foligno, Assisi and every other possible town, including Spoleto, from which he took his title of Duke. Later came the charge of the patrimony of St Peter in Tuscany. In 1457 Don Pedro was also made Prefect of the City. The saintly Cardinal Capranica alone ventured to protest, but in vain.

The aged Pope had even wilder schemes for the advancement of his nephew, which must have raised a smile among those who heard them. His good relations with Alfonso of Naples did not survive his elevation. Calixtus never forgave him for his indifference to the Crusade, and it is but natural that the change in their positions should produce an instinctive reaction in the Pope. Alfonso had no legitimate son, but the barons and Pope Eugenius IV had, out of affection and respect towards the King, recognized his natural son, Ferrante, once the pupil of the Borgia, as his heir. But Naples was a fief of the Church, and Calixtus announced that he did not intend to accept this arrangement; indeed, he openly declared that he would do his best to deliver future Popes from bondage to Naples by preventing the succession of Ferrante, and he appears to have seriously thought of conferring the crown upon Don Pedro Luis. Hence his eagerness to prove that there was royal blood in his own veins.

So violent was his fury when, on Alfonso's death, Ferrante announced the event in the style of one already king that the Neapolitan ambassador only escaped arrest by a timely flight. However, the change released another batch of fat Catalan benefices,

9

which had remained vacant during the life of the late king, owing to the inability of himself and the Pope to agree upon the appointments. Chief of these was his own See of Valencia, the richest in Spain, which fell to Rodrigo. Other ecclesiastical members of the family and of the grasping brood of Catalans were enriched to such a degree that " the whole palace laughs ", for the Pope's health warned them that there was no time to lose. The crowning act of nepotism of one who had himself steadily refused to hold any benefices *in commenda*—by deputy—and had set an example as rare as it was admirable by declining all preferment except his bishopric, was to confer upon Don Pedro Luis the duchies of Benevento and Terracina, if, indeed, he was still really capable of controlling his actions; for by now he was altogether in the hands of his family.

The approaching end of the Pope created unusual excitement. It threw the whole country into confusion, we are told, for there was a general determination to make an end of Catalan rule. Rodrigo had too much sense to agree to his brother's wild schemes. No Papal relatives ever had so complete control, both military and ecclesiastical, of the resources of the Church in Rome as these two young nephews after the three short years of the reign of Calixtus, but, as always, their power collapsed on the Pope's death. The Church proved stronger than any of the holders of the See of St Peter. Rodrigo may have found it hard to convince his brother, who was bitterly hated as the chief of the Catalans, that his day was over and his life far from safe. However, when approached by the cardinals whose duty it was to ensure order during the Conclave, Don Pedro Luis consented to give up the castles, including S. Angelo, on receipt of the 22,000 ducats Calixtus had bequeathed him. All these negotiations went on without the knowledge of the sinking Pope.

Meanwhile the Catalans, with whom were classed Spaniards and even Neapolitans, were paying the penalty. Such had been their behaviour that many officials of other nationalities had been forced to resign their posts at the Vatican. The mob murdered them and sacked their houses whenever possible. The Orsini were prepared to stick at nothing in order to be avenged upon Don Pedro for his insolence. They were using their control of the country round Rome to cut off all possible ways of escape ; nor had his Italian troops any love for him. His one chance lay in flight. Rodrigo played no small part in the arrangements made for getting him out of Rome. He had the pluck to go with him in disguise, as also did Cardinal Barbo, afterwards Pope Paul II. Leaving Rome by the Porta S. Angelo, they went round by the Ponte Molle, then back to the Porta del Popolo and across the city by quiet streets to the lonely Porta S. Paolo, for Ostia. Here the cardinals left Don Pedro, while his troops and even his grooms refused to go further with their master. The ship chartered at Ostia did not wait for him and he had to be content with a boat to take him to Civita Vecchia. Here, some six weeks later, he died of fever and all his considerable wealth passed to his brother Rodrigo.

The young Vice-Chancellor showed both courage and heart on this occasion. He was the only person who did not desert the dying Pope and, Catalan though he was, he went openly to St Peter's to pray for him, just as he afterwards built him a worthy monument. He was also genuinely fond of his brother. He never forgave the Orsini the part they had played in driving him from Rome and he remained grateful to Barbo for his support. He lived to repay both debts. Thus he already showed that strong family affection which was so marked a characteristic of the Borgias and which they probably brought with them from their more simple Spanish home. Unfortunately, it proved anything but a virtue in a Pope.

CHAPTER II

CARDINAL RODRIGO BORGIA

DURING the Conclave the young Borgia cardinal showed himself able to uphold the dignity of the high office that had been thrust upon him by his uncle. For a moment it looked as if the wealthy Estouteville, Archbishop of Rouen, stood the best chance. But there was a strong feeling against another foreign Pope, and an even stronger one against the proud, vain Frenchman. From the first Piccolomini was the favourite, but there seemed small chance of any candidate receiving the needful two-thirds majority. The scene preceding his election is vividly described by the Cardinal of Siena in his memoirs. " All sat pale and silent, as if absorbed in the presence of the Holy Ghost (" if ambition and jealousy are attributes of the Holy Ghost," comments Gregorovius, with a rare flash of irony). No one spoke : every mouth was set firm : only the eyes moved." At last Cardinal Borgia, who had been promised the Vice-Chancellorship by both parties, but warned by the astute Piccolomini during his round of canvassing that Estouteville had also promised it to his countryman, Alain, the Cardinal of Avignon, felt moved to make sure of his own interests by rising and solemnly declaring, " I accede to the Cardinal of Siena ". For it had been decided in the seeming impossibility of securing an election in the usual way to adopt this method of accession. The other necessary accessions quickly followed.

The move was masterly. Pius II never forgot to

whom he owed the turning of the tide. Borgia remained Vice-Chancellor and retained all his other lucrative posts and benefices. Indeed, he now begins to stand out as a definite character, already one of the leading personalities in the Church, keeping himself well to the front by his affability, his brains, his energy and conscientious hard work and his wealth. His tutor, Gaspare da Verona, had described him as a young man richly endowed by Nature with eloquence, looks and engaging manners. His cousin, Juan de Mila, could not hold a candle to him. Obviously, too, he possessed the physical vigour, the sheer animal strength of the great personalities of that day. No Pope ever warmed both hands more eagerly before the fire of life. Possessed of a fine, dignified presence, his early experience of high office gave him a corresponding manner which soon became second nature to him. In summing up his character after his death, Guicciardini, who hated him, says that he possessed extraordinary cunning and sagacity, excellent judgment, with a wonderful persuasiveness, great diligence and real ability in handling difficult questions. It was remarked that he rarely missed a Consistory, and this regular attendance gave him every opportunity of increasing his influence among his fellow-cardinals and with the Pope of the moment.

Nor was there anything cold or sceptical about Borgia. He had nothing in common with the Humanists and their pagan leanings. His eager exuberance implies as much. He may not have been religious or devout in the highest sense of the terms, but his faith and piety were, in their way, sincere, difficult though it may be to realize it in the case of one who has become a byword. " We have always felt and feel a special affection for the Virgin," he once declared, and he also regarded St Anne and St Catherine as among his special protectors. It was natural for such a man to turn to the women saints. He was also a stickler for Church discipline and a strict upholder of dogma.

By this time he had long entered upon his successful career with the fair sex, which is said to have begun at Valencia. His tutor, Gaspare da Verona, noted his extraordinary fascination for women. "He is of a most genial countenance and happy appearance, a charming and most winning talker," able to fascinate and excite women in an astonishing manner and drawing them to him as irresistibly as a magnet; but, he adds with more tact than probability, it is generally thought that he lets them go unharmed. No one at that time expected a handsome young cardinal to keep his vow of chastity with absolute rigidity. It was only the delicate and sickly ones who were thought to be marked out for saints. The age was corrupt and the Church was naturally affected. But they were expected to behave with some regard to decorum and decency, especially when they held high office. In the Commentaries of Æneas Sylvius, as one would expect in the work of one who touches life at so many points, the Vice-Chancellor begins to come into prominence, and it is from them that we get the most damaging evidence concerning his conduct at this time. The Pope himself had sown his wild oats. He would have given much to be able to destroy some of his early writings. But he had a high ideal of the duties of a great churchman, or at least a far higher ideal than was then usual in the Sacred College, as we see in his denunciation of the luxury and vice then prevalent in the Curia in contrast with the qualities that had made the Church great.

Such was the scandal which the Vice-Chancellor's conduct had aroused in the Pope's own town of Siena, a fact which may have moved him to take action, that he felt compelled to address to his " dear son " a letter of admonition (June 11th, 1460). A number of ladies, dressed in the height of fashion, had gathered in the gardens of Giovanni de Bichis and he had been informed that the Vice-Chancellor had shown himself very unmindful of the dignity of his office by keeping company with them from the seventeenth to the twenty-second hour. Report said that there had been " dancing with complete absence of restraint, that flirting and love-making had been indulged in, and that you behaved just as if you belonged to a set of young laymen. Decency forbids me to repeat in detail all that is said to have occurred there. Not merely what took place, but even the very mention of it is unworthy of the position you hold." To allow greater freedom, admission was refused to the husbands, brothers and other male relatives of the women, which doubtless did more than anything else to increase the scandal. He and his friends and a few servants had presided over the feast and even led the dance. The Pope learns that nothing else is talked of in Siena and that everyone is laughing over it. Even at the baths of Petriolo, where Pius then was, his behaviour is the subject of general gossip. He is more displeased than he can say. Such conduct is the cause of the contempt in which princes and potentates hold churchmen. " Hence the daily jibes of the laity ; hence, when we wish to reprove them, they throw our own lives in our faces ; and even the Vicar of Christ is blamed, because it is thought that he shuts his eyes." Is it becoming for one of your rank to flirt with girls, pelt them with fruit, send round cups of wine that you have tasted to a favoured beauty and spend the whole day amusing yourself watching every kind of frolic ? " We are blamed on your account, the blessed memory of your uncle is blamed [and this is worth noting, considering from whom it comes], whom many people thought to be doing wrong in heaping offices upon you." If he pleads youth in excuse, he is certainly old enough to understand the dignity of his office. " A cardinal should be without blemish, a true mirror of unsullied life, a model to all who behold him." If he does not mend his ways, "we shall be compelled to make it plain that these things are done without our consent, or rather with our strongest disapproval; and to be rebuked by us would certainly bring you no honour. We have always loved you, and because we have seen that you are a model of earnestness and modesty, we have thought you deserving of our protection."

The letter is worth giving virtually in full for the light it throws on the men and their times. There is also another letter, dated in 1476, from the Cardinal of Pavia, Ammananti, a cultivated, pleasure-loving nephew of Pius, written in an affectionate tone and urging that they should both put on the new man, so that the laity may no longer have cause to laugh at them. He bids him not give it to his secretaries, but keep it by him, read it occasionally and think of it at least once a year. These kindly warnings produced little effect. The amusements of the cardinal of thirty continued to be those of the Pope of seventy, when he indulged in them quite as openly.

The way of life of a cardinal differed little from that of a noble of the time. Both as Cardinal and as Pope Rodrigo was fond of hunting. He appears to have struck up an early friendship with Ludovico Gonzaga of Mantua and his wife, Barbara of Brandenburg. They were among the first to be informed of his appointment as Vice-Chancellor. But the Mantuan chronicler, Schivenoglia, was not favourably impressed, saying that at twenty-five he looked capable of doing any evil. The Gonzagas sent him some of their admirable falcons and hunting dogs, and he tells them, in 1460, that without them he would have been bored to death at Siena, where he was with Pius II, compelled to stay in his room with nothing to do and no amusements but "to endure the suffering of our journey through these wild and wooded valleys".

Clearly the fondness of the restless, curious Pius for
travelling and for being in the country struck no answering cord in the breast of his Vice-Chancellor.
The Gonzaga saw the wisdom of keeping in the good
books of this rising young cardinal.

Pius continued to love and appreciate him for his
good qualities as also for the good side of the qualities
he felt bound to reprove. If his Vice-Chancellor was
the richest of the cardinals, with the exception of
Estouteville, he was always willing to use his wealth
for the glory of the Church. Æneas Sylvius understood the value of a good show, none better, at a
time when the wealth and luxury of Italy made such
displays the natural expression of the brilliant, if
corrupt court life, and on such occasions he knew
that he could count upon Borgia. In 1461, the year
after the letter of reproof, there were great doings
for the arrival of the head of St Andrew, the priceless
treasure which had been saved by Thomas, the last
of the Palæologi, when he was driven from the Morea
by the Turks. It was welcomed with the greatest
ceremony. Pius would have liked to bring the heads
of Peter and Paul to meet it, had not their cases been
too heavy. Thirty thousand candles were carried in
the procession and altars with burning incense were
set up all along the streets. The decorations were
splendid, but all, even those of the Procurator of the
Knights of Rhodes and the richest nobles, were
outdone by the Vice-Chancellor. Not only was his
palace completely draped with rich and splendid hangings, but the street in front of it was covered in with
an imitation sky, adorned with many and various
marvels, and he also decorated some of the neighbouring houses. The whole district was like a Para-
dise, filled with sweet music and singing. Again, in 1462,
when Pius decided to celebrate Corpus Domini with
special magnificence at Viterbo, Borgia outdid everyone else in the portion of the route entrusted to him.

Yet, two years later, when the dying Pope went to Ancona in order to embark for the Crusade which it had been the dream of his life to inspire, the Vice-Chancellor took the opportunity of amusing himself in his usual way, and with his usual indecent shamelessness. The Mantuan ambassador wrote that he had not slept alone. He was ill before the Conclave, which he entered at the last moment with his head tied up. Pietro Barbo had stood by his brother after the death of Calixtus and the election of this able, vain, pleasure-loving ex-merchant of Venice who, but for the protests of the cardinals, would have called himself Formosus, was doubtless to his satisfaction. It was Paul II who gave the cardinals their purple robes, for he wished to be surrounded by a splendour worthy of himself, just as it was he who organized the carnival as it long remained, with its races of old men, young men, boys, Jews, horses, asses and buffaloes, thus introducing a strong pagan element, which shocked the more puritanical cardinals. No one enjoyed the fun more thoroughly than His Holiness. Doubtless, also, he was satisfied with a Vice-Chancellor who could play his part so well. We find him receiving guests of distinction, such as the Emperor Frederic III or Federigo of Naples.

Borgia was a prominent figure in the next Conclave, from which Francesco della Rovere came out Pope as Sixtus IV, and he was rewarded with the great abbey of Subiaco. This was a notable addition even to his revenues. It fell to the lot of the Vice-Chancellor to crown Sixtus. In early days, before the advancement of his worthless Riario nephews became the ruling passion of his life, all the efforts of the restless, eager, impulsive Pope were directed to the hopeless task of rousing Christendom to a Crusade. Borgia was naturally chosen as Legate for Spain. It was a proud moment for him when he set foot once again in his native Valencia, now his bishopric. But the splendid state he kept, though true to his reputation and the traditions of his great office, did not raise him in the eyes of the sterner, more simple and ascetic Catholics of Spain. The attempt to kindle enthusiasm for a Crusade failed, as it was bound to do, but the journey was of great service to the Legate. He handled the delicate question of the marriage of Ferdinand and Isabella with a tact and skill that did much to win over all parties in Castile, as well as in his own Aragon, to an acceptance of the union of the crowns. Borgia always instinctively leaned towards Spain and Naples and he now made Ferdinand his firm friend. The King had welcomed him in almost royal style in Madrid, honouring him by walking at his side in the procession, and Borgia was made godfather to his eldest son. Ferdinand was fully alive to the value of the support of so prominent a cardinal, a Spaniard to boot.

After a year's absence Borgia sailed for Italy with a couple of Venetian ships. All went well till they were off Savona, when they ran into a storm so violent that one of them foundered. His baggage, including 30,000 gold ducats, and 180 souls, among them three bishops and six knights, were lost. Borgia, with his mobile character, was deeply affected by the disaster. He proceeded incognito to Siena and thence post-haste to Rome, where, in spite of his unexpected coming, all the Sacred College turned out to meet him in state, as was but fitting for one returning from a mission of such importance. With his no less habitual buoyancy he quickly recovered his spirits.

On the death of Sixtus, such was the state of Rome owing to the bitter feeling against the hated Girolamo Riario and to the vigour of his wife, the redoubtable *virago*, Caterina Sforza, who seized the Castel S. Angelo, that both the Vice-Chancellor and Cardinal Giuliano della Rovere fortified their houses and provided armed defence. However, the Conclave was, as usual, held in peace. Borgia now began to make a serious bid for the tiara, offering handsome bribes in the right quarters. But the Florentine envoy saw that he had no chance owing to his reputation for falseness and pride. When it became clear that none of the big men could obtain the two-thirds majority, Cardinal Giuliano della Rovere threw all his weight into the scale of Cardinal Cibo, a gentle, well-meaning man who owed him everything. He was the father of at least a son and a daughter, born before he became a priest. The satirists, who had not yet become accustomed to Papal families, gave him one of eight boys and eight girls. So successful was Rovere that Borgia, seeing that his election was inevitable, ended by acceding to Cibo.

Thus Giuliano, who had had no influence with his uncle, Sixtus IV, became "Pope and more than Pope" under the feeble Innocent VIII. He lived in the Vatican, and his brother, Giovanni, was made Captain-General of the Church. He and Borgia were on opposite sides, Rovere for France, Borgia for Spain. At a Consistory in 1486 Borgia made a long speech urging the Pope to reject the French offers of help and make peace with Naples. Cardinal La Balue replied vigorously and effectively. The scene that followed gives a vivid picture of these fiery princes of the Church, whose language differed, if anything, less than their lives from those of a hard-living, hard-fighting soldier of the day. Borgia lost his temper and heaped every kind of abuse upon the Frenchman, saying, among other things, that no notice should be taken of his words, as he was drunk. The Frenchman retorted by calling him a *marrano*, a renegade Jew or Moor who had been baptized— the word is Spanish—and the son of a prostitute, whose private life was an outrage upon decency. So violent were they that they were on the point of coming to blows and the Consistory was hastily adjourned.

By this time Borgia was famous for his wealth and

the luxurious state in which he lived. Jacopo da Volterra talks of his plate and his pearls, his tapestries and his richly embroidered vestments and his learned books of all kinds, which would not disgrace a king or a pope. He will not linger over the sumptuous fittings of his litters and the trappings of his horses, his ample wardrobe and his hoards of gold. By 1470 he had moved into the magnificent new palace he had built, half-way between the Bridge of S. Angelo and the Campo dei Fiori, on the site of the old Mint. It is now the Palazzo Sforza–Cesarini. There is an interesting description of it by Cardinal Ascanio Sforza in a letter to his brother, Ludovico Sforza, soon to be Duke of Milan.[1]

When we remember that the Cardinal of Pavia was himself one of the most magnificent churchmen of the day and the greatest sportsman in the Sacred College, astonishing all Rome with his horses, hawks and dogs, his testimony carries weight. He went with Giuliano della Rovere and two other cardinals to dine with the Vice-Chancellor. The dinner was good, well-served and sumptuous and the house splendidly appointed. The entrance-hall was hung with tapestries of historical subjects. Beyond this was a reception-room, also hung with very fine tapestries, the carpets on the floor going well with the rest of the decorations. There was a divan of crimson satin and over it a canopy, such as every cardinal had over his throne. Here was the *credenza*, the plate chest, which was then the chief pride of a man of position. It was beautifully carved and loaded with gold and silver vessels of every kind, a really noble sight. Beyond were two other reception-rooms. The first was hung with fine arras and covered with carpets equally fine with a state divan and canopy of Alexandrine (i.e. blue) velvet. The other was much more sumptuously fitted, the divan being covered with gold brocade and the canopy lined with sable

[1] Pastor, *History of the Popes*, V, 528.

and fringed with gold. The table in the middle was also covered with blue velvet and the elaborately ornamented stools harmonized with it.

It was well known that the Vice-Chancellor had no love for banquets. The Popes then kept the simplest tables, however splendid their state, as their accounts show, none more simple than Pius II. Borgia was no exception. Even when Pope he required only one dish, though it must be an ample one. Anyone who has seen a Neapolitan, after making the same profession, fall upon a great bowl of macaroni will understand that such a habit does not necessarily imply abstinence. But the younger members of the Curia, even his son, Cesare, and his nephew, Cardinal Monreale, came to regard it as a penance to dine with His Holiness. He never allowed amusement to interfere with business. Always a hard worker, he would remain at his desk till far into the night. Cardinal Sforza's letter implies that it was the first time he had dined with the Vice-Chancellor. Such an event may be explained by the fact that the heir to the Neapolitan throne was then in Rome and his brother, the Cardinal of Aragon, among the guests.

Like Calixtus, Borgia appears to have had little taste for literature or poetry, but he was fond of music and had a veritable passion for dancing. He was one of the leaders of the more worldly of the cardinals, who were never more powerful, more wealthy or more corrupt than at this time. " Surrounded in their splendid palaces with all the most refined luxury of a highly developed civilisation, these cardinals lived the lives of secular princes and seemed to regard their ecclesiastical garb simply as one of the adornments of their rank. They hunted, gambled, gave splendid entertainments, joined in all the rollicking merriment of the carnival-tide and allowed themselves the utmost licence." No wonder Lorenzo dei Medici warned his son Giovanni, afterwards Pope Leo X, in his famous letter of advice to the youngest cardinal ever appointed, that "the less your conduct resembles that of the men who now compose the Sacred College, the more loved and respected you will be". He advised him to steer his course midway between the Scylla of sanctimoniousness and the Charybdis of profanity. The cardinals, Gregorovius assures us, wore swords, had a small court of their own, where they lived with their nephews (or sons) surrounded by several hundred retainers. They made far more display than the old Roman nobles. As for play, Cardinal La Balue lost 8000 ducats to Cardinal Riario in a single night.

The barefaced secularization of the Papacy began with Sixtus IV. His spiritual authority was for him a useful means of escaping the consequences of his political crimes. Indeed, in political morality Sixtus stands even lower than the Borgia, whom he rivalled in his nepotism. The vulgar brutality and coarseness of the lives of his spendthrift Riario nephews, or sons, is far more revolting than anything we know of the Borgia children, in whose redeeming qualities they were altogether lacking. Sixtus, we must remember, was privy to the conspiracy of the Pazzi against the Medici, to which Giuliano succumbed. In other ways his outlook differed not a whit from that of other secular princes of the day. On being told that two of his guards were to fight a duel to the death, he gave orders that it should take place in St Peter's Square. He blessed the combatants and crossed himself as a sign that the fight should begin and watched it to the finish.

The gentle Innocent bought the tiara almost as openly as Alexander VI or Julius II were to do. In his day all crimes could be compounded for money, the heavier fines going to his nephew, Cardinal Cibo. As the Vice-Chamberlain put it, the Lord did not desire that the sinner should die, but that he should live and pay. Life was never held so cheap in Rome.

Infessura tells us that a father compounded for the murder of his two daughters with 300 ducats. It was left for Innocent to shock public opinion and to scandalize even Ferrante of Naples by keeping his children at the Vatican and celebrating their marriages and those of his grandchildren with royal splendour. This was the school in which the future Alexander VI graduated. He was merely following in the footsteps of his predecessors and carrying their principles to their logical conclusion : indeed, he has become, to some extent, their scapegoat. In common fairness, before passing judgment upon him and his children, the reader should know something of the popes who preceded him and the cardinals with whom he mixed. Burchard, whose diary is our best source of information, remarks, in describing Lucrezia Borgia's first marriage, that all the clergy are turning their energies with due diligence to the procreation of children. All classes of them keep mistresses as though they were married and, but for the grace of God, the corruption will spread to the monasteries ; those in Rome are little better than brothels and no one raises a protest.

This cold, formal, meticulous, wholly admirable Master of the Ceremonies, an Alsatian by birth, is a typical specimen of the type of man who made German influence so unobtrusively powerful at the Vatican, in his gift for work, his thoroughness and his detailed accuracy. Such a man had little sympathy with the weaknesses of the South. He was, however, a man of his day, quite ready to pick up any piece of ecclesiastical preferment that might be going, or even a cast-off cloak of ceremony, when opportunity offered. He had, in accordance with custom, bought his office of Master of the Ceremonies. Possibly his weakness lay in another and more German direction. We find him complaining, when invited to dine with the Pope, that the dinner was very ordinary and there was no good wine.

CHAPTER III

By this time, in spite of occasional lapses, Cardinal Borgia had settled down into something like regular family life with Vannozza, as she is always called. She was the mother of the children to whose advancement he devoted himself with the passionate family affection that was so marked a feature of the Borgias. The lady's name was Giovannozza dei Catanei. Nothing certain is known of her. She is generally said to have been a Roman, but both Siena and Mantua have been suggested as her birthplace. Her three husbands were all from the North and Luzio, arguing from her name, makes her a Mantuan whom Rodrigo met at Mantua during the Council of 1461, when she was eighteen. However this may be, she must have possessed both character and tact, as well as charm and beauty, to have retained the affection of such a man for so long. Whether the portrait given by Buggelli[1] from the Congregazione di Carità in Rome—" Vannozza Cattanea Benefatt "—is authentic or not I do not know. It is not a great work of art, but the resemblance to the traditional portraits of Cesare is striking. The deep-set eyes, the nose and the mouth and the brows are the same and there is the same almost sinister strength in the face. Lucrezia also had her mother's nose, almost straight, but her mouth and chin were obviously her father's. Possibly it was from her that Lucrezia got her fair hair and light eyes, and the boys the tinge of red in their hair, for

[1] *Lucr. Borgia*, p. 41.

Rodrigo is known to have been dark. Obviously, too, she was a very strong character. Rodrigo was just the type of man who might easily be dominated by a woman.

Vannozza was born in 1442, as was recorded on the inscription on her tomb in S. Maria del Popolo. This, like most of the monuments of the Borgias, has disappeared. She is there described as the mother of four children, Cesare, the Duke of Gandia, Gioffredo and Lucrezia, Duchess of Ferrara. Cesare is now known to have been born in 1475, when she was thirty-three, possibly in 1474. Juan, second Duke of Gandia, seems to have been born in 1476, Lucrezia in 1480 and Gioffredo in 1482. Rodrigo's eldest son, the first Duke of Gandia, named, after his brother, Pedro Luis, was born between 1458 and 1463. He had two other children, Girolama and Isabella, who married into great Roman houses in 1482 and 1483 respectively. Girolama died young, as probably did Isabella. Had she lived, we should certainly have heard something of her. The names of these three children do not appear in Vannozza's epitaph and they have been assigned to a different mother or mothers. But the omission is probably due to the fact of their early deaths. Italian women age early, and it is natural to suppose that Vannozza captivated Rodrigo in the prime of her youth. Nor is it likely that, with her strength and temperament and with such a lover, she would remain for so many years without being pregnant. Vannozza could hardly have been one of the fashionable courtesans of the day, good though their position often was at this time, or the fact would have been known ; nor does she seem to have been a woman of the people. It is usually held that she belonged to the middle classes, and everything we know about her tends to confirm this belief.

Vannozza lived in a house of her own on the

Piazza Pizzo di Merlo, now Sforza–Cesarini, quite close to the palace of her cardinal lover. Not till 1474 was a husband found for her in Domenico d'Arignano. He lived long enough for Cesare to be born in lawful wedlock, but not long enough to confer the same privilege upon Juan. By 1480 she was married again to Giorgio S. Croce, a Milanese, who was an apostolic secretary to Sixtus IV. Like his predecessor, he was probably a man advanced in years. He possessed some property, and it was through him that she came to own the vineyard near S. Pietro in Vinculi where the supper was held on the night of the murder of the Duke of Gandia. She brought him a dowry of 1000 gold florins and went to live with him in a house of her own on Piazza Branchis. She also presented him with a son, who died in the same year as his father, 1486. The Bishop of Mantua stood godfather.

By then she had ceased to be Rodrigo's mistress, but he always treated her with respect as the mother of his children, who were all genuinely attached to her. In June, 1486, she was again married, this time to Carlo Canale, a Mantuan. He was a man of some repute in the world of letters and scholarship. The youthful Politian submitted his *Orfeo* to him. He had been chamberlain to Cardinal Gonzaga. Canale appears to have been proud of his position. He refers to Gandia as his stepson in a letter in the Gonzaga archives, and once, in a fit of enthusiasm, he signs himself Carolus de Cattaneis. He also quartered the Borgia arms upon his own. He gladly placed all the influence he had at the Vatican, of which he doubtless made the most, at the disposal of the Gonzaga of Mantua.

Rodrigo early set about remedying any disadvantages which their birth might bring to his children. Not that they were serious in the case of a layman. This was the age of bastards. Æneas Sylvius notes that

most of the rulers of Italy were then born out of wedlock. Not one of the seven princes who received him
at Ferrara in 1459 was legitimate.[1] But even the
Renaissance found the son of a priest a little difficult
to digest. Ferdinand the Catholic was delighted to
show his gratitude to the Vice-Chancellor by removing
all disabilities in Spain. Not only were the children
naturalized, but they were legitimized and expressly
exempted from any disabilities their birth might cause
them there.

As cardinal, it was to Spain that Borgia looked
for the future of his family. Cesare was from the first
meant for the Church. Why, we do not know.
Possibly on account of the early promise he showed, or
perhaps because he was, like Rodrigo, the second son.
Gioffrè was also at first destined for the same career.
Rodrigo was only following fashion in beginning to
provide Cesare with benefices at an early age. At
seven he was Protonotary Apostolic, Prebend and
Canon of Valencia, Rector of Gandia and Archdeacon
of Xativa. These were gifts from Sixtus IV, all, be
it noted, in the diocese of Valencia. To them Innocent VIII added the See of Pampeluna, as a present
for his sixteenth birthday. Sixtus IV had already given
him the necessary dispensation for holding benefices,
in spite of his birth. There could be no more trouble,
unless he aspired to the cardinalate.

There is no doubt that Cesare showed unusual
promise. In the dedication of his *Syllabica* to him
Paolo Pompilio calls him the hope and glory of the
Borgia family and he praises him for a wisdom beyond
his years. This is a handbook on the writing of Latin
verse, compiled specially for Cesare, who never lost
his early fondness for poetry. A year later he was
studying law at the Sapienza of Perugia with Francisco de Ilerda, who remained his friend for life. His
tutor, Giovanni Vera, was, like Pompilio, a Catalan,

[1] Pastor, *Popes*, V, 114.

One day, after walking in the delightful garden of the Dominicans with the Prior, he went into the church, where he witnessed a so-called miracle by a hysterical Sister Colomba. The Dominicans thought highly of her, but even the monk who tells the tale was, according to Alvisi, sceptical in this case. In 1495, when Alexander VI was visiting Perugia, he asked to see her. Way was made for him with difficulty through the crowd that was round her. When he proceeded to question her upon the divine mysteries, the poor creature became silent and confused, as well she might, and the Pope became sceptical. Cesare then came forward and related what he had seen, saying that, since the Prior was then doubtful, he deserved more credence now. This intervention was characteristic. Unlike his father, Cesare talked little, but when he did intervene, his words were to the point. Also, they carried weight with his father. Alexander was always wisely sceptical in such cases. We find him sending his doctors to examine Suor Lucia da Narni, a rising saint patronized by the Franciscans, who was said to have received the stigmata.

In 1491 Cesare went to Pisa to continue his legal studies under Filippo Decio, then a famous teacher of law. The brilliancy of his *disputatio* for his degree in both civil and canon law is admitted even by that bitter enemy of his house, Paolo Giovio. It was here that he was made Bishop of Pampeluna.

Don Pedro Luis was identified even more closely with Spain. He became a soldier and fought well at the siege of Ronda in 1485, so well that Ferdinand conferred upon him the title of Egregio. Not only did he make him the first Duke of Gandia, but he betrothed him to his youthful cousin, Donna Maria Enriquez. He it was who began the building of the Gandia palace at Gandia. He died in Rome in August, 1488, before the marriage took place, possibly of Roman fever. Don Pedro left Lucrezia a handsome sum towards her dowry. Surely this makes it more probable that he was also a son of Vannozza. His brother Juan, whom he made his heir, succeeded him in his duchy and was even allowed to marry Donna Maria.

Juan appears to have been troublesome from the first. In Spain he neglected his wife, spending his evenings roystering in the streets. He was also an inveterate gambler. So extravagant was he that Alexander put him in the charge of two men whom he could trust, with orders not to allow him a penny, only to pay his debts. He wrote him long letters of excellent advice and severe reproof. Even Cesare, now a Cardinal, was called in to admonish his brother. " His Holiness is deeply distressed," he told him, and added more admirable advice.[1]

Vannozza remained discreetly in the background. She played no active part in the lives of her children, for whom their father's doting ambition was planning brilliant careers, but, to their credit, they always remained attached to her. Her name never appears in the diaries of the time, except incidentally. She was a stranger to the Vatican and the court life there. Clearly Rodrigo removed his children from her care as soon as possible and had them brought up under his own supervision. With the boys this was easy, but Lucrezia must have stayed with her mother rather longer ; not much, however, for it was not long before the Vice-Chancellor entrusted her education to his cousin, Adriana de Mila, who had married Ludovico Orsini, lord of Basanello. She naturally lived with her husband's family, probably in the chief Orsini stronghold in Rome, at Monte Giordano, in the old-fashioned Ponte region, not far from Rodrigo's own palace. He was on very intimate terms with Adriana, especially after her early widowhood. She played a notable part in his relations with Vannozza's successor.

1 Suau, *St François de Borgia*, p. 19.

This was Giulia Farnese, a magnificent girl with a figure of classic beauty, to whom Borgia fell an easy victim. In 1489, when she was nineteen, she was married to Adriana's own son, Orsino Orsini, with great splendour in the " star-chamber " of Rodrigo's own palace. They had been betrothed as children. Adriana continued to favour the intrigue which gave her increased influence. The cardinal's unfortunate young cousin had no choice but to play the complacent husband. " Giulia bella " remained Rodrigo's mistress long after he became Pope. She appeared at his side at entertainments and both Burchard and Infessura call her " the Pope's concubine." Sanudo talks of the Pope's favourite, " a young bride of great beauty, intelligent, tactful and of a sweet disposition." Ambassadors often refer to the relationship. Later Giulia and her husband lived with Adriana and Lucrezia in the Palazzo di S. Martino, close to the steps of the Vatican.

There is nothing surprising in Rodrigo winning this lovely girl, brought up in such surroundings, with all the advantages his position could ensure, and her family had to thank the relationship for its rise to distinction. So well known was it that her brother, Alessandro, afterwards Pope Paul III, owed his hat to the Bride of Christ, as the Romans called her,—it was conferred in spite of considerable opposition by the cardinals—that he was dubbed the Petticoat Cardinal, " il cardinale della gonnella."

Vasari records that, when he decorated the Borgia apartments in the Vatican, Pinturicchio painted Giulia as the Virgin in a round fresco over one of the doors, with the head of Alexander in an attitude of adoration in the same picture. The Madonna is certainly there, over the door, surrounded by angels, but the kneeling figure of the Pope, probably the most speaking likeness we have of him, is in another room. Vasari's story has lately been completely

31

discredited. It is said that he had never seen the apartments, though others have suggested that the Pope's head was removed. But Luzio points out[1] that the Farnese themselves did all they could to have the fresco covered up. When, in 1612, the Gonzaga asked their agent in Rome to procure them a copy of a " pittura stravagante," he suggested this. He found, however, that " on the fresco is nailed a cloth fastened with a number of nails, then comes taffeta and on it a Madonna." It was in the room where Cardinal Borghese slept in winter, and he managed to bribe his Master of the Robes with a pair of silk stockings to let him have it copied. Venturi says that the Madonna differs little from Pinturicchio's favourite type and cannot therefore be Giulia, but a comparison with Raphael's striking portrait of Cardinal Alessandro Farnese in the Naples museum reveals a distinct similarity of features, notably the eyebrows, the nose and the chin. I have not seen the original of the Pinturicchio.

Tradition says that the splendid figure of Justice, which was originally nude, by Guglielmo della Porta, on the tomb of the Farnese Pope in St Peter's, is a portrait of his sister, Giulia. Rodrigo was the father of her daughter, Laura, born just before he was made Pope, and it is possible that she was also the mother of Giovanni Borgia, the " infans Romanus ". The Pope was particular about Giulia. When the Gonzaga of Mantua were advised to send presents, not letters, to the ladies of the Vatican, they sent some jewellery in the hope of increasing their chances of having a red hat in the family. Alexander refused to allow Giulia to accept any, but he laughingly permitted her to take some of the carp and cheese they sent to Rome for Lent, adding in Spanish that some must be given to the Cardinal of Valencia and the other women.

There was something fateful about the year 1492.

1 " La Galleria del Gonzaga venduta all' Inghilterra," p. 45.

32

Every other event pales before the discovery of America, which, for a contemporary, must have appeared a trifle to the capture of Granada by Ferdinand on January 2nd. The news was received with wild rejoicing in Rome. The Spanish ambassadors who brought it were entertained with a representation of the conquest, including the entry of Ferdinand and Isabella, by Cardinal Riario. Cesare Borgia gave the Romans a bull-fight, the first to be seen in Rome, on St Peter's Square.

Hardly less enthusiasm was awakened by the arrival of the point of the holy spear with which the side of Christ had been pierced, though unfortunately it had rivals both in Paris and Nüremberg. The reception was worthy of the occasion. Innocent VIII owed this priceless relic to the fact that the brother of Sultan Bajazet, Prince Djem, as he is usually called, was now in his keeping. Defeated by Bajazet in the civil war after the death of their father, the conqueror of Constantinople, Mahomet II, he had given himself up to the Grand Master of the Knights of St John, the most heroic of his father's enemies. A hostage so precious was treated with every courtesy. No one understood his value better than Bajazet, who paid the Knights of St John 45,000 ducats a year to ensure his safe keeping. Djem was placed in a château in Poitou belonging to the Knights under the protection of Charles VIII.

Every Power in Christendom, to say nothing of the Sultan of Egypt, was anxious to get possession of an asset so valuable, no one more so than the Pope. In a crusade he would be of the utmost importance, as Bajazet's enemies would rally round him. Innocent was able to bring sufficient pressure to bear upon the King of France and a red hat was promised the Grand Master, but only when Djem was safe in the Vatican.

Djem made his entry into Rome on March 3rd, 1485, through a dense crowd. Mounted on a white palfrey, wearing turban and veil, he rode between the Grand Master and Franceschetto Cibo. He barely nodded to the important deputation sent to meet him and was equally indifferent to the abject salutations of the Egyptian ambassador, who bowed to the ground and embraced his leg and that of his horse. Surely no stranger procession had ever made its way along the Tiber to the Vatican since the passing of the old Roman world. He did not deign even to glance at the rich gifts sent him by the Pope.

On the following day Innocent received the son of the conqueror of Constantinople, whom Charles VIII of France had declined to meet, in full Consistory. The stout Oriental figure, turbaned, as before, with the hawk-like nose and the bright blue eyes, impassive as ever, again made but the slightest of bows, placing his hand under his chin as he went up to the Pope, whom he kissed on the shoulder.

Djem was given a splendid suite of apartments in the Vatican. He became a familiar figure in Rome. His characteristic features stand out vividly from Pinturicchio's fresco in the Borgia apartments. He was a man of intelligence, fond of hunting and music, but he spent much of his time, like a true Oriental, dozing or in impassive abstraction.

In 1490 an attempt was made to poison the well in the Vatican by an Italian noble, with the consent of Bajazet, but he was caught and executed. In the same year, when the Sultan sent an embassy with the money to the Pope, the ambassador insisted on seeing Djem, who received him in full state. He declined to accept the letter from Bajazet till the ambassador had licked it all over, both inside and out, from fear of poison. He took no more notice of the gifts brought him than he had done of those of the Pope.

In 1492 died Lorenzo dei Medici, the acknowledged peace-maker of Italy, barely a month after his son, Giovanni, afterwards Pope Leo X, had made his official entry into Rome as cardinal at the age of seventeen. It also proved fatal to Innocent VIII. Three boys at a ducat ahead are said to have succumbed in an attempt to effect a transfusion of blood into the sinking Pope by a Jewish doctor, who fled. Innocent may also claim to have been one of the peace-makers of Italy.

Over Innocent's death-bed the rivalry between the Vice-Chancellor and Giuliano della Rovere, Cardinal S. Pietro in Vincula, or Vincula, as he is often called, flamed up once more. We must remember that the hatred of the olive-skinned, thin-lipped, fiery-tempered, dominating Ligurian peasant, with the deep-set eyes, for his successful rival was not due to moral causes. Though a finer character, and possessed of a fundamental seriousness, he was one of the most worldly of the cardinals. He hated Borgia as his personal enemy and successful rival to his dying day. Passionate and impetuous, he was outspoken to a degree. On November 26th, 1507, Vincula, now Julius II and already one of the strongest of the Popes, moved out of the Borgia apartments because he could not endure to have the portrait of his enemy always before his eyes. He called Alexander a *marrano* and, when Paris de Grassis laughed, he lost his temper with him because he did not believe that he was circumcised. De Grassis suggested that he should have the portrait destroyed and the other frescoes boarded over, but he refused, one is thankful to say, adding that it was not right, though he would not live there himself, to be reminded of that evil and criminal memory. Yet he allowed his nephew, Niccolò della Rovere, to marry Laura, Alexander's daughter by Giulia Farnese.

The envoy from Ferrara tells us that the dying Innocent was nodding his consent to the Vice-Chancellor's suggestion that the Castel S. Angelo should be handed over to the College of Cardinals, when Vincula broke into the room and bade him remember that the Vice-Chancellor was a Catalan.

He implored him to leave the castle to his successor alone. " If we were not in the presence of His Holiness, " burst out Borgia, " I would teach you who is Vice-Chancellor." Rovere retorted and they were soon calling each other *marrano* and white Moor. Cardinals Ascanio Sforza and Colonna witnessed the scene.

CHAPTER IV

THE ELECTION OF ALEXANDER VI (1492)
HIS NEPOTISM

THE mortal illness of Innocent VIII had, as usual, weakened authority in Rome, and the cardinals dreaded serious disturbances. These fears, however, proved groundless and the vigour shown by Cardinal Raffaele Riario, the Camerlengo, kept the city at least as quiet as usual during the election. On August 6th, 1492, the large number of twenty-three cardinals went into the Conclave, which was held in the Sistine chapel. The Vatican was duly barricaded, the leading Roman nobles mounted guard at the head of the troops, and the ambassadors, as usual, assisted in securing the inviolability of the Conclave. The most favoured candidates were Ascanio Sforza, who thought that he could count on seven votes, with possibly four others, and Giuliano della Rovere, who could dispose of nine. They thus checkmated each other. Rovere was the French candidate. Rumour said that Charles VIII had paid 200,000 ducats into a Genoese bank to support him, and the Republic of Genoa another 100,000, which shows how it was expected that the election would be conducted. Ferrante of Naples also appears to have looked upon Rovere with favour, a rather strange combination. For a moment the tiara hovered over the learned and saintly Neapolitan, Carafa. It was not by saintliness, but by the means and methods of which Borgia could dispose, that papal elections were decided in the Cinquecento, when, in any case, strength of character was far more necessary for the head of the Church, and still more of the Papal States, than the passive and cloistered virtues.

Few candidates can ever have had as many wealthy offices with which, if elected, they could reward their friends as Borgia. In Italy he was Vice-Chancellor and Bishop of Porto, besides holding four good abbeys, as well as Subiaco, with its income of 1200 ducats, and the towns of Nepi and Civita Castellana. In Spain he held sixteen bishoprics, including, of course, Valencia, and a number of abbeys and lesser benefices. Yet before the Conclave his Spanish birth was thought to have eliminated him as surely as his French sympathies did Giuliano.

The Spaniard Carvajal delivered the customary sermon, in which he deplored the state of the Church and urged his brother cardinals to choose wisely and choose quickly. On the 10th nothing had been decided, though there had been three scrutinies, or votings. By that time Ascanio realized that he had not a chance, and that he had most to gain from Borgia's princely bribes. He was to have not only the Vice-Chancellorship, but the Bishopric of Erlau, with an income of 10,000 ducats, Borgia's own palace, which he had described in a letter to his brother at Milan, and which has thus come to be the Sforza–Cesarini, as well as the town of Nepi with its castle. Borgia had removed all valuables from his home, as, in case of his election, or even on a persistent rumour of his election, it would be pillaged by the mob; and Burchard tells of four mules laden with gold being seen on their way from Borgia to Ascanio's palace for safe keeping during the Conclave; or was it another bribe? Ascanio's chances were good enough for his own palace to be in danger.

Sforza now began to work for Borgia, whom Giuliano would not have at any price, for all he was worth, and proportionate bribes were offered to other possible supporters, among whom Orsini was one of the most active. By thus securing the Sforza party Borgia had fourteen votes, one less than the two-thirds required. The better type of cardinal, such as Carafa or Piccolomini, was no more to be bribed into voting for him than his enemy, Vincula, or the boy Giovanni dei Medici. There was still the Patriarch of Venice, Gherardo, ninety-five years old and almost in a state of senile decay, who was coaxed and bribed into giving the favourite the Papacy.

Late on August 10th Borgia was elected. " We are Pope and Vicar of Christ," he is said to have exclaimed in Latin, with the eager zest with which he habitually threw himself into everything he undertook, beaming with delight at the crowning success of his long efforts. He was sixty-two years of age. Ascanio, with unconscious irony, said that the election was God's work and promised great things for the Church. Borgia answered that God would help him, and he hoped He would give him strength, for he was well aware of his own weakness. His words were undoubtedly sincere. When it was suggested that he should call himself Calixtus, after his uncle, he answered that he chose the name of the unconquered Alexander. Men remarked his eagerness to put on the Papal robes.

Early on the following morning the window of the Conclave was thrown open, the cross appeared, and Alexander VI was proclaimed Pope. The bell of the Capitol was rung and the dregs of Rome rushed to sack the palace of their new sovereign. A few hours later the old St Peter's swallowed an even larger crowd, eager to see the late Cardinal enthroned in the great basilica. A loud cheer went up as he appeared with the Sacred College, and gigantic young Sanseverino, who had been elected, but not proclaimed by Innocent, and had yet been admitted to the Conclave, stepped forward. He was brother to the famous condottiere Gasparo Sanseverino, known as Fracassa, who was to be intimately associated with Cesare Borgia, and a match for him in strength. Picking up the solid figure of the Pope, who was dropping with fatigue, he placed him upon the throne behind the High Altar and proclaimed him. The cardinals then approached and did him homage, with the mixed feelings inevitable on such occasions. Alexander astonished the onlookers by the effusive charm with which he received each of them in turn. On hearing the result young Medici had whispered to Cibo, "We are in the jaws of the wolf. He will devour us if we don't escape." Perhaps he feared he might pay for his unwillingness to support him at the Conclave.

Devout people, on looking back, may have been inclined to see in the elevation of Borgia a proof of the wrath of God, as prophesied by Savanarola, hardly less striking than the invasion of Charles VIII of France. The Florentine envoy says the result caused little joy in Rome, where another Spaniard was not likely to be popular. But this was not the general feeling, even in Rome. Alexander was thought to be just the man needed for the crisis. Indeed, considered from the purely temporal side, he would have made an admirable prince. In judging Alexander we must always remember that this was in no small measure the point of view from which he looked at his great office, and as temporal prince he compares favourably with many of his contemporaries. Able and experienced, a hard worker, a thorough man of the world, a good diplomatist, strong and possessed of a rare charm, dignified, an eloquent and ready speaker, he had much to recommend him. The satisfaction in many quarters was perfectly genuine. Ludovico il Moro was unfeignedly pleased, doubtless thinking that the important part played by his brother in the result augured well for him in Milan. So was Florence, where it was known that Borgia had worked hard to secure the red hat for young Giovanni dei Medici.

POPE ALEXANDER VI, BY PINTURICCHIO

Venice was openly disappointed, but the story that Ferrante of Naples shed tears at the news is highly improbable, though he may have been troubled at the success of a man whom he had vigorously opposed. He soon sent him a letter of hearty congratulation.

Recent experience had made the world at large comparatively indifferent to a Pope with a family. But the flagrant simony, the barefaced bribery by which Alexander secured the tiara was too much even for fifteenth-century Italy. Yet it is noticeable that only the Princes who were his enemies professed to be shocked, realizing how useful the charge might be against him. " As soon as he became Pope, he dispersed and distributed his goods among the poor," say both Burchard and Infessura, so that the remark may be a *mot* current in Rome at the time.

The *possessio*, the procession from the Vatican to the Lateran, and the coronation on August 26th was one of the most splendid ever seen, in every way worthy of the handsome, genial Pope. The streets were lavishly decorated with hangings, triumphal arches, flowers and even altars and statues. The cardinals and other dignitaries vied with each other in display. The Borgia arms, a bull grazing on a gold field, were everywhere. Outside the Palazzo S. Marco was an arch with a bull spouting water from its mouth, nostrils and ears, while from its forehead flowed a stream of delicious wine. On the arches were Latin inscriptions, for which there was always a brisk demand. A protonotary, who erected a *cosa stupenda* of an arch over his house, had the following under the vault in gold letters : " Rome was great under Cæsar, now is she greatest : Alexander VI reigns : Cæsar was a man ; he is a god."[1] Such paganism was a matter of course at this time. Never did it go to such lengths in glorifying a Pope as in the honour done to

[1] Cæsare magna fuit, nunc Roma est maxima : Sextus
Regnat Alexander : ille vir : iste deus.

the Borgia bull in the decoration of the Borgia apartments at the Vatican. It is everywhere. We even see
it deified as Apis. And it is certainly effective.

In appearance at least the man was worthy of the
occasion. " He was riding a horse white as snow, with
brow serene and majestic dignity," wrote Fermo.
Every glance of his brought joy to all beholders,
every look was an omen of good import. Marvellous
was the ease and freedom of his gaze, the nobility of
his face. How could his exuberant vigour, the natural
charm of his bearing, his strength and health fail
to increase the veneration he inspires ? It would
be difficult to find a more genuine tribute to Alexander's personal magnetism, the perfect, healthy
balance of the whole man. His was unmistakably a
lucky face in the eyes of all beholders, and the Borgia
luck soon became a commonplace. Jeronimo Porzio,
who liked to think that the name Borgia was a corruption of his own and that they both traced their descent
from the old Roman family of the Portii, describes
him as tall, with a complexion neither too dark, nor
too fair, his eyes black, his lips rather full. He was
remarkably eloquent and had a well-bred man-of-the-
world's instinctive repulsion for bad manners.

When the procession reached the Lateran, says an
eye-witness, the Pope, half dead with fatigue, lost
consciousness, and there was some delay before he
could enter the basilica. At last, supported by two
cardinals, he advanced to the altar of the chapel
Sancta Sanctorum, but as soon as he took his seat on the
Papal throne, he leant his head upon the shoulder
of Cardinal Riario and fainted away. Water was
sprinkled on his face, but it was some time before he
came round.

This is the first we hear of the fainting fits to which
Alexander was subject, as he probably had been when
cardinal. Burchard often records these attacks, from
which, however, he speedily recovered. During the

three successive Corpus Domini celebrations (1498–1500) he was taken ill, and in 1500 he was obliged to sit through the Mass, which he asked to be finished as quickly as possible, without his mitre. Cesare often came forward to help him on these occasions. This weakness may help to explain his wish, often mentioned in Burchard, to make ceremonies, and still more, sermons, as short as possible. It may also account for the mistakes in the ritual which he sometimes made and which deeply distressed his Master of Ceremonies. At Easter, 1498, Burchard found a consecrated wafer which the Pope had dropped in front of the altar. On another occasion he dropped a fragment of the wafer, for which Burchard looked in vain after the ceremony, coming to the conclusion that he must have inadvertently crushed it with his foot.

The period of the Conclave was always marked by an increase in crimes of violence. No less than two hundred and twenty murders had been committed during the last days of Innocent and the days of *sedia vacante*. The new Pope's vigour in putting down crime was a welcome change. He had the house of a murderer destroyed by the mob and the culprit's brother executed on the day after the crime. Such exemplary justice made a great impression. He appointed officials to visit the prisons and four commissioners to hear complaints, while he himself gave audience to all who had special cause for complaint on Tuesdays.

Indeed, with his sanguine temperament, he began with excellent intentions. Ambassadors report that he meant to reform the Papal court, and he declared that he would restore peace to Italy and, following in the footsteps of his uncle, unite Christendom against the Turk. For a moment it looked as if he meant to keep his family away from Rome. Cesare was still at Pisa, studying law. On his father's election he did not come to Rome, but was sent to Spoleto. During his stay at Pisa he met both Lorenzo dei Medici and his son Piero, and on October 15th we find him writing to Piero, recommending his friend Remolines, who felt that he had no vocation for the Church, for a Chair in Canon Law at Pisa. Piero saw the wisdom of propitiating the son of the new Pope, who declared himself ready to help him in any way he could in Rome, and Remolines was given the post.

Nature, however, soon asserted herself. A great crisis more than once galvanized Alexander into forming admirable resolutions, which he proclaimed to all the world with his habitual impulsiveness and set about putting into effect with an almost boyish enthusiasm. The most that can be said for them is that they show, at bottom, that he knew that his way of life was not an ideal one for a Pope. One account says that, while he was being carried up to the Vatican from St Peter's after his election, he talked to Ascanio about seeing that he changed his way of life. But as soon as the novelty wore off he recovered and resumed his normal habits. Everything was as before, and his resolutions went the way of most of their kind.

It would have been too much to expect a father so affectionate to keep his children away from Rome, even had public opinion expected him to do so. People were beginning to understand that it was well for a Pope to have relatives round him, since he needed men upon whom he could depend absolutely amid the intriguing, ever-shifting world of the Curia. Rome was even growing accustomed to a Papal family, though no one quite realized the lengths to which Alexander's paternal affection would carry him. An envoy writes that ten papacies would not suffice for the swarm of relatives and Spaniards that flocked round him. This is, however, an exaggeration. Every new Pope brought a number of his friends into the Vatican. Alexander, being a Spaniard, naturally brought a

number of Spaniards. Both his secretaries and his
datary were at first Spaniards. But in later days it
cannot be said that he showed undue favour to his
own countrymen. Had they been Italians, nothing
would have been said. But the Romans characteristically reacted against a fresh invasion of Catalans.

Alexander's nepotism soon began to show itself.
At his very first Consistory he gave Cesare, the youthful Bishop of Pampeluna, his own great See of
Valencia. Ferdinand, angry that one of the wealth-
iest bishoprics in his dominions should thus be
treated as an appanage of the Borgias, long opposed
the appointment, about which he had not been
consulted. The Pope also bestowed a red hat upon
his sister's son, Juan Borgia-Lançol, the Bishop of
Monreale.

Then there was the question of the marriage of
Lucrezia, which was very near the Pope's heart. His
first idea had been to find a home for her in Spain.
Marriage was then purely a matter of business or
politics or both. Lucrezia was quite ready to accept
the husband chosen for her by her father, with her
easygoing good nature, probably more ready than
most of the girls of her day. She was but a child of
eleven. All she expected was a settlement that would
satisfy her ambition. Nor was her life in the Palazzo
S. Maria in Porticu likely to give her an exalted view
of the state of matrimony. She must have been a
frequent witness of the attentions of her father to
the lovely Farnese, whose golden hair rivalled her
own.

This, the year of his accession, was the year of the
birth of Laura, the first and probably the last child
to be born to a future Pope within the precincts of the
Vatican. For the Palazzo S. Maria in Porticu stood on
the left of it, till it was swept away to make room for
Bernini's arcades. As early as December, 1493, there
was talk of betrothing Laura to Astorre Manfredi of

Faenza, who was to cross swords with Cesare and, in an evil hour, trust him. Gregorivius tells the story.

The Florentine ambassador, Lorenzo Pucci, writes to Piero dei Medici what he has heard from Cardinal Farnese about this " daughter of the Pope, niece of the Cardinal and putative daughter of Orsini," and in the course of his letter gives a vivid picture of Giulia and Lucrezia. On Christmas Eve he went with Farnese to attend Papal Vespers and, while waiting for the Pope, they paid Giulia a visit. She had been washing her head and was sitting by the fire with Lucrezia and Adriana. They all received him with loud demonstrations of joy. " Madama Giulia insisted on my sitting beside her. . . . I reminded her how much I owed her ladyship for what she had done for me. . . . She answered that such trifles did not need thanks, adding that she hoped to do even more for me on more important occasions, as I should see when the time came. Then Madama Adriana answered that I might rest assured that it was not to Messer Antonio, or to his efforts, but to Signora Giulia that I was indebted for the benefices I had received.

" I pretended to believe her in order not to contradict her, and I thanked her ladyship again. Then Madama Giulia questioned me closely about Messer Puccio, remarking : ' We will ask him here and though, in spite of all our efforts, we could not get what he wanted when he was here, we shall succeed now without any difficulty.' . . . She also wanted me to see the child ; it is already a good size and, I think, like the Pope, so that it may really be said to be his own. (This remark is in Latin.) The Signora Giulia has grown fatter and become very beautiful. She undid her hair in my presence and had her hair and her head dressed. It came right down to her feet in a way I had never seen before. She wears a large cap of the finest linen, and over it a net that produced the effect of smoke, ornamented with gold threads, so that she really looked like the sun. I would have given a good deal to have had you there with me, so that you could have found out what you have long wished to know. She had on a dress lined in the Neapolitan style, as also had Signora Lucrezia, who soon went to change hers, returning shortly afterwards in one almost entirely of purple satin, also lined." It is clear that Giulia's beauty completely put Lucrezia in the shade.

Such an atmosphere was not calculated to raise the moral tone of an impressionable girl who was the illegitimate daughter of the Pope; but at least she learnt the art of pleasing, of making herself agreeable to the visitors in an admirable school. These would be mostly priests, more pressing than ever in their attentions now that Alexander had so much to give, for the influence of his daughter over him was well known. In 1494, when she was only fourteen, their envoy informed the Gonzagas of Mantua that he hears that Lucrezia has the readiest access to the Pope. She has ability above her years and most of those who want anything go through that door. They should apply to her. She had inherited her father's bright, happy temperament. Her charm is universally admitted, and doubtless did not a little to increase the instinctive jealousy felt for her by her own sex.

It does not seem that Lucrezia was highly educated, or that she shared the intellectual interests of the great ladies of the best and most cultured Italian courts. Living as she did in surroundings where Latin was the lingua franca of the priests of all ranks and all nations who frequented the Vatican, she naturally picked up a smattering of it. She spoke Spanish as well as Italian, for the Borgias habitually used their native tongue among themselves. Two of her letters to Cardinal Bembo are in Spanish. The biographer of Bayard, who met her at Ferrara in 1512 and was duly captivated, assures us that she spoke Spanish, Greek, Italian,

47

French and a little Latin of the purest quality ; also,
that she wrote poems in these tongues. Obviously
this is a chivalrous exaggeration. The Greek we may
well doubt, and the verse, if she wrote any, has not
been left for the cooler judgment of a more critical
posterity. Her letters suggest a rather commonplace
intelligence. They cannot compare with those of her
rival and sister-in-law, Isabella d'Este, the Marchesana
of Mantua. But in the more strictly feminine accom-
plishments she could hold her own with the best.
She was an excellent dancer, as we should expect,
considering her father's passion for dancing. She
could sing and play, accompanying herself on the lute,
as could most educated women of the day, and her
embroidery was long admired at Ferrara. Also she
was genuinely religious, like Vannozza, and in later
life even *dévote*.

Lucrezia was betrothed in 1491 at the age of eleven,
by no means early for one of her rank. The first
husband chosen for her was Don Cherubino Juan
de Centelles, of Valencia, brother of the Conde de
Oliva. He was in Valencia and they never met.
Considering that her dowry was to consist of 100,000
sols Valencian, it is not surprising that she was looked
upon as something of a prize. This sum was to include
the trousseau and to be paid partly in jewels. In it
were counted the 11,000 left her by Don Pedro Luis
and another 8000 given her by Cesare and Gioffrè.
The bride was to be conveyed to Valencia at Rodrigo's
expense within a year of the signing of the contract.

For some unknown reason this marriage fell
through. Gasparo de Procida, another Spaniard,
was chosen for her later in the same year. His father,
the Count of Aversa, lived at Aversa, in the kingdom
of Naples, but the son was also in Valencia. The
contract was regularly signed.

When he became Pope Alexander felt that he could
look higher. He might even give his children the

48

positions his ambition craved for them in Italy. Ascanio, to whom he owed the tiara, was now all-powerful with him, and it was due to his influence that for a moment he turned a willing ear to Ludovico Sforza, who was proposing to call Charles VIII into Italy to claim the throne of Naples as the heir of the Angevins. He was thus about to bring disaster upon the peninsula in order to prevent Ferrante of Naples from supporting the rightful heir to the Duchy, Gian Galeazzo, for he was determined to oust his nephew and himself become Duke of Milan. Gian Galeazzo had been married to Ferrante's grand-daughter, Isabella, who was appealing to him for help.

Giuliano della Rovere, who was, if possible, more afraid of Ascanio than of the Pope himself, had withdrawn to his bishopric at Ostia, where Giuliano da S. Gallo had built him the formidable castle we can still admire. This was in December, 1492.

Then the Pope turned again to Naples. There was even talk of the young Bishop of Valencia throwing up the priesthood, marrying a Neapolitan and being created Prince of Salerno. The Ferrarese ambassador describes a visit he paid to Cesare about this time at his house in Trastevere. He was just starting out hunting in lay costume, that is to say, his clothes were of silk and he was armed. " He had only a tiny *clerica*, like a simple tonsured priest. We talked a good deal as we rode together. I am on very intimate terms with him." Doubtless Cesare's manner gave many others the idea that he was on intimate terms with them. " He is possessed of quite exceptional abilities. He carries himself like the son of a prince; he is of a remarkably cheerful, happy temper, always apparently in good spirits. His manner is admirable and he cuts a far better and more distinguished figure than his brother, the Duke of Gandia, who is, however, well endowed. The archbishop has never had the slightest inclination for the priesthood, but his benefices bring him in more than sixteen thousand ducats." In the case of the suggested marriage coming off, these were to go to his brother Gioffrè.

Cesare owed not a little of his popularity to the bright, sunny charm he shared with his sister. Under it, however, lay a much stronger character than that of Juan and genuine ability, which were already showing themselves. He took no pains to conceal his dislike for the career which had been thrust upon him against his will.

There was certainly a proposal, welcomed by Ferrante, that Gioffrè should marry one of his daughters. But the Pope again changed his mind and joined the League, of which Venice and some of the smaller states were members. Ferrante, the last of the old generation of peace-makers and the most far-sighted statesman then living in Italy, wrote both to Alexander and to Ludovico, warning them of the danger of disturbing peace by calling in a powerful foreigner whom they would be quite unable to control. In a letter to Ferdinand of Aragon he describes Alexander in terms which come ill from such a man with his record of cruelty, treachery and debauchery. Alexander, he says, leads a life that is a scandal and abominated by all. He shows no respect for his throne. "His one aim is to aggrandize his children at all costs. Fraud and dissimulation mark all his dealings, for such is his character."

Ascanio was anxious to strike while the iron was hot. A match was soon arranged with a member of his own house. This was Giovanni Sforza, lord of Pesaro in the Romagna, himself a bastard, the son of Costanzo of Pesaro. He was twenty-six, just twice the age of his bride and a widower. But all was not yet plain sailing. There were rumours of another Spaniard. Not till February, 1493, was the contract signed, for there was still the other contract, duly signed and sealed, and legally binding, to be got over. Gasparo da Procida, now in Rome with his father, did not accept his fate without a struggle. He blustered, like a true Catalan, saying that he would lay his cause before all the courts of Europe. However, he ended by accepting the poor compensation of 3000 ducats, and undertook, in writing, not to marry for a year. Possibly he hoped there might still be a chance for his suit.

The news of the signing of the contract was received with wild rejoicing in Pesaro. Sforza gave a splendid banquet in his castle. During the ball that followed the guests, led by Mons. Scaltès, the Papal representative, danced right through the streets of the town, to the delight of its inhabitants.

The bridegroom made his official entry into Rome on June 9th, by the Porta del Popolo. His first wife was a sister of Elisabetta Gonzaga, Duchess of Urbino, and of the Marquis of Mantua ; the sisters were married on the same day. Now the Gonzagas lent him jewels for the occasion, as it was of the utmost importance that he should impress the onlookers in a manner worthy of an event so auspicious. Lucrezia watched the entry from a balcony. Giovanni bowed gallantly to her as he passed, and she returned his greeting with one of her most winning smiles.

The wedding on June 12th was a great affair of state and occasioned no little scandal in many quarters. Sforza, who had the family belief in astrology, insisted that the ceremony should not take place till the astrologers found that the favourable moment had come. The Pope was annoyed, but Ascanio was firm.

All the officials and their wives, the ambassadors and everybody of importance in Rome, received invitations. As on the notorious occasion at Siena, only the wives and daughters were admitted. The men had to wait an hour before the doors were opened for them and then the ceremony was over. Fifty silver bowls of sweetmeats were thrown, amid great merriment, into the laps of the women, especially the pretty ones, "and this to the honour and glory of Almighty God and the Church of Rome". A number of ladies were present, including Giulia's sister-in-law, the Countess of Pitigliano, Adriana Orsini and Giulia herself, "about whom there is so much talk," says Boccaccio, the Ferrarese envoy. They dined at the same table as the Pope and the cardinals, each of whom had a lady beside him. Afterwards the ladies danced, "a worthy comedy" was given and there was much playing and singing. "We spent the whole night there," adds Boccaccio, who enjoyed himself thoroughly. "I leave it to Your Excellency to judge whether well or ill." The chief ambassadors of the League, France, Milan and Venice, were also present. Burchard, who was not, hears that the comedy was scandalous. To a bishop from Germany it may well have been. Not a word is said of Lucrezia's brothers.

The Pope actually accompanied the couple back to the palace of S. Maria in Porticu and played the part of a good father of the day in all that followed, "and many things are reported which I am not writing down and which are either false, or, if true, incredible", says Burchard. It did not take long for Alexander to make it plain that the Pope of sixty-three in no way differed from the gay cardinal of twenty-eight. Such entertainments soon became a regular feature of the life at the Vatican.

Ferrante of Naples made every effort to win the Pope, who was becoming alarmed at his threatening attitude and at the closeness of his relations with Cardinal della Rovere at Ostia. Once, when Alexander went out to spend the day at a villa near Ostia, a gun was fired by way of a salute of welcome on his approach. So alarmed was he, thinking that it was the beginning of an attack upon him by Vincula, that he rode back to Rome at full speed. Hence, when

Ferrante suggested a marriage between Gioffrè and his own illegitimate granddaughter, Sancia, the natural daughter of Alfonso, Duke of Calabria, he jumped at the idea, especially as Gioffrè was to be made Prince of Squillace and Count of Cariati. He was only thirteen and the betrothal was not to be made public till Christmas. Great amusement was caused when Ferrante's second son, Don Federigo, who had come to Rome from Ostia, acted as proxy for Sancia and accepted the ring from Gioffrè. The result was a reconciliation with Vincula, who came to Rome, dined with the Pope and had all his privileges confirmed, receiving permission to live out of Rome, if he chose. It is inconceivable that the fiery cardinal could have remained there in peace while his enemy was Pope.

In this same month of August, Juan, Duke of Gandia, sailed for Spain to marry Donna Maria Enriquez, taking with him a quantity of jewels upon the mounting of which the jewellers of Rome had been busy for months. The Pope meant that he should appear in a style that would impress his new relatives.

There was still Cesare, the unwilling priest, who must have watched his younger brother's brilliant departure with bitter jealousy, to be provided for and Alexander was not long in taking the obvious step. He was made Cardinal on September 20th of this year. The Sacred College was not pleased. One account says that when the Pope announced what he was going to do, the cardinals got up and left in a body. It was not enough that Sixtus IV had by a bull of October 17th, 1480, and by another of two years later, openly proclaimed Cesare's parentage and freed him from any difficulties it might cause. A bull of Alexander's own now declared that he was born in wedlock to Vannozza during the lifetime of her husband, Domenico d'Arignano, but by a second secret bull, addressed also to Cesare, he declared that the first bull was issued to prevent any injury his birth might do him. The Pope there says that he was not responsible for the statement that he was born in wedlock. The bull was found by Woodward.[1] Cesare was thus guarded in every possible way.

Cesare was just eighteen. The other nomination which awakened universal comment was that of Alessandro Farnese, Giulia's brother, who had, however, some position in the Church. Ippolito d'Este, who was also given the hat, was only fifteen.

Thus, within a year of his accession, Alexander had settled all his children satisfactorily.

The Pope had been called on to make a momentous decision in May, little though he probably thought of it at the time. In March Columbus had returned to Lisbon from his great voyage of discovery. Spain and Portugal at once began to quarrel about these new territories and appealed to Alexander. Then it was that he drew his famous line through the globe a hundred leagues west of the Azores and assigned all lands west of it to Spain on condition that she set about converting the natives.

[1] *Cesare Borgia*, p. 47.

CHAPTER V

ALEXANDER VI AND CHARLES VIII OF FRANCE
(1494–1495)

It was left for Alexander to bear the brunt of the quarrel over the disputed succession to the throne of Naples. Charles VIII of France, the heir of the Angevins, was a young man of twenty-three, so badly educated that he could hardly read, ungainly and vicious, but fired with a passion to become a great conqueror, above all to lead Christendom in a crusade against the Turk. Meanwhile there was Naples, which might be taken on the way. The cruelty and treachery with which Ferrante and Alfonso had put down the rebellious barons had raised up a host of enemies against them. The Neapolitan exiles at the French court, like the Sanseverino, urged him to seize the chance. He was soon proclaiming that his rights to Naples were as good as his claim to France. The project roused no enthusiasm among his courtiers, but he clung to his dream with the characteristic obstinacy of a weak man.

As Naples was a fief of the Church the support of the Pope was of the utmost importance, and his attitude at first encouraged Charles to think that he might count upon it. But Alexander can never really have hesitated when it came to the point. Now, as always, he stood by Spain and, in spite of differences between them, Ferdinand had no desire to see Ferrante replaced by Charles. When Ferrante died in January, 1494, the Pope at once granted investiture to Alfonso, as Innocent had promised to do : he even admonished Charles not to disturb the peace of Christendom when war against the Turk was the first duty of a Christian prince. After the marriage of Gioffrè, what else was to be expected? The devoted father reaped his reward. The young Prince of Squillace was given an income of 10,000 ducats, as well as a *condotta*, a military command, worth another 10,000, while Alexander was to allow him a similar sum. Gandia was to receive estates worth 12,000 a year, and a *condotta* bringing in 33,000 ducats, which was to cease with the Pope's life. He was also to be made Captain-General of the Church. Cesare, who was granted benefices worth a mere 4000 ducats, noted the rising fortunes of his brother, whom he felt to be his inferior in the profession for which he longed, with ever-growing jealousy. He had none of the kindly good nature of Alexander, who was genuinely fond of his own brother, Don Pedro Luis, and could take delight in his success. This Gandia was clearly destined to rival, since he had been chosen to perpetuate the family. Nor had he Alexander's taste for an ecclesiastical career. Cesare's admission to the minor orders, all that he ever received, can only have served to increase his bitterness. He showed himself as reluctant as ever to take part in ecclesiastical ceremonies.

Burchard had the time of his life when he went to assist Cardinal Monreale, the Pope's nephew and right-hand man, at Naples in the coronation of Alfonso II, whom he duly instructed in the part he had to play. Three days later, on May 11, Gioffrè was married to Sancia d'Aragona. Burchard gives the most intimate details of the undressing and bedding of the young couple, the King and the Legates staying and chatting in the room the whole time. The thoroughly sophisticated Sancia, who had enjoyed all the freedom of what was probably the most corrupt court in Italy, already felt nothing but contempt for the boy, some years younger than herself, who had been given her as husband for political reasons.

It is said that for a moment Charles VIII thought of abandoning his expedition and even recalled some of the troops which had started. Then it was that Giuliano della Rovere appeared upon the scene. When in February Alexander formally recognized Alfonso, his fury knew no limits. Once again he withdrew to Ostia and then took ship to France, where his appointment as Legate had been confirmed, and hastened to the Court. The effect of such a personality, armed with all the power of a Prince of the Church, upon a character like that of Charles can be imagined. The vehemence and authority of this fatal instrument of all the woes of Italy, to quote Guicciardini, soon fanned to a flame his flagging spirit. But it was not of Naples that Vincula was thinking. He was determined to bring the King to Rome, make him call a Council and depose the man he hated above all others. Nor is there any doubt that he was supported by a considerable body in the Sacred College, among whom were to be found the best of the cardinals, such as Carafa, who were actuated by higher motives.

The advance began in the autumn. On September 9th Charles reached Asti with S. Pietro in Vincula, Ludovico il Moro of Milan and Ercole d'Este, Duke of Ferrara, in his train. Here the King fell ill of small-pox. " The snake has its tail in Italy," wrote the able Florentine ambassador at the French court, who had seen all along that the *impresa* was inevitable. " It is the Italians who are pulling it with all their might. Ludovico would have liked to defeat Naples and remain cock of the walk, but rage led him into the trap "; and he was soon forced to realize, as old Ferrante had warned him, that the *impresa* would end in universal disaster. The French began to talk of making Milan their objective. Louis d'Orléans, who was to succeed Charles as Louis XII, even styled himself Duke of Milan, claiming the Duchy through his grandmother, Valentina Visconti.

The Italians now had a taste of what war could mean in the sack of Rapallo by d'Orléans. The condottieri, professional soldiers who were almost as careful of the lives of their enemies as of their own, seeing that dead men could pay no ransom, were as horrified at the fury of the attack and the ruthless slaughter as the civilians. Charles entered Florence as a conqueror, lance in rest, and Savonarola, who was already beginning to speak freely about the Papal court to his crowded audiences in the Duomo, regarded his coming as a fulfilment of his own prophecies—the Cyrus who was to ride through Italy without breaking a lance and without meeting any serious resistance.

Late in the autumn Charles began his advance on Rome, demanding a free passage through the Pope's dominions for his army. He refused to receive the Papal envoy, saying that he meant to negotiate with him in person in Rome, where he proposed to pass Christmas ; and Alexander was warned that there was talk of a Council and of his own deposition. He was much perturbed at the news.

Luck was against the Pope. When the Sultan delayed sending the subsidy for Djem, Alexander wrote to tell him that Charles was about to seize Djem and embark upon a crusade. He even begged him to use his influence to keep Venice quiet. Bajazet saw the danger. Not only did he write four letters in Turkish for Alexander, which he gave to his messenger, but he sent an envoy of his own with the 40,000 ducats. By ill-luck they were both captured at Sinigaglia by Giovanni della Rovere, Prefect of Rome, and lord of Sinigaglia. He sent them to his brother, Giuliano, who lost no time in publishing the letters. The Sultan readily complied with the Pope's requests, but suggested that Djem might be delivered from the miseries of this life and his soul sent to another and better world, where he would be at peace, to prevent his falling into the hands of the French. If the Pope consented, the Sultan would send him on receipt of the body 300,000 ducats with which to buy estates for his children. Obviously he was well supplied with information about His Holiness. Other princes in Italy were quite ready to turn to the infidel in time of trouble, but the revelation of the intimate terms upon which the Head of the Church was corresponding with him came as a great shock to the Christian world, more especially outside Italy.

Then the French actually captured Giulia Bella and her Duenna, if we may so call her, Adriana Orsini, when they were on their way to visit Cardinal Alessandro Farnese at Viterbo. Charles refused to see them. Giulia wrote that she was well treated, but begged Alexander to send the 3000 ducats demanded for them by their captor. The Pope was in a great state of agitation and complained to the King of the insult. Their release was soon effected, and they were escorted back to Rome by four hundred French troops, who must have thoroughly enjoyed the incident.

Il Moro, like other Italians of the day, had little of the chivalrous feeling of the countrymen of Bayard towards women. He was indignant at Giulia being thus set free, saying that Alexander might have been made to grant anything, so long as the women were prisoners. He informed Trotti, the envoy of the d'Este, that the Pope went out to meet them dressed in a black doublet embroidered with gold and a handsome baldric in the Spanish style, wearing sword and dagger. " He also wore Spanish boots and a velvet cap." And he asked the ambassador, laughing, what he thought of it.

Probably there is not a word of truth in the story. Alexander was a favourite butt of Ludovico, who would say whatever he liked about him, even in full

Council. Thus he told Trotti that he was hourly expecting news that he had been arrested and beheaded and repeated stories like the following. The Pope had three women brought to him; one had been a nun in Valencia, another was a Castilian and the third a lovely young bride of fifteen or sixteen.

The mere fact that such things could be said and half believed speaks volumes. Also it shows the kind of gossip to which Alexander's habits, combined with his success, his ability and his supreme indifference to public opinion, laid him open. Thus in 1496 it was widely rumoured that the Duke of Gandia had brought him back a handsome woman from Spain for his harem.

The Pope was in great perplexity, quite unable to decide what to do. The surrender of Ostia, Vincula's town, to the Colonna, who already controlled much of the Campagna, increased his troubles. Ascanio, after Cesare had been sent as a hostage, came to treat with him. On December 14th he scandalized Burchard as he has done many later writers, by talking earnestly with him right through Mass, even after the elevation, remaining seated when he should have stood up. Long habit may have made Alessandro a little indifferent about forms, as it sometimes does excellent priests of all denominations, but the circumstances were so exceptional that we should not attach too much importance to this single incident. The negotiations failed, as the Pope said that he would lose his life and his crown rather than be false to Alfonso of Naples, for Charles insisted that he was to be recognized as the rightful king of the Regno. It soon became clear that the Neapolitan army could make no serious defence of Rome and it was suggested that the Pope should withdraw under its protection. Plans were already drawn up, but ultimately the Pope decided to await the coming of Charles, who insisted that his intentions were wholly peaceable.

On December 19th he addressed the Roman people, saying that he knew they would not submit to the dictates of a foreigner, and he hoped that, like himself, they would rather die than yield. Overawed by the police, they declared themselves ready to follow him. But they only laughed at another speech he made them. Indeed, the magistrates threatened to open the gates to the French, if he refused to do so. Then the Pope broke out into contemptuous abuse of the Italians, soldiers good for nothing but a review. His Spaniards would show them how they should behave ; France owed her easy success to the poor quality of the people. This was perfectly true. The Italians of that time were quite incapable morally of standing up either to Spain or France. The King should pay for having come, he assured the French ambassador. All Italy was behind him. Alexander's impulsiveness and his irritation under the difficulties of his position come out clearly in such outbursts as these, which soon became familiar to the diplomatic corps.

Cardinal Monreale duly saw Ferrante, Duke of Calabria, off from the Porta S. Lorenzo with his Neapolitans, and then rode post-haste out of the Porta del Popolo to Bracciano, the great castle of the Orsini, who had now joined the enemy, to welcome Charles. Burchard was also sent to arrange the order of his coming, but Charles disappointed him by saying that he wished for no ceremony. Charles then called to him and made him ride with him for a good four miles, plying him ceaselessly with questions about the Pope and the Cardinal of Valencia and other matters, as he ambled beside him on his episcopal mule through the deep winter mud, which Burchard found it hard to answer.

On the advice of the astrologers the King had chosen the last day of 1494 for his entry. The long stream of soldiers began to file down the Via Lata—now the Corso—at three, and the last of them had not passed

61

before nine. They made a formidable appearance, especially by the flickering light of the torches, as they splashed through the mud. No such army and, indeed, no foreign army had been seen in Rome within living memory. There were a number of bonfires and the French lilies were on most of the houses. Charles himself entered the Porta del Popolo about seven and was given the keys of the city. As he passed there were loud cries of " Francia ! Francia ! Colonna ! Colonna ! Vincula ! Vincula ! " For beside the King rode Giuliano della Rovere, thirsting for revenge, and disappointed Cardinal Sforza, to whom Alexander owed his tiara, with other opposition cardinals following. It was the thirty-six big guns that most impressed the spectators, far more than the Swiss and Germans and Gascons, the hundred Scotch cross-bowmen, or the 5000 heavy cavalry, the flower of the chivalry of France. Once more Charles was in full armour, lance in rest. He took up his residence in the Palazzo S. Marco, the guns being parked in the square in front. The troops were the finest Tedaldini had ever seen, but the King was the ugliest man upon whom he had clapped eyes, small, hunchbacked and altogether hideous ; how different from their Pope, thought the Romans, who set much store by grace and beauty. The French army was quartered all over the city, except on the right bank of the Tiber, the Vatican quarter. The men gave endless trouble, plundering and murdering wholesale. Both Vannozza and Burchard were robbed.

Alexander, seriously alarmed, shut himself up in the Castel S. Angelo. The fall of a large portion of the upper wall was looked upon as a divine warning by the Romans. He steadily refused to grant the King's demands or to hand over the castle, though the guns were twice trained on it. Charles had by now abandoned any idea of calling a Council, if, indeed, he had ever really intended to do so. His success was raising up too many enemies against him, chief of whom were Ludovico il Moro and Ferdinand of Spain, for him to be able to dispense with the Pope's aid. He was not of the stuff of which reformers of the Church are made. Ludovico Sforza remarked that he had better reform himself before reforming other people. Even Commines saw that such talk was merely a weapon of Alexander's enemies, one of the chief of whom, Ascanio Sforza, had profited next to the Pope himself by the simoniacal character of his election. The Pope was adamant in refusing to grant Charles the investiture of Naples.

However, terms were arranged by January 15th, the King being as relieved as the Pope, and Charles came to reside in the Vatican. The meeting was to be informal. The King was in the gardens when the Pope appeared from the covered way leading to S. Angelo. Charles knelt twice and the Pope pretended not to see him. When he was about to kneel for the third time the Pope prevented him, removed his mitre and kissed him. Before the reception in the Camera del Papagallo Alexander had another of his fainting attacks, several of which are recorded during these anxious weeks, but he quickly recovered. He celebrated Mass for his guest in St Peter's, making a number of mistakes which the perturbed Master of the Ceremonies let pass uncorrected so as not to draw attention to them, probably because he was again feeling unwell. Charles made due submission to the Vicar of Christ, but he was careful to assert himself. He had received the first deputation of cardinals that waited on him in Rome, among whom was Cesare, very haughtily, remaining seated. On this occasion he should have taken his place with them. Instead, he not only kept them waiting an hour, but remained standing by the Pope during the whole ceremony.

As a memorial of his stay in Rome he founded the Church of S. Trinità, above the Piazza di Spagna.

The King's change of attitude awakened great indignation among the opposition cardinals. Ascanio left Rome at once and Vincula refused to be comforted, though the King twice endeavoured to console him in person, and the Pope restored all his offices to him, as well as Ostia. He declined to reside in Rome with his enemy and left in high dudgeon with Charles when he started for Naples on the 25th.

The King had two valuable hostages. Before him, under a strong escort, had started Djem, whom the Pope had reluctantly been forced to surrender. Alexander had engaged Pinturicchio to begin his work in the Borgia apartments in the Vatican by the end of 1492. There we can see the melancholy, impassive face of the Sultan's brother in the fresco of St Catherine of Siena, where is also the portrait of Gandia in Turkish costume. Like his brother, whom he much resembled in general appearance, he looks decidedly a Spaniard, with his Spanish beard. Once, when the Pope went in procession to visit the Lateran, Gandia rode right through Rome in Eastern costume, even turbaned, beside Djem, in front of the Cross, and they visited the Church together. One likes to think that he had been posing for Pinturicchio. St Catherine in the same fresco is generally held to be Lucrezia. Cesare is not there as a priest, but he is often said to be the Emperor Maximilian, presiding over the group.

On the left of the King also rode Cesare, who was to remain with him at his royal pleasure, being treated according to his state and dignity, but none the less a hostage. On the second day they reached Velletri. The next morning the nineteen-year-old cardinal was nowhere to be found. He had slipped out during the night, mounted a horse which was waiting for him outside the walls and ridden post-haste to Rome.

This flight is the first example we have of Valentino's way of doing things. He acted with the careful, deliberate, silent preparation and attention to detail which were later to make him so sinister and inscrutable a figure in popular imagination. He had no intention of remaining with Charles and probably he was acting in concert with his father, as he was often to do later. He had even arranged that his baggage-waggons should disappear almost as soon as they had left Rome. He took refuge with a friend, Antonio Flores, an auditor of the Rota, but quitted Rome at once in order to avoid complications. Charles was annoyed, but he accepted the apologies sent him by the Pope and the City. Cesare went to Spoleto for a while.

Back in Rome, he once more made his presence felt in characteristic fashion. When some of the Switzers in the service of the French were about to leave, they were attacked on St Peter's Square by the Spaniards, with whom they had long been at feud. A number, including a woman, were killed and more wounded, while others were taken to the Vatican and stripped and robbed. The remainder were at last got safely away by the Pope's troops. This was Valentino's method of reprisal for the 800 ducats' worth of property which the Swiss had carried off from his mother.

With the conquest of Naples we are not concerned. It was the crowning success of Charles VIII's triumphant march through Italy " with a piece of chalk (to mark the billets) and spurs "; for, as Savonarola had prophesied, he had met with no serious resistance. Here Djem, who was lodged in the Castel Capuano, died in February. It was persistently rumoured that the Pope, or Cesare, had had him poisoned. This rumour is entirely in accordance with the times. Anyone who has read something of the history of the Renaissance knows that a person of position had only to die, when someone to whom his death was an advantage would at once be accused of poisoning him, especially if the death had been sudden. Ludovico il

Moro was accused, with more probability, of having poisoned his nephew Galeazzo; and Giangaleazzo Sforza of poisoning his mother, Bianca Maria Visconti, as well as his fiancée, Dorotea Gonzaga. Many other instances could easily be adduced, and naturally, as the reputation of the Borgias became more sinister, especially after the turn of the century, such rumours became more frequent till at one time they created something like a panic. The probably mythical slow Borgia poison must have been wonderful indeed if it could prove fatal a month after it had been administered to Djem by Cesare.

Burchard says that " Gem " died from eating or drinking something that did not agree with him. The Mantuan envoy believed that he died a natural death, though many people said that he had been given something to drink, an ominous phrase that crops up only too frequently in later despatches from Rome. The Council of Ten at Venice, who were no friends of Alexander, wrote to their ambassador at Constantinople that Djem had a bad throat when he left Rome and then the cold went to his chest. This sounds reasonable in the case of one who had made a long journey in winter after a lengthy confinement. Even Ludovico il Moro had no doubt on the subject. Nor is it easy to see what the Pope had to gain by Djem dying in the power of Charles.

When Charles was compelled to retreat post-haste in face of the dangers threatening him from the new League, in which Ludovico Sforza and Ferdinand the Catholic were the prime movers, he eagerly pressed for another interview with the Pope as he passed through Rome. This Alexander had no intention of granting. To avoid it he left for Orvieto, of which Cesare was Governor, with the whole Papal court, escorted by a large force. He invited Charles to take up his residence in the Vatican, declaring that he had left it in order not to incommode his guest in his free enjoyment of his palace. When the French army had made good its retreat by the hard-fought battle of Fornovo, after which Ludovico Sforza once more betrayed his friends and allied himself with Charles, the Pope returned to Rome.

One of Cesare's first acts as Governor of Orvieto had been to make some appointments there which were outside his province. Protests were made and Cesare's reply, which is quoted by Yriarte,[1] already shows the tact and the respect for the rights of his subjects, which were to make his memory long cherished in the Romagna. He addresses the officials as his very dear friends and ends: " If at any time it should happen that I do anything to violate your customs, statutes or privileges, rest assured that it is because I have been led into error by some interested person, for I am a man and therefore liable to be deceived and make mistakes." He even signs himself " C. Cardinalis Valentinus . . . qui vos ex corde amat."

[1] *César Borgia*, Vol. I, p. 97.

CHAPTER VI

THE MURDER OF THE DUKE OF GANDIA (1497)

THE Pope now set about gathering his family round him. Henceforth a gathering of the Borgia clan, if Cesare were present, generally foreshadowed a family tragedy. Lucrezia was usually in Rome, where her influence with the Pope was well known. Never was there seen a more affectionate father, " un più carnale uomo ". The four new cardinals, all Spaniards, among whom was Juan Borgia, nephew of Monreale, visited her immediately after their official calls on the rest of the Sacred College and were entertained by her. In 1494 the Mantuan envoy had warned the Gonzagas that money, not letters, were needed with her. It was to her that the Pope asked Pesaro to give the letter stating that Sigismondo Gonzaga would pay 15,000 ducats for his red hat for safe keeping. Hence she was not pleased when the Pope sent for Gioffrè and his wife, whom he had never seen, for it was rumoured that it was for her looks that Sancia was being summoned to Rome. Her sister-in-law might prove a dangerous rival.

Lucrezia was to receive her. She rode out to the Porta S. Giovanni, preceded by a couple of pages, one of whose horses had trappings of gold brocade, the other of crimson velvet, and accompanied by a dozen ladies. She met the pair outside the gate and gave them a charmingly affectionate welcome. The ambassadors and other officials were waiting by the Lateran church. Here the principals and a few ladies dismounted and offered up a prayer, after which the

68

procession reformed, headed by twenty-eight carts marked with the arms and loaded with the luggage of Squillace and his bride. The two girls rode together, escorted by the Spanish and Neapolitan ambassadors. All eyes were turned on Sancia, a young lady of twenty-two, dark of skin, with an aquiline nose and a complexion carefully made up, who was already turning her own lively grey-blue eyes in every direction as she chatted with Lucrezia. She was dressed in black in the Neapolitan style, with long, wide satin sleeves, embroidered in the Spanish way. She rode a grey jennet. Squillace, not yet fifteen, was also in black, dark complexioned and full of life, his hair long, and with a reddish tinge, like others of his family. He was wearing a black velvet cap. He rode in front of his wife, between the Governor of Rome and the ambassador of the King of the Romans, but the Mantuan envoy describes Sancia first. Burchard was more than satisfied with his procession as it made its way through a district so studded with ruins that the old world might still claim it for its own, past the Coliseum and on to the Campo dei Fiori towards the river—here the narrow streets and the gaunt, gloomy mediæval houses became continuous—then over the Tiber to the Castel S. Angelo.

Alexander eagerly watched for the arrival of his children from a window in the Vatican. As soon as he caught sight of them, he left his place and took his seat upon his throne with his cardinals round him, among whom stood Cesare, in no way distinguished from the rest. Gioffrè kissed the Pope's foot and then his hand. The Pope took his head in his hands and bowed his head, but did not kiss him. The others were similarly received. Gioffrè then kissed the hands of the cardinals in turn, and was kissed by them. The women did likewise. After this ceremonial the two girls took their seats on cushions by the Pope and chatted and laughed with him. It would be difficult to find

a parallel to this scene of domestic felicity in the
annals of the princes of the Renaissance. Even
Burchard forgets to be shocked, perhaps because he
had staged it all so well. Unfortunately this loving
father was the celibate head of the Christian
Church.

From the first Gioffrè was a nonentity. As the
Romans put it, he fastened on Cesare's spurs. Lucrezia
had nothing to fear from Sancia, who soon became
a centre of scandal. Both Cesare and the Duke of
Gandia were known to be her lovers and her intrigues
with other young nobles and cardinals became
notorious. At a later date Cardinal d'Este is said to
have fled from Rome for fear of Cesare on her account.
Her behaviour ended by outraging the Pope himself.
The ladies in her suite had no better reputations. She
was the only person who was not afraid of Cesare.
She flouted him openly, as a woman often will a man
who has enjoyed her favours. In 1500, the Jubilee
year, when he was Duca Valentino and a warm
champion of France, there was a duel in Rome between
a French soldier and a Burgundian, who had been
insulted by the Frenchman, and had refused to accept
the Duca's proffered compensation. It was said that
Valentino would rather have lost 20,000 ducats than
that the Frenchman should be beaten. When the
Burgundian won, Sancia decorated twenty of her men
with the cross of St. Andrew in honour of Burgundy
and took them about Rome with her.

The next day, May 21st, was Pentecost Sunday, and
Burchard, like the rest of the congregation, was terribly
scandalized at seeing Lucrezia and Sancia take their
places in the marble pulpit, where the canons usually
read the Gospel and the Epistle, with a number of
other young women, those who could not find room
grouping themselves underneath. Doubtless the
Pope had given them permission in order that his
daughter-in-law might have a better view of the

70

ceremony, her first in Rome. But it is not surprising that good Christians were shocked.

On the 10th August the Duke of Gandia arrived from Spain. He was met at the Porta Portese, whither he had come from Civita Vecchia, by Cesare and escorted with full state to the Vatican along the ominous route by the Island of St Bartolomeo and the Piazza degli Ebrei to the Campo dei Fiori. Cesare rode on his right.

His father had great plans for Gandia. Like other princes of Italy the Pope saw that, if he was to have any real authority in his states, he must reduce the powerful and factious clans of the Roman barons, notably the Colonna and the Orsini, to some kind of order. The Colonna had sided with the French from the first, but the desertion of the Orsini, who voluntarily surrendered their great castle of Bracciano to Charles, was a stab in the back which he never forgave. Like others of their kind, they were held by no ties of loyalty towards their sovereign or their country, fighting only for their own hands. On June 1st a bull outlawed the chief of the Orsini, among them Virginio, the head of the clan, with Giangiordano, Paolo and Bartolomeo d'Alviano, of all of whom we shall hear again.

Virginio had been captured by the Spaniards when they had driven out the French, for which purpose El Gran Capitàn, Gonsalvo de Cordova himself, had been sent to Naples by Ferdinand. In accordance with the terms of the agreement the Spaniards were about to release Virginio. The Pope, however, would not hear of it, threatening to excommunicate them, as he declared that he meant to destroy the Orsini root and branch. Virginio was therefore imprisoned in the Castel dell' Uovo, where he died. The Orsini attributed his death to the Pope, and the usual charge of poison was made in some quarters.

Doubtless Alexander also hoped by this means to

carve out a territorial principality from the Orsini possessions for Juan. On the next day, August 11th, by the Pope's express orders, Gandia was placed on the highest step of the Papal throne during the celebration of High Mass, and thenceforth he was always given the first place. He was, in fact, "the Pope's right eye", as a contemporary put it, the son to whom he looked for the future glory of his house. He was the more docile of the two elder sons, not unlike his father, possibly garrulous and certainly blessed with his full share of the Borgia charm. Though quarrelsome and self-assertive, he was tall, handsome and well set up, and he was generally popular.

A preference so marked was dangerous when there was a rival like the young Cardinal of Valencia, who knew how to conceal his feelings. He may well have believed that Juan was safely out of the way in Spain. As we casually turn the pages of Burchard's diary, we are continually running across incidents which must have proved galling in the extreme to the elder brother. Thus one Easter Tuesday the Pope went to S. Maria sopra Minerva for Mass, riding a white horse, preceded by the cardinals (*et male*, comments Burchard, since they ought to have followed). The Cardinal of St Denys had arranged a representation of the Annunciation outside his palace, a very humble affair, but the procession stopped a little to watch it, for the Pope loved a show. Gandia was riding in front of his father, after the cardinals, on a magnificent horse, which was covered with silver bells on bridle, cloth and chest-piece. He was wearing a priceless collar of jewels, including a number of pearls, while on his hat was also a fine string of gems. He had the family taste for such things. Then Don Gonsalvo de Cordova joined the procession and rode on Gandia's left, while Cesare was, as usual, inconspicuous among the cardinals.

The Pope meant to give the command against the

Orsini to Juan, but as he was quite inexperienced in
war, he sent for Guidobaldo d'Urbino, a condottiere
of note, to act with him. The Duke of Urbino made
a splendid entry into Rome. Three days later the
Pope blessed the standards, one bearing the arms of the
Church, the other two the Borgia bull, before presenting them to his son as Gonfalonier of the Church,
and then gave the two commanders their white batons.
Scalone wrote to Mantua that he was beside himself
with joy at Gandia being Gonfalonier. " It is said that
on the morning he arranged the plumes and fastened
a jewel of great value on his hat with his own hands."

Ten castles quickly fell before the Papal forces, but
they could make no headway against Bracciano. So
ineffectual was the siege that Cesare was nearly taken
prisoner while hunting near the Tre Fontane. If he
had been, there would have been a new Pope, wrote
Scalone; though he had never applied his head to
business, " he holds the Pope in his fist ". Such was
the impression the Cardinal of Valencia had already
made. His behaviour suggests one who is biding his
time. He was going his own way, not pretending to
take an interest in a career for which he had no vocation, but planning a way of escape from it.

At Christmas, 1496, the Pope was unwell and did
not attend Mass, says a Venetian envoy. " He was
also depressed because his expedition against the
Orsini did not go as well as he would have liked.
Twice were his people roughly handled and many
killed at Bracciano." Bartolomeo d'Alviano, aided by
Virginio's *virago* of a sister, put up a spirited defence.
One day he drove out an ass " molto bello e grande ",
having tied round its neck a notice in large letters :
" Let me go my way, for I am sent as ambassador
to the Duke of Gandia ". Under its tail was a letter
to the said Duke couched in scurrilous terms. This
because he offered deserters from the Orsini half as
much again as they were being paid.

73

Thanks to French help, Bracciano was relieved, and then the Papal forces were caught unawares at Soriano and completely defeated. Guidobaldo was captured and Gandia, slightly wounded in the face, only escaped by riding at full gallop to Rome. The campaign was a complete fiasco. The Orsini recovered their castles on payment of a fine of 50,000 ducats, but, as they fixed the ransom of Guidobaldo at 40,000, they got off very lightly. The Pope made his luckless general pay up. Already it was whispered that Alexander wished to give Urbino, which was a fief of the Church, to one of his sons, since Guidobaldo was childless.

Ostia was restored to the Pope by Gonsalvo de Cordova himself, who was summoned to Rome for the purpose. He returned to Rome in triumph, being received by Gandia and Giovanni da Pesaro and riding through the city with Menaldo de Guerra, the late commander at Ostia, in front of him. On Palm Sunday the haughty Spaniard refused to take the place offered him on the steps of the Papal throne or to receive a palm. Gandia and Giovanni da Pesaro were on either side of His Holiness and it afterwards transpired that Gonsalvo had taken umbrage at Gandia being given precedence over himself. This is the last occasion upon which Giovanni Sforza appears in Rome. Before the end of the month he went to pay a visit to the church of S. Onofrio. Here he had mounted a swift Arab horse, which was waiting for him, and ridden without drawing bridle to Pesaro. He covered the distance in twenty-four hours and his horse fell dead as he entered the gates.

The lord of Pesaro does not seem to have got on well with the difficult Borgia household. He quarrelled with Gandia, who was intolerably overbearing. Nor did he win the affection of his girl-bride, now sixteen, who complained that " non le faceva buona compagnia ", a phrase upon which various interpretations have been put. Then Pesaro was no longer of any political use to the Borgias. If Alexander had begun to turn his thoughts to Romagna, such a son-in-law would be distinctly in the way. Undoubtedly Lucrezia's hand might be bestowed to much greater advantage.

It is quite likely that Gandia threatened him when they quarrelled; possibly Cesare had done the same, since Sforza showed no inclination to help them in depriving him of his wife and her dowry. The story current in Pesaro was that a lackey of her husband chanced to be in Lucrezia's room one day when Cesare came to see her. She bade him hide behind the arras. Cesare then told her that orders had been given for the murder of Giovanni. At her request the lackey repeated what he had heard to his master. That gentle, good-natured Lucrezia had no wish for blood-shed, even though she was not particularly fond of her husband, we can well believe. She may even have advised him to fly. But it is inconceivable that Cesare would have talked to her in such a strain. The story obviously grew up in accordance with the later Borgia legend.

The Mantuan envoy speaks of the difficulty of allaying the jealousy among the Pope's sons by giving Cesare sufficient to compensate him for all that was being done for Gandia. Doubtless he was far from sorry that his younger brother, whom he knew to be his inferior in ability and strength of will and character, had failed in the field and hoped that he would soon be on his way back to his Spanish duchy. Then Ferrante died and his uncle, Don Federigo d'Aragona, wished to obtain the investiture of the kingdom of Naples. Alexander at once seized the chance. Federigo's position, both political and financial, was so desperate that he was powerless to do without the Pope or to oppose him effectively. Alexander decided to resume the Papal rights to the Duchy of Benevento, and at a secret Consistory

announced his intention of conferring it upon the
Duke of Gandia and making it hereditary in his family.
To it he should add Terracina and Pontecorvo. The
Spanish ambassador and one cardinal, Piccolomini of
Siena, who was to succeed Alexander as Pius III,
alone had the courage to protest against this wholesale
alienation of the rights of the Church in favour of
a son of a Pope. At the same time the tribute paid by
Naples to the Church was to be remitted. Alexander
hoped in this way to put Juan in a position eventually
to lay claim to the throne of Naples, but in all probability he was signing his death-warrant. Cesare had,
as in duty bound, supported these proposals in favour
of his brother. His feelings can be imagined. On
the next day, June 8th, though many of his brother-
cardinals disliked the appointment, he himself was
nominated Legate to crown the King of Naples.

The two brothers were about to start together for
Naples, Cesare to crown Federigo, Gandia to receive
the investiture of his new Duchy. For the first and
last time Vannozza steps into the limelight in the history
of her children, to play a part in the most mysterious
of all the Borgia tragedies. On June 14th she invited
her two sons to supper at her vineyard on the Esquiline,
near S. Pietro in Vinculi. Their cousin, Juan, Cardinal
of Monreale, and a few others, intimate friends, were
also present. The relations between the brothers
were well known to her; so well known, indeed, were
they that in one of the bulls, quoted by Woodward,
in which Alexander acknowledges Cesare for his son,
he expressed a wish that they might live together in
greater amity. In their mother's presence, with her
easier manners, these differences may have been allayed
for a time. No one was better able to understand
the sinister young cardinal, who was obviously a
true son of his masterful mother. One can imagine
her, fifty-three now, full-figured, still handsome,
loaded with jewellery, the stones in her rings flashing

76

FIGURE IN TURKISH COSTUME SAID TO BE THE DUKE OF GANDIA,
BY PINTURICCHIO

on her dimpled hands as she ate and drank, proud of the honour of entertaining her sons on the eve of such a journey. It was cool and pleasant under the pergola, as they sat sipping their wine. During the evening a masked man appeared and whispered a few words to Gandia and then went away. No one asked any questions.

It was late when they rose to go. The brothers rode off together, Cesare on his ecclesiastical mule, Juan on his horse. They had but few servants with them. They parted near their father's old palace, which had been given to Ascanio Sforza as part of the price of his vote. Cesare went on his way towards the Ponte S. Angelo, Gandia through the narrow alleys towards the Piazza degli Ebrei, telling his brother with a smile that he had an appointment with a lady. Behind him, on his crupper, was the masked man who had appeared at dinner, and who had visited him several times recently at the Vatican. Gandia left his servant—he took only one with him—at the Piazza degli Ebrei, telling him to wait for him there for an hour and, if he did not appear then, to go home. He was found where he had been left, seriously wounded and quite unable to give any information. When last seen the Duke was still with the Mask, but it was noticed that there were some ugly-looking roughs, obviously interested, in his neighbourhood. As it was after midnight such company awakened no surprise in such a quarter.

His absence next day troubled his servants. The Pope was anxious too, but guessed that he had gone wenching. When he did not return on the day following the Pope grew seriously alarmed. With his temperament, Burchard's phrase " moved to the depths of his vitals " is not too strong. Every effort was made by the police, under the directions of the Governor of Rome, to find the missing Duke, but in vain.

At last one Giorgio Schiavone, who was lying in

a boat moored along the Tiber, guarding some wood that had been unloaded, was questioned. He said that he had seen two men on foot come out of the street to the left of the hospital of S. Jeronimo degli Schiavoni, on the road that leads from the Castel S. Angelo to the Church of S. Maria del Popolo along the river, close to the modern Ponte Cavour, near the fountain. It was just after sunrise. They looked round to see whether all was clear, then went back. They were followed by two others who, after also glancing round, made a sign. A man on a white horse then came out of the alley with a man's body across it. Two men on foot walked beside it, holding it so as to prevent it from falling. Thus they came down to the river, to the point where the dung carts were emptied. The horse was turned with its back to the Tiber, the two men took hold of the body by the hands and the feet and flung it out into the stream with all their strength, as far as they could. The horseman asked them whether it had sunk and they answered, " Yes, sir." He then looked round into the river and noticed that the dead man's cloak was floating and asked what that black thing was. Stones were thrown till it sank. Then they all went off, including the first two, who had stood looking on. When asked why he had not said anything before, he answered that he had seen a hundred bodies thrown into the river there at night and no questions asked.

Some three hundred boatmen and fishermen were set to drag the river. About the hour of Vespers the Duke's body was found with the throat cut and eight other wounds. He was fully dressed, his gloves still at his belt and thirty ducats in his purse, which proved that he had not been killed by thieves but for private reasons. His hands were tied.

" Lest we should not think thee a fisher of men ", wrote Sannazzaro, in what is, perhaps, the cruellest of the epigrams with which he pursued the Borgias for their part in the overthrow of his masters, the Aragonese kings of Naples, " lo, thou fishest for thine own son with nets ".[1]

The body was covered with a cloak, and rowed to the Castle of S. Angelo. Few tragedies of the day appear to have made a deeper impression than the murder of this rather commonplace bastard son of the Pope, who was just twenty-four. That evening, clad in the full uniform of a Captain-General of the Church, Gandia was borne along the Tiber, his face uncovered, looking as if he were asleep, by the light of two hundred torches. Priests and officials of the Vatican, with large crowds of the general public, accompanied the procession. A Venetian on the bridge of S. Angelo says he never heard such lamentations. He declares that the agonised cry of the Pope, who was watching from a window, was audible above the rest. The Spaniards went through the streets with drawn swords, vowing vengeance, but the Pope's enemies rejoiced almost openly. Many looked on the murder as a judgment from Heaven.

Alexander was prostrated with grief at the thought of the son upon whom he had set all his hopes for the future glory of his house being thrown into the Tiber " like dung ". He shut himself up in his room and wept bitterly, refusing either to eat or drink for three days.

On June 19th he appeared in Consistory, where all the cardinals and ambassadors were assembled to condole with him. By a strange irony, Alexander's love for his children was, perhaps, the best and most genuine trait about him. His speech, as given by Sanudo, has a dignity and a sincerity that show how deeply he was moved. " The Duke of Gandia is dead. His death has caused us the deepest sorrow. It would be impossible for us to experience a greater grief, for

---

[1] Piscatorem hominum ne te non, Sexte, putemus,
  Piscaris natum retibus ecce tuum.

we loved him dearly. We set no more store by the
Papacy, nor by anything else. Had we seven Papacies,
we would give them all to bring the said Duke back
to life. Perhaps God has willed it so on account of
some sin of ours. We do not know who killed him
and threw him into the Tiber." And he went on to
exonerate by name not merely the Duke of Urbino,
but Squillace and Pesaro. Rumour had already been
busy and suggested these two, owing to the reported
relations of Gandia with Sancia and even with his own
sister. Malipiero suggests Pesaro on these grounds.
That the Pope found it necessary to make such a
statement in full Consistory sheds a lurid light upon
conditions in the Borgia family.

Ascanio Sforza was the only cardinal absent. The
Spanish ambassador rose to make his excuses, saying
that he was afraid to come owing to the report
that he was responsible for Gandia's death. They had
quarrelled at a dinner at Ascanio's, and Ascanio had
complained to the Pope of his son's insolence. Alexander replied that such a thought never entered his
head. He looked on Ascanio as a brother. The
Pope also announced that he would, in future, have
no thought but for the Church and that he was
appointing a commission of six cardinals to reform it.

With one of Alexander's temperament emotions
pass quickly. The very violence of his grief was a
sure sign that he would soon get over it. He was too
sanguine, too healthy and well-balanced for any
emotion to have more than a passing effect. As
Capello put it, his troubles never survived the night.
For a month Alexander worked regularly with his
commission of reform, then, growing tired of it, he
resumed his normal life and was soon busy with new
schemes. He suppressed the commission on the
specious ground that it would impair the Pope's
authority. In any case a genuine attempt to reform
the Church effectively at that time, with a Sacred

College so constituted, would have been as hopeless as, let us say, an attempt to reform Chicago to-day.

Meanwhile, he informed all the courts of Christendom of what had happened and received suitable condolences and even more sincere congratulations on his proposed reforms. Among the most interesting letters of sympathy is one from Savonarola, but he too wrote rather to urge him to be strong in his resolve to repent and lead a godly life and, above all, to persevere in the reform of the Church than to console him for the loss of his son. At the same time he begged him to look favourably upon his own work and remove the excommunication that had been launched against him. At first the Pope showed no resentment, but when he recovered he spoke angrily about it, declaring that Savonarola had actually blamed him for his son's death ; the letter in Villari shows how false was the charge.

Every effort was being made to find the murderer. By June 23rd the Florentine envoy, Bracci, writes that he has heard on the best authority that the Pope had all the information he required, but was making no move, as the guilty people were of importance and he wished to lull their suspicions. By August 5th the search was abandoned. The Pope is declared to have said some time earlier that he knew who the murderer was.

For myself, I am convinced that Cesare was responsible for the murder of his brother. The very fact that no evidence was forthcoming against him only increases my conviction. Those who do not believe this usually hold that the murder was the work of the Orsini, and among these are Höfler and Woodward. Sanudo wobbles. In August it is Cardinal Ascanio, in December the Orsini, while in February, 1498, he talks about the Orsini trying to compass the Pope's death, adding that they were boasting of having had his son murdered. Had they been guilty, it is inconceivable that Alexander would not have used the charge against them in the campaign of extermination that Cesare was to initiate in the Romagna, when he actually spared more than one of the clan. Alexander's remark in 1503 to Louis XII that he would never spare them, that it was " casa Ursini contra Borgia e poi Borgia contra Ursini ", is sufficiently explained by the Orsini's desertion of the Pope during the invasion of Charles VIII, and by the part they had played in driving his brother, Don Pedro Luis, from Rome. Nor had they any particular reason for wishing to get rid of Gandia, seeing that they had defeated him, unless, conceivably, in order to avenge the death of Virginio, the head of the clan, at Naples, which some people attributed to Alexander.

The Orsini could never have planned such a murder, still less executed it without betraying themselves. They were good fighting men, but possessed of little ability or character. " The man who did the deed has brains and pluck ", wrote Bracci. " It is the work of a master hand." It bears the sinister stamp of Cesare's swift, silent ruthless way of doing things—no word before or after. Such a man had the personal magnetism that attracts efficient tools and keeps them loyal, as much from respect and affectionate admiration as from fear. He had the qualities of a great brigand chief, wedded to the insinuating manners of a Prince of the Church. It is noteworthy that he always employed Spaniards. We do not know whether Don Michelotto or Micheletto was yet in his service, Don Michele Corella, of Valencia, who became notorious as his executioner-in-chief. We know that he had every reason to be jealous of his brother. According to Zurita, quoted by Woodward, Cesare, in setting forth his motives for desiring to abandon the cardinalate, declared that he would have gladly murdered his brother when, though the younger, he was chosen to succeed to the dukedom of Gandia. We do not

know what was Zurita's authority for this statement,
but it is not like Cesare to talk so unguardedly, unless
he thought that such openness would divert suspicion
for the murder from himself. Had this remark really
been made and become common gossip, it would
probably have found its way into the despatches of
one of the ambassadors. Cesare could not hope to
obtain his freedom till Gandia was out of the way.
Jealousy of Sancia would have little weight with
him. Women played but a secondary part in his life.
He was sensual, but no passionate, devoted lover.

Moreover, only a man whom the Pope dared not
punish could have escaped scot-free, a man in a higher
position than one of the Roman barons. On the other
hand, had Gandia been murdered by a jealous husband
—and, as we have seen, he was a good deal of a royst-
erer—some trace of the crime must have been forthcoming. It is incredible that the son of the Pope
could have been killed in such circumstances and no
one brought to justice.

Yet, such was Alexander's paternal affection, his
absorbing passion for the advancement of his children,
that he gradually forgave even this crime. Murder
was too common in those spacious days for men of
the Cinquecento to see it as we do, but even then
fratricide awakened horror. It must have required
an effort, once he had realized the lengths to which
jealousy between the brothers could go, even for the
Pope, with his power of sloughing off the dead weight
of the past, to adjust himself and accept the inevitable.
One of the effects of the moral reaction caused by the
murder was that he packed the Squillace couple off to
Naples ; and the fact that he is said not to have seen
Cesare again till July 22nd, when he also started for
Naples, may be due to his momentary determination
to make an end of nepotism, put his children from him
and devote himself wholeheartedly to the reform of
the Church. They did not exchange a word when

the Pope received Cesare on his return : he merely kissed him in silence. This struck Burchard as so unusual that he records it in his diary. And there is also the suspicious gap in the diary from the day after the murder till August 8th. Had Burchard's holiday in Germany begun so opportunely, he would not in ordinary circumstances have broken off thus abruptly, but given us other information obtained from his assistant.

This terrible secret explains the completeness with which Alexander now came under the influence of his strong-willed, ruthless son. After such a crime he grew more and more afraid of him and Cesare, for his part, can have felt little fear or even respect for a father who had forgiven so much, even though he were the Pope himself.

The first to mention Cesare as the murderer was Pigna, the Mantuan envoy in Venice, on February 2nd, 1498. He says that he has again heard that the cardinal, his brother, was the cause of the death of the Duke of Gandia. It would have been unsafe to make such a charge at that time in Rome. In 1499 the Mantuan envoy there speaks of " the danger there is in writing the truth ". Not till Cesare showed himself in his true colours by exchanging his cardinal's hat for the sword and by murdering the Duke of Bisceglie did the belief that he was guilty of murdering a brother to compass his own ends become general, and this belief grew into conviction with the increasing number of crimes attributed to the Borgias after the turn of the century.

Such an event was bound to have a supernatural accompaniment. A priest was awakened by loud noises in the Vatican and saw torches and lights moving, though there was no one to hold them. In December a terrible voice that frightened all those in the palace of the Pope was heard in the Castle of S. Angelo more than once and was said to be the ghost of the Duke of Gandia. These facts are recorded in Sanudo.

CHAPTER VII

LUCREZIA'S DIVORCE AND SECOND MARRIAGE
(1497–1498)

Lucrezia withdrew to the convent of S. Sisto after
Pesaro's flight. This step naturally gave rise to many
rumours, as that she had left the Vatican without
saluting her host or even that she was about to take the
veil. Here it was that she heard the news of her
brother's murder.

Meanwhile her divorce was being pushed forward.
The marriage had proved childless and the Borgias
declared that it had never been consummated, even
that Giovanni da Pesaro was impotent. The latter
charge was absurd on the face of it, seeing that his
first wife had died in childbirth and Lucrezia's successor lost no time in giving him an heir. Since
Lucrezia was but thirteen when she was married, it is
not surprising that the marriage was not consummated at once, but the Mantuan envoy, Cattaneo,
announced that it had been consummated in 1493.[1]
As such events were given a publicity commensurate
with their importance at that time, especially in great
houses, it is improbable that he should have been
mistaken. However, the yielding Lucrezia was ready
to swear that she had never been Giovanni's wife
in fact, and in December the two cardinals presiding
over the enquiry announced that the marriage had
never been consummated, that Giovanni was " impotent and cold by nature " and that Lucrezia was
a virgin. The decision caused no little amusement,

[1] Luzio e Renier, *Isabella d'Este e i Borgia*, p. 30.

85

Lucrezia was not happy with Giovanni, and it is just possible that this was one of those cases where a man proves impotent in relation to a particular woman, but with a couple so healthy and full-blooded this is very unlikely.

Sforza went to Milan in disguise and appealed to Ludovico to help him. Il Moro suggested that he should give proof of his virility before competent witnesses. Such trials were by no means unknown during the Renaissance. But Giovanni objected. Finally, Ludovico and Ascanio anxious not to forfeit the Pope's friendship, induced him to make the best of a bad business. He made himself ridiculous by signing a statement that he was impotent, adding, however, that he did so in obedience to Ludovico and Ascanio, and that he had been Lucrezia's husband only in name. Yet in June a Ferrarese despatch from Milan relates that he was openly boasting that he had frequently cohabited with his wife. He even declared the Pope was acting as he did in order that he might enjoy his daughter himself—not that he had done so, be it noted, as Creighton points out. This monstrous charge, which clearly originated in Sforza's not unnatural resentment and bitterness at the way in which he had been treated, has been the chief source of the accusations of incest that have been made against Lucrezia. It was eagerly seized upon by the Pope's enemies.

Meanwhile Cesare went to Naples in July to crown Federigo. It is probable that he took with him the magnificent sword which is still in existence. It came into the possession of the witty Abbé Galiani in the eighteenth century and fired him with a desire to write the life of its owner, for which he began to collect materials. He left it to the Duke of Sermoneta and it is still in the Caetani family in Rome. By the handle is the significant motto " Cum numine Cæsaris omen ", and elsewhere, " Jacta alea est "—the die is cast

86

—an obvious allusion to the crossing of the Rubicon, taken from Suetonius's *Life of Cæsar*, where the words are, " Alea jacta est ". The Roman Emperors were always in the minds and on the lips of the men of the Renaissance, who never tired of reading Suetonius. The beautifully engraved decorations on the sword are nearly all of a warlike character and include a triumph of Cæsar. It is hardly fanciful to see in this handsome weapon a symbolical reference to the career which Cesare meant to hew out for himself, once his path was clear. He shared the superstitions of the day, including a respect for astrology, and, like other successful and ambitious men of the Renaissance, believed firmly in his star. He liked to play with his name. His father had chosen the name of the invincible Alexander on his election to the Papacy, and possibly his second son had been given the name of the great Roman conqueror of set purpose. Alexander would doubtless remind him of the fact, for Cesare is not a common name in the fifteenth century. " Aut Cæsar, aut nihil ", was the motto he chose for his banners in later days—either Cæsar, or nothing. We cannot say with certainty that the sword was made for the coronation, but this would be the first important occasion upon which the young cardinal would have to use one. Among the decorations is a bull, doubtless the Borgia bull, upon an altar, with the word " hostia ", victim, upon it. Before it lies a figure, which Portigliotti suggests may be Gandia. Yriarte, however, tells us that it is the figure of a woman, and once more Cesare was the last man to give himself away by an allusion so palpable.

He reached Capua on August 1st, where the coronation was to take place because of an outbreak of plague in Naples. Here he fell ill. Sancia and Gioffrè came to nurse him and also to appear at the coronation, which had been boycotted by the great nobles of the kingdom. The Prince of Bisignano, one of the greatest of them, withdrew his promise to appear. Cesare soon recovered and the ceremony took place. The Pope, possibly in order to allay suspicion, had appointed him trustee for his dead brother, an appointment which Donna Maria must have resented bitterly, as she was convinced of his guilt from the first. Hence, after the coronation, he went on to Naples, to receive the investiture of Gandia's new duchy. Cesare always travelled in state and on this occasion he had 300 horses with him. The drain on Federigo's slender purse was serious and he heaved a sigh of genuine relief when his expensive guest left on August 22nd. As he had been on an official visit he received an official welcome on his return. It was then that Burchard noted that father and son did not exchange a single word. He would not have mentioned the fact had it not struck him as unusual.

This was the year in which Cesare's trusted physician, Gaspare Torrella, dedicated to him his treatise *De Pudendagra*. Since the French invasion syphilis had become extraordinarily virulent in Italy, where it was henceforth known as the *mal francese*. Torrella considers his patron a benefactor to the human race for enabling him to discover a cure for this terrible scourge.

Cesare shared to the full the sensuality of the Borgias and his life was very much that of other young nobles of the time. Though we read of his mistresses, there is no instance of a woman really affecting or influencing him. In this he was unlike Alexander, who would always have been amenable to a woman's influence. There is no Vannozza in Cesare's life. The famous courtesan Fiammetta, who gave her name to the Piazza Fiammetta in Rome, was one of his loves, rumour says the first. One of Lucrezia's ladies was another. We do not know the name of the mother, or mothers of his illegitimate children. With him ambition came first. It is inconceivable that he would have murdered any man for love of a woman, though it is possible that he might have felt an animal jealousy of a man to whom she also gave her favours, especially if, like Gandia, fortune appeared to pour into his lap all that he himself most coveted. Such jealousy might be a contributory cause, but never in itself a sufficient cause for such a crime as a deliberately planned fratricide.

The only women to whom he appears to have been really attached were his mother and his sister. Such affection for a sister was then so unusual and so unlike all else that was known of Cesare that it helped to awaken suspicions of incest, just as did his paternal affection in the case of the Pope himself. The suspicions were almost certainly false in both cases.

Cesare was by no means the only member of the Sacred College to catch syphilis, which also proved fatal to a number of priests. Burchard records that the Cardinal of Segovia sat last among his brethren owing to the severity of his attack, on account of which he was also excused from bowing to the Pope. In December, 1499, Cardinal Monreale, Juan Borgia–Lançol, made his first public appearance at Mass for some two years, having at last recovered. Giuliano della Rovere, afterwards Pope Julius II, also had it severely. Hence there is nothing surprising in a Professor at the University of Padua dedicating his treatise upon the disease to Ludovico Gonzaga, Bishop of Mantua.

There was no mistaking Cesare's intentions. Already there were persistent rumours that he and Gioffrè were to change places, Gioffrè taking his red hat and he marrying Sancia. As early as January, 1498, the Gonzagas learnt that Mons. di Valenza was exercising himself daily in arms and meant to make himself a good soldier. In strength and fighting qualities Cesare was the living incarnation of the Borgia bull, as the Romagnol peasants were to learn

with astonished admiration. He could jump into
the saddle with one hand on the horse, and he was an
expert bull-fighter.

A wife must also be found for him. Once again
the Pope turned to Naples. The desperate state of
Federigo made him believe that there was most chance
of his fishing up the crown, which had been predicted
for his son in a prophecy he liked to believe, from the
troubled waters of the Regno. Naples was a fief of
the Church, and the investiture lay in his hands, so
long as he remained Pope. First there was talk of the
widow of Ferrante. Finally, Alexander proposed that
Cesare should marry Federigo's daughter, Carlotta.
But in spite of his financial troubles and the heavy
clouds on the political horizon, this was more than the
pride of the last and the finest in character of the
Aragonese kings could stomach. The idea of giving
his daughter, born in wedlock, to the bastard son of a
priest, himself a cardinal, who was to be unfrocked
for the occasion, revolted him, even though his father
was the Pope. Anyone who knows anything of Italy
will understand his feelings. He said that he would
lose his children, his kingdom and his life rather
than thus sully the honour of Aragon. "Make
it possible for a cardinal to marry and keep his
hat and I will give him my daughter," was his
answer.

We read of father and son going on the hunting
expeditions they both loved. To the very end of his
days the Pope would be up at dawn and back late at
night if there was a chance of a boar hunt. Or
Cesare goes out to the wild country round Ostia for
some sport, dressed as a layman in the French style,
with his favourite cousin, Cardinal Juan Borgia the
younger. He appears more rarely now at ecclesiastical
ceremonies, but it is interesting to find him accompanying the Pope on a visit to S. Maria Maggiore,
to inspect the roof, which was being redecorated.

Tradition says that the gold used there was the first to be brought from the New World to Europe.

There was still Lucrezia to be consoled for Giovanni da Pesaro. In March, 1498, according to the Venetian Capello, the Ferrara envoy at Venice and others, the Pope's daughter, who had been solemnly pronounced a virgin by the two cardinals, brought an illegitimate child into the world. Even her loyal, but fair champion Gregorovius feels bound to admit the fact, realizing that it would hardly be possible for her to escape taint in such surroundings and, we might add, with such blood in her veins. The question of the paternity of this child is another of those quite insoluble problems which face one in the history of the Borgias.

On February 14th Burchard says that the body of Pedro Caldes, generally known as Perotto, a favourite chamberlain of His Holiness, was found in the Tiber, into which he had fallen " not of his own free will ", as well as that of a serving maid of Lucrezia's, named Panthesilea. Many hold, with much probability, that this Perotto was the father of Lucrezia's child. Cristoforo Poggio told the Marchese di Mantova that he had heard that this was why he was killed. It was said that Cesare killed him with his own hands, pursuing him into the Pope's presence and stabbing him in his arms, so that the blood spurted into his face.[1] The body found in the Tiber is more like Cesare's way than the spectacular stabbing in the Pope's arms recorded by Capello, the Venetian ambassador.

The question is further complicated by the appearance upon the scenes about the same time of the *infans Romanus*. Just before Lucrezia left Rome to marry Alfonso d'Este, on September 1st, 1501, the Pope issued two bulls legitimizing his beloved son, the noble Giovanni di Borgia, *infans Romanus*, then about three years old. A bull of Leo X (April 30th, 1515) makes him a year older. In the first of

[1] Portigliotti, *I Borgia*, p. 223, for the evidence.

these, which was published, he is described as son of Cesare Borgia of France, Duke of Romagna and of Valence, and an unmarried woman; in the second, which was to be kept secret, he acknowledges him as his own son, which for good reasons he did not wish to do in the first document. He thus adopted exactly the same procedure as in the case of Cesare himself. The two bulls together made everything safe from the legal point of view, as an able canonist like the Pope was well aware. Burchard describes the boy as the son of a Roman woman; so also does Sigismondo dei Conti.

The connexion with Lucrezia is a curious coincidence. Not only was the child born about the same time as Lucrezia's alleged illegitimate child, but the object of the bulls was to enable him to share with Rodrigo, Lucrezia's legitimate child by her second husband, the estates belonging to the Colonna which the Pope had confiscated. He was even made Duke of Nepi, a favourite castle of the Borgias and of Lucrezia herself. Moreover, copies of the documents concerning his legitimacy were found among Lucrezia's papers.

Yriarte and others make the *infans Romanus* the son of the Pope by Giulia. The fact that the mother was a married woman, not *soluta*, as described in the bulls, is not an insuperable difficulty in the case of the Borgias; they would not trouble about trifles where it suited their interests. In the Latin dialogue between Death and the Pope, Guilia is said to have borne him three or four children, but one cannot take such a satire at its face value. Others hold that the child was the son of the Pope by an unknown woman.

The strangeness of the coincidence that both father and daughter should have illegitimate children of about the same age is such that others have sought to identify the *infans Romanus* with Lucrezia's son. Gregorovius suggests that Alexander may have taken

upon himself the paternity of his daughter's boy.
It is conceivable that a father so devoted might have
done so to save his daughter's name and to increase
the boy's chances of maintaining his hold upon his
duchy. Cesare also would not have been likely to raise
any difficulties. Creighton suggests that Alexander
was doing the same for a bastard of Cesare's, but this
is far less probable.

Lastly, there is the theory that the Pope himself
was the father of Lucrezia's child. The charge of
incest was freely brought against the Borgias by their
many enemies. Machiavelli suggests that jealousy of
their own sister was the reason why Cesare murdered
Gandia. Peter Martyr, who was in Spain, repeats the
charge, as also does Capello. Sannazaro assailed this
sore point in the Borgia bull with some of the nastiest
of his epigrams, but the great humanist and true
poet, Pontanus, who was also in the service of the
Aragonese kings of Naples, is neater. " In this
tomb sleeps Lucrezia in name, but Thais in fact,
Alexander's daughter, bride and daughter-in-law."[1]
Many later writers have believed the charge, but we
had thought that Gregorovius had virtually killed
it in his classic work on Lucrezia. Portigliotti, however, who cannot allow the Borgias a single redeeming
feature, firmly believes it. " Unquestionably the idea
of incestuous relations in the shadow of the Throne
of St Peter must be profoundly repugnant to everyone.
But this feeling must not be allowed to obscure our
objective weighing of historical documents and facts.
Nor, above all, must we forget that in the case of the
Borgias we are brought face to face with one of those
families of non-moral people who are not conscious
of the repulsion of blood relationship. Their instincts,
and especially their sexual instincts, which were extraordinarily strong in all the members of the family,

[1] Hoc tumulo dormit Lucretia nomine, sed re
Thais, Alexandri filia, sponsa, nurus.

seek and find their satisfaction within the family itself."
Freud has taught us to look on such matters rather
differently. For myself I cannot see that the Borgias
were in any way abnormal, judged by the standard of
the times, and it was only the fact that Alexander was
Pope that has made people think so. For men with
such abnormal tendencies they were remarkably
self-sacrificing in looking elsewhere for the satisfaction
of their appetites. Compared with a Francesco Cenci,
who was as a last desperate resource falsely charged
with incest by his unhappy daughter, Alexander
might almost be regarded as a good man. Portigliotti even explains the two bulls by the fact that
Alexander knew of the incestuous relations existing
between Lucrezia and Cesare. But at least, in spite of
the boy's name, he excludes the Duke of Gandia from
his charge.

One can but leave it at that. The most one can say
is that the *infans Romanus* was, in all probability, the
child of the Pope by an unknown woman. There is
nothing surprising in this. He was father of a son
called Rodrigo in the last year of his life, who became
a monk in the days of Leo X.[1]—surely the only case
of a child being born to a reigning Pope. The name
of the mother is unknown.

Had Giovanni's mother been Giulia Farnese, we
should almost certainly have known it. That the
Pope gave him an equal share in the estates with little
Rodrigo does not seem to me to imply necessarily
that he was a child of Lucrezia. When Giovanni came
to Ferrara in 1518 he was treated as Lucrezia's brother.
Had there been the least suspicion that the boy was
her illegitimate son, he would hardly have ventured to
appear there.

Seemingly it was in the hope of drawing the
Neapolitan connexion even closer and of increasing
Cesare's chances of marrying Carlotta d'Aragona that

[1] Woodward, *C. Borgia*, p. 391.

94

ST. CATHERINE, GENERALLY HELD TO BE LUCREZIA BORGIA,
BY PINTURICCHIO

the Pope went to Naples for a husband for Lucrezia. Federigo had no objection to allowing the bastards of his house to marry the children of a Pope, and he readily consented when Alexander proposed a match between his own daughter and Alfonso d'Aragona, Duke of Bisceglie, who was Sancia's brother. The match was not a particularly brilliant one for Lucrezia, but it was useful for the moment, or at least her father and brother hoped that it might be. Perhaps, after the story of the illegitimate child, she could look for nothing better at that time. She brought with her the handsome dowry of 40,000 ducats, an addition of 10,000 to the 30,000 which the unfortunate Pesaro had been compelled to refund.

By the Pope's wish the Duke entered Rome without any ceremony. He dined with Ascanio Sforza, and was welcomed by the Cardinal of Valencia with every sign of affection. The marriage was celebrated very quietly on July 21st, when Ascanio was one of the witnesses. On the 22nd there was a merry family gathering, Alexander throwing himself into the fun as gaily as anyone. The supper lasted till daylight. In the masquerades Cesare appeared as a unicorn. The proceedings were marred by a violent quarrel between his men and the servants of the Princess of Squillace in the early part of the evening. Swords were drawn in the Pope's presence and a couple of bishops were a good deal knocked about with fisticuffs in the scuffle. Cattaneo describes the scene, adding (August 8th) that Lucrezia was very well satisfied with her husband, who was a year younger than herself and the handsomest young man of his day in Rome.[1]

As there was talk of the possibility of Gasparo da Procida, though a married man with a family, once more pressing his claims, Alexander had, with characteristic legal caution, made all safe by a bull in which he absolved Lucrezia from the sin of having

[1] Pastor, *Popes*, Vol. VI, 611–12.

broken troth to marry Sforza and pronounced her at liberty to take another husband.

Savonarola ended his remarkable career in 1498. It was a strange freak of destiny that placed his fate in the hands of such a Pope. Savonarola had defied Alexander, first, by not going to Rome, as ordered, to explain the divine origin of his mission, upon which he insisted, then in preaching when he had been forbidden to do so ; and the Pope had shown his utter inability to understand him by trying to bribe him with a cardinal's hat. The Pope's quarrel with him was more political than religious, for it was principally due to his influence that Florence refused to join the league against France. Savonarola and many of his followers always regarded the coming of Charles VIII as a fulfilment of his prophecies. Indeed, Alexander let it be understood that, if the friar would avoid politics and cease his attacks upon himself and upon Rome, he might continue preaching. Alexander was tolerant and had no wish to be driven to extremes.

In 1497, when Bracci, the Florentine ambassador, had informed the Pope that Florence would not give up the French alliance, he exclaimed angrily that he supposed their obstinacy was due to the prophecies of their babbling friar, " quel vostro parabolano ". In May he excommunicated Savonarola. When he so far defied Alexander as to say Mass in S. Marco at Christmas and preach in the Duomo, there could be only one end. Florence did her best to defend him, pointing out the wonderful moral effect of his work. Alexander told Bracci that it was not for his teaching, but because he persisted in preaching after being excommunicated that he was condemned. He even said that, if Savonarola would submit for a time and then humbly ask for absolution, he would grant it and allow him to go on preaching. He added, truly enough, that, if he allowed such conduct, all apostolic authority would be at an end. Alexander acted with great caution. He was well aware of the profound impression the great Dominican had made upon Charles VIII and there was always the bogey of a Council which Savonarola, in desperation, tried to raise by writing to the chief princes of Christendom. Nor was Alexander unaware of the odium he would incur by condemning one who had exercised a moral influence so extraordinary. He was naturally delighted when the Florentine government arrested him. By an odd coincidence Charles VIII was stricken with apoplexy on April 7th, 1498, the day on which occurred the fiasco of the proposed ordeal by fire in Florence. On May 23rd Savonarola was strangled and burnt in the Piazza della Signoria. One of the commissioners who tried him was Francisco Remolines, Bishop of Ilerda, Cesare's lifelong friend, who had thought better of his youthful idea of abandoning the priest-hood. A prophet with such a profound belief in his own divine inspiration would certainly have been driven into opposition to almost any Pope in the fifteenth century, but his end might have been different had the Pope been of a different stamp from Alexander.

CHAPTER VIII

THE death of Charles VIII proved a blessing to the
Borgias.   Alexander saw his chance, for Louis XII
needed his help.   He meant to assert his claim to the
Duchy of Milan as well as to Naples, and he wished
to marry the widow of Charles, Anne of Brittany.
His attachment to the capable Anne, who was not
without charm, seems to have been sincere, but the
purpose of the marriage was to unite Brittany per-
manently with France.   In order to do this he would
have to divorce the unattractive daughter of Louis
XI, with whom he had never lived, or, at least, so he
said.

Alexander was quite ready to grant the dispensation;
indeed, he set up a commission at once; for it gave
him the chance of providing for Cesare.   The Cardinal of Valencia was to resign his hat and be made
Duke of Valence, the district in the Avignon region
which had long been in dispute between Rome and
France, and which would thus become part of France.
Louis was also to use all his influence to win him the
hand of Carlotta d'Aragona, Federigo's daughter, who
was at the French court.   Louis gladly consented.

On the death of the Cardinal of Parma in December,
1497, the Pope had bestowed his benefices and his
estate upon Cesare as a parting gift from the Church.
Decisive steps were now taken towards making him a
layman.   On August 17th he explained his reasons
for desiring to be allowed to abandon an ecclesiastical

career to a special Consistory. He had no vocation for it and was ill fitted for it. From early youth, he said, he had been drawn to a secular career. His Holiness, however, had insisted upon his embracing an ecclesiastical life and had heaped benefices upon him. He could not oppose his wishes. Moreover, he had been permitted to accept the red hat under false pretences, under the belief that he was born in lawful wedlock, whereas it was well known that this was not so. Wherefore he begged that His Holiness would of his great clemency deign to grant him the dispensation necessary for his laying aside the ecclesiastical habit and dignity and returning to the lay state and contracting marriage. He begged the Right Reverend cardinals to consent and to join him in imploring His Holiness to grant the necessary dispensation. One can imagine the charm with which he pleaded his cause. The cardinals unanimously referred the matter to the Pope, who granted the dispensation that very day.

Ferdinand of Castile had from the first disapproved of the step. The giving of a French title to Cesare and the *rapprochement* between the Pope and France which this involved began to alarm him. His ambassador, therefore, protested to the Pope. Alexander replied that he would not oppose Cesare's taking the course contemplated for fear of jeopardizing his immortal soul, since his way of life was not suitable to an ecclesiastic and he had no vocation for a spiritual career. The answer, however sound, must have amused anyone who knew anything of his brothers in the Sacred College. But it is quite possible that Alexander, with his gift for seeing only the side of the question which suited his purpose, really meant what he said. He was the Vicar of Christ relieving a cardinal who felt he had no vocation from his vows, not an ambitious father who would stick at nothing in order to promote the interests of his children. He went on to assure the ambassador that the late cardinal's benefices should be conferred upon Spaniards. As these were worth 35,000 ducats a year, Cesare was sacrificing a solid advantage. The Pope kept his promise. The Archbishopric of Valencia and the other benefices were duly conferred upon a Spaniard, Juan Borja–Lançol, a great-nephew of the Pope. This step annoyed Ferdinand still further, for he resented the Pope keeping this wealthy See in the Borgia family and appointing to it without consulting him.

The whole affair had been admirably staged and timed. Hardly was the Consistory over when there arrived at the Porta Portese, and was received with the customary state, Louis de Villeneuve, Baron de Trans, the representative of the King of France, who was to escort Cesare to France. With him he brought the patents transforming the Cardinal of Valencia into the Duke of Valence—Valentino, or Valentinois, as he was henceforth called. Louis undertook that the income of the Duchy, which included the counties of the Valentinois and the Dinois, should be 20,000 gold francs. To this was added an annual allowance of the same amount. The new Duke was to have the command of a hundred French lances, which were to be at his own disposal, and these might be increased to 200 or even 300. Owing to the number of men attached to each lance, according to the custom of the day, Cesare might thus find himself in command of a force of French cavalry 1800 strong.

Cesare was determined to impress the French with a luxury which astonished even the Italy of that day, and which would outstrip the greatest splendour of the Duke of Gandia. Money had to be found and, just as it was for the good of his own soul that he should be released from his vows, so it proved for the good of sundry heretics that they should be compelled to supply funds for the journey of this son of the Pope in search of a wife. As early as April Pedro de Aranda,

Bishop of Calahorra, Alexander's major-domo, had been arrested with his son on a charge of being a *marrano*, secretly a Jew. He was now deprived of his considerable property of 20,000 ducats. Like other Popes, Alexander was tolerant of the Jews and had allowed a number of those expelled from Spain to settle under his wing, for they paid a tax. There was quite a colony of them round the tomb of Cecilia Metella. Three hundred more *marrani* were arrested and heavily fined. A number of them did public penance on July 29th in yellow gowns, carrying candles. The ambassadors saw that the real reason for this unwonted zeal was to obtain money. Henceforth they were left in peace. If Aranda really held the views attributed to him by Burchard, it is not surprising that he got into trouble. He was imprisoned in S. Angelo till a fall of the roof of his cell released him. Many, of course, insisted that he had been poisoned. Why the Pope should have troubled to poison him in the circumstances it is difficult to see.

Public feeling against the Borgias was growing. The sudden peace and alliance between the Colonna and the Orsini after the crushing defeat of the latter in their war for the possession of Tagliacozzo was followed by the finding of an epigram on the door of the Vatican library urging them to unite in slaying the bull that was wasting Italy, throw his calves into the Tiber and send his soul to hell.

A huge fortune was squandered in order to " far bello " this Pope's bastard. He had written to Mantua to ask for one of the famous Gonzaga horses on which to make his entry and to Ferrara for some viol players for which that city was noted. The ships sent to fetch him by Louis were long in coming. Not till October 1st could he start, the Pope watching his departure with a swelling heart from a window in S. Angelo. He wore a doublet of white damask, says the Mantuan ambassador, trimmed with gold, a cloak of black velvet, also trimmed, in the French style, and a plumed hat of black velvet, adorned with large rubies. Even on his boots were cords of gold and pearls. The trappings of his horse were of red silk and gold brocade, while the stirrups and other appointments were of silver. So many gold chains and so much brocade went with him that a second Papacy would not pay the bill, which, with the money that he took with him, amounted to 200,000 ducats. Every yard of silk, every ounce of gold and silver that could be found in the shops, as well as all that came from Venice, had been commandeered.

With him went Don Ramiro de Lorqua as his steward, Torrella, his physician, and his secretary, Agapito. Among his suite, which consisted of thirty gentlemen, chosen from the chief Roman families, was Giangiordano Orsini, who was thus to win the support of the King of France, which was later to stand him in good stead against his present chief. In September Fabio Orsini, son of the foolish Paolo, had married a niece of the Pope. This sudden *rapprochement* may have been due to fear of the danger of their alliance with the Colonna. It is hardly credible that they would have ventured to trust Alexander if they had murdered Gandia.

Cesare took with him a secret dispensation enabling Louis to marry Anne at once, a cardinal's hat for d'Amboise, Bishop of Rouen, soon to be well known as Rohan, brother of the King's chamberlain, the Sieur de Chaumont, and a letter from the Pope, introducing " *cor nostrum*, our beloved son, Duke Valentino, dearer to us than all else ". He reached Marseilles on October 12th and proceeded to Avignon, where he was met by Giuliano della Rovere, who was bishop there and also Papal legate. Since the French alliance he was once again reconciled to the Borgias. He had been doing all he could to further Cesare's projects, as he was to continue to do during his stay in France. He entertained him royally for a fortnight, at a cost of 7000 ducats. He was soon writing to the Pope, saying that Cesare was in high favour at court. Everyone liked him and thought highly of him; everyone was captivated by his tact, charm and ability, his mental and physical gifts. The Mantuan who had witnessed his departure was less complimentary, fearing that his projected wife might refuse him on account of his face " peggio che francese ". Indeed, Cesare appears to have been disfigured with blotches and sores for the rest of his life. This may be one of the reasons why he was so fond of going masked.

We can follow his progress in every detail. He wisely refused all honours offered him in the capital of his new duchy of Valence, as he had not seen the king. He even declined to accept the Order of St Michel from the official sent for the purpose by Louis, thus offending him grievously. Indeed, his haughtiness, insolence and great pretentions speedily estranged the French nobles. The court was, as usual, in Touraine, at Chinon, for Blois was not yet ready. Hither Rovere preceded him. Cesare was careful not to arrive there till the commission had pronounced the nullity of the royal marriage. As the new duke's position was distinctly equivocal, Louis arranged to meet him informally, outside the town, while hunting, treating him with an easy familiarity which completely disarmed him.

On December 17th took place his circus-like entry into Chinon, which has been described by Brantôme, who took his description from a popular poem. He was escorted to the bridge by a number of French gentlemen. First came two dozen handsome mules laden with chests and coffers, with red covers bearing the arms of the said Duke; then 24 more mules, caparisoned in red and yellow, the royal colours, which Cesare had now adopted as his own; then 22

more with covers of yellow satin or cloth of gold.
After them came 16 splendid horses, led, with covers
of red and yellow cloth of gold ; then came 18 pages,
each on a noble charger ; 16 of them were in crimson
velvet, the other two in rough cloth of gold. Think
who these two boys must be, said people, who are so
much finer than the others. Next, led by six lackeys,
came six magnificent mules, with their sumptuous
saddles, bridles and harness, all in crimson velvet,
and the grooms likewise. After them came two
mules, bearing coffers, all covered with cloth of gold.
Think, said people, how much more precious must be
the loads of these two, lovely rich jewels for his mistress or for someone else, or bulls and fine indulgences
from Rome, or maybe some holy relic. Thus people
talked.

Then afterwards came thirty gentlemen dressed in
cloth of gold or cloth of silver, all with gold chains.
Great importance was attached to gold chains at that
time. Too few, said the Court, after all that has gone
before. There should have been at least a hundred,
or six score, dressed in the mode of France, others in
that of Spain. Also there were three minstrels, to wit
two tabourers, and a rebec player, such as were much
in use in that day. . . . The two tabourers were
dressed in cloth of gold, in the costume of their
country, the rebec players accoutred with gold
trimmings ; also the instruments were of silver, with
great chains of gold. The said minstrels went between
the said gentlemen and the Duc de Valentinois,
playing continuously. Also four trumpets and clarions
of silver, richly dressed, playing continuously. There
were also 24 lackeys, all dressed in parti-coloured
crimson velvet and yellow silk; and among them came
the Duke, and by him was the Cardinal de Rohan,
who was entertaining him.

" As for the said Duke, he was mounted on a
handsome, noble courser (the Gonzaga dapple grey),

very richly caparisoned, dressed in a parti-coloured
doublet of black satin and cloth of gold, embellished
with very precious stones and large pearls. On his
hat, which was in the French style, were double rows
of five or six rubies of the size of a large bean which
flashed brilliantly. There were also a number of
stones on the border of his hat, among them a pearl
as large as a nut, while even on his boots was a quantity
of gold cord edged with pearls.

> " Et un collier, pour en dire le cas,
> Qui valait bien trente mille ducats.

So runs the rhyme of the said writing."

The horses of himself and his suite were shod with
silver. The Duke's horse was loaded with gold and
good jewellery, including a quantity of pearls and
stones. On the crupper was a pearl as big as an arti-
choke. Cesare also had a beautiful little mule to ride
through the town, which had all its harness, as well as
its saddle, its bridle and its chest-piece, covered with
rosettes of fine gold as thick as a finger.

The Duke's breast flashed like a mirror with diamonds ; in his doublet were a dozen gold studs with
a ruby set in each.

The procession was closed by a dozen carts, loaded
with travelling beds, plate and the like.

> Aisni entra, pour avoir grand renom,
> Le dit Seigneur au Château de Chinon.

" There you have the turn-out of this gallant, in
which I have not changed the purpose of the original,"
says Brantôme. " The king, being at the window, saw
him come and said that it was too much for a little
Duc de Valentinois." But it is not surprising that the
entry found its way into popular ballads.

Valentino went to the castle, where Louis awaited
him with Vincula and the gentlemen of his suite.
He bowed down to the ground as he entered the

banqueting hall, and then again in the middle of the room, whereupon the king raised his hat. When he was close to the king, he made as if he would kiss his feet, but the king would not permit this, so he kissed his hand.

There we see the son of the Pope behaving to Louis as he would have done to his own father. But it is more than this. It betrays the *parvenu* as surely as the display of his entry, for Cesare had himself crowned a king. Alexander would never have behaved in such a way. This is not the pride of Spain, but the cringing of the Italian peasant before his superiors. The son of Vannozza shows his origin as surely as he was to do after his father's death, betraying the weakness which Machiavelli noted and of which we may see a trace in the almost gushing politeness he could assume so readily, the politeness of the insinuating ecclesiastic. The French nobles doubtless mocked, after their wont, as Brantôme says, just as they mocked at the " vain-glory and foolish bombast " of the entry, for the French court was simple and severe when compared with the Italian courts of that century, and such lavish display was as unknown there as it was unnecessary, even absurd. Nor was it likely to increase the Duke's popularity with the nobles.

However, he was too valuable to be neglected. Louis showed him every honour, even sending him his guard, an attention which the ex-cardinal, new to arms, would know how to appreciate, and treated him with the intimacy of an equal. Doubtless, too, he felt the influence of his charm and intelligence and winning manners. A cynical Spaniard in his suite compared these attentions to the honours paid to Christ on the Mount of Olives. The French might crucify him on Friday.

Ferdinand was angry and troubled at this complete change of front on the part of the Pope. Special envoys were sent to Rome, who insisted on being received in full Consistory. The Pope, however, would only receive them in the presence of a few intimate cardinals, and at last they were obliged to be satisfied with this. They demanded that Cesare should be recalled at once and raked up the old charge of simony and talked of a Council. The Pope, who never lost his dignity, said that he declined to believe that their royal master and mistress had instructed them to use such language. It had been prompted by their Orator in Rome, Garcilaso, a sworn foe to the Borgia. He was, not unnaturally, angry and so were the ambassadors. High words passed. They bade him see the hand of God in the murder of the Duke of Gandia. He retorted that the hand of God had fallen far more heavily upon their master and mistress in depriving them of all hope of a family because they insisted on meddling in Church matters. He was furious at such impertinence and is said to have threatened to have one of them thrown into the Tiber.

But the altered attitude of Spain, his own country and hitherto his best friend, clearly troubled Alexander, especially as his complete change of front did not seem likely to turn out to his advantage. Cesare's courtship was progressing anything but favourably. Carlotta d'Aragona, doubtless in obedience to her father's instructions, would not hear of the match. She said that nothing would induce her to run the risk of being called *La Cardinala*. The Pope wrote bitterly to Giuliano della Rovere that the King was making him the laughing-stock of Europe, since everyone knew that Cesare had gone to France to find a wife. He begged Ascanio to see whether he could do anything to influence Federigo, only to be told that it was hopeless. In February, Valentino was talking of returning to Rome. Rumour said that he thought of resuming his red hat. As a last resource Louis placed Carlotta, who was said to be in love with somebody else, opposite Valentino at dinner, but in vain. She said she would agree only if the Neapolitan ambassador told her with his own lips that her father consented to the match.

This was unlikely, as the Neapolitan envoy had informed Louis that the king would not give a bastard to the Duke, much less his own daughter. Possibly the Duke's malady had something to do with the vehemence of this refusal. Valentino turned to Villeneuve, who was present, and said that Alfonso had been a bastard and that he was the son of the Pope and proud of it; and he proceeded to abuse the King of Naples roundly. Cesare had a long memory, and was anything but forgiving and he treasured up this deadly insult, which was also a blow to his hopes of establishing a claim to the throne of Naples.

Louis was no less disappointed, as he was preparing to enter into an alliance with Venice for an attack on Milan. Valentino's talk of leaving alarmed him, as it was probably meant to do. Louis sought to soothe him by lodging him in his own palace and giving him his guard. The Pope indulged in one of his characteristic outbursts against the King, accusing him of breaking his promises. Louis now proposed either the daughter of Gaston de Foix, his niece, or Charlotte d'Albret, sister of the King of Navarre. Charlotte was the most beautiful and lively of the charming ladies of Anne de Bretagne, who had done much to raise the tone of the court, at least among the women, in the reign of Charles VIII, her first husband, by her piety, her own example and the high standard she expected, without in any way detracting from its brilliance or its charm. Cesare unhesitatingly preferred Charlotte d'Albret. Her father, Alain d'Albret, Duc de Guyenne, was at first opposed to the match, as was the lady herself. Carlotta d'Aragona's contemptuous rejection of the ex-cardinal must have lowered his value in the eyes of the best-born ladies at court. Doubtless they helped her sharpen her tongue upon

him, and Charlotte was one of the wittiest of them.
Nor had Alain any desire for a foreign son-in-law.
But he had no wish to offend the king and he was soon
persuaded to make the best of the proposal and raise
his price as high as possible. He insisted that the
dowry should be 120,000, not 100,000 livres, to which
the king assented, though he never paid a farthing of
the money promised. To this d'Albret added 30,000
livres. Cesare's duchy was to be settled upon his wife
and her brother was to be made a cardinal. To the
last proposal Valentino at first strongly objected, saying he had no authority, but he knew perfectly well that
his father would not hesitate a moment. The contract
was signed at Blois. His witnesses were Agapito and
Ramiro de Lorqua, the faithful secretary and one of
the best of his henchmen, who were both to serve him
loyally. It was generally thought that Cesare was to
be congratulated on his new choice.

The marriage was celebrated on May 12th. Custom
allowed no secrets on such occasions. Cesare wrote
a very frank letter to his father, the Pope,[1] doubtless
to the old man's delight and amusement ; he wrote in
Spanish, the language the Borgias used among themselves. The letter was soon public property in Rome.
Louis wrote to the Pope in much the same tone. He
also sent him 100 casks of Burgundy. Anne of Brittany
gave the bridegroom a horse and a gold ring worth
a hundred ducats, bidding him wear it for love of her,
a pretty speech which pleased the Pope into a happy
chuckle. The bride wrote him a dutiful and charming
little letter, saying that it was her great wish to come
and see him in Rome and that she was delighted with
her husband. She was now mistress of the magnificent
gold and silver plate, such as could then hardly be
made in France, brought in handsome Italian *cassoni*,
which is described in the still existing inventory of her
goods, and of a quantity of valuable jewels. Robert

[1] He told him that he " hizo ocho viajes ".

de la Marck has a very different tale to tell of the wedding night, which the French nobles, who considered this son of a priest fair game, thoroughly enjoyed circulating, as did also the ladies in attendance, upon whose authority it rested.

At Pentecost, on May 19th, Valentino was invested with the Order of St. Michel, founded by Louis XI, the highest in the realm.

The Pope was beside himself with delight. There were many bonfires and illuminations in Rome, especially among the Spaniards, " as a sign of joy, but to the great disgrace and shame of His Holiness and of this Holy See ", sighs Burchard. Every available farthing was now sent to Cesare, and a letter overflowing with gratitude was written to Giuliano della Rovere by his old enemy.

The Pope had been obliged to make some concessions to Spain and had thought it wise to give back Gandia's duchy of Benevento to the Church. Now, however, he threw himself unreservedly into the arms of France, announcing that the Sforzas must be expelled from Milan. Ludovico first learnt the fate in store for him from papers seized upon a messenger returning from the Pope to Cesare. Ascanio thought it wise to fly from Rome, and in August Bisceglie followed his example. His wife was six months with child and did nothing but weep. A few days later the Pope, perhaps to console her, made her Governor of Spoleto. She set out with Gioffrè and Fabio Orsini, her cousin by marriage. The Pope watched them start, a gay cavalcade, and blessed them from the Vatican balcony. Mercurial like her father, she quickly recovered her spirits. The Pope had sent ahead a mule carrying a litter with mattresses and a cover of flowered crimson, cushions of white damask and a handsome canopy, as well as a second mule with a specially comfortable saddle. She had had a miscarriage recently owing to a fall. Bisceglie joined her at Spoleto and, by the Pope's orders, they came on to Nepi, which he now took from Ascanio in order to give this town also to Lucrezia. Here he himself joined the family party for a short while. When she returned to Rome in October he sent his fools and jugglers to meet her.

On November 1st her child was born. The delighted grandfather had the news sent to the cardinals and the diplomatic corps before daybreak. There was a splendid christening in the old Sistine, the baby being wrapped in a covering of gold brocade lined with ermine. The Sacred College gave Lucrezia two silver bonbonnières, containing 6000 ducats. Burchard gives full details, even recording that the little Rodrigo cried lustily before entering the chapel, but the trumpets drowned his voice as the procession left.

The Squillace couple were not proving a credit to the family. In June Gioffrè, with a large party of Spanish friends, had come into collision with the police while on a frolic and had been wounded with an arrow in the thigh. Cattaneo writes that he had just missed being sent to join the Duke of Gandia. The indignant Pope declared that he could not possibly be a son of his. Donna Sancia, pleased for once to have a grievance of her own against her stripling husband, had words with His Holiness upon the subject. Her own conduct was such that in August the Pope packed her off to Naples. He threatened to turn her out by force, if she did not start at once, and refused to give her a farthing when she asked for money.

CHAPTER IX

VALENTINO remained with his wife till early in
September when, on joining Louis, he made her his
legal representative for all his property in France.
They never met again, nor did he ever see his daughter,
Louise, born early in 1500. As he was on Louis'
staff, he took no part in the easy conquest of Milan.
Cesare was with the King when he entered Milan
on October 6th, a ceremony of great splendour, in
which he knew how to make a worthy appearance.
Louis was under a gilded canopy, splendidly dressed.
After him came in pairs d'Amboise and the Duke of
Savoy, Cardinals Vincula and young Juan Borgia,
the Venetian ambassadors, the Dukes of Ferrara and
Valence, the Marquises of Monferrat and Mantua.
Baldassare Castiglione, who was there, says in a letter
that it was good to see Valentino's carts, only a dozen
of them, but outdoing all the others in their rich
trappings of velvet and gold brocade, and he notes
that the Duca was " molto galante ". His Italian
heart rejoiced to see him more than holding his own
with the French in a way that meant so much in Italy,
for the historian Prato says he was " una cosa stupenda ". Castiglione was not the only one to be
saddened at the sight of the castle filled with drinking
booths, with horses stabled in it and smelling of dung.
There were many who remembered the great days
of the Sforza and his brilliant court with Beatrice.
Ludovico had fled to the Emperor Maximilian and the
castle was surrendered without a struggle. For the

next two months Cesare played his part in the gay days that followed, with their endless feasting and the merry hunting parties.

Henceforth Valentino becomes Cæsar Borgia of France, beloved son of the Royal House, and the lilies of France are added to the Borgia bull and the d'Oms bars in his coat of arms.

Valentino was now about to embark upon the career of conquest in Romagna which, thanks not a little to his association with Machiavelli, has done more to rivet attention upon him than any other incident in his career. In his anxiety to find a means of carving out a principality for his son Alexander, like other popes before him, had turned his eyes towards this turbulent province of the Church. In the case of a man so *carnale* this was almost certainly the main motive, but the subjugation of the petty tyrants who lorded it in most of the towns, like the crushing of the great Roman barons of the Campagna, was an essential part of the police work of the Papacy, if the Pope was ever to be master in his own house. The elective character of the Papacy and the shortness of the reigns of the individual popes, combined with the general corruption, put a settled policy out of the question. The little despots in their powerful castles perched upon lofty rocks, always nominally the Pope's vassals, were quite beyond the control of the Papal vicar instituted by the great Cardinal Albornoz who was responsible for the system under which the Romagna was governed. Machiavelli describes Romagna as " a nursery of all the worst crimes, the slightest pretext giving rise to wholesale rapine and murder. This resulted from the wickedness of these lords, and not, as they asserted, from the dispositions of their subjects. For these princes, being poor, yet choosing to live as though they were rich, were forced to resort to cruelties innumerable and practised in various ways. . . . Whence flowed many mischiefs, and particularly this, that the people, being impoverished and not corrected, sought to make good their injuries at the expense of others weaker than themselves." The misgovernment was a byword in Italy.

The one thing upon which the Romagnol insisted was his independence, the maintenance of the rights, privileges and statutes of his town. These also the Papacy, with its essentially legal outlook, rigorously upheld. Alexander had several of the municipal charters, if we may so call them, published. The terms on which the governances of the various townships had been granted varied greatly. The conditions existing in the days of the Borgias were in no small measure due to Sixtus IV, who had given Imola to his Riario nephew and added to it Forlì on the death of its Ordelaffi lord. Of recent years the *census*, the yearly tribute to the Pope, had been allowed to lapse. The one outstanding exception was Ferrara, where the d'Este had paid their dues honourably since their duchy had been granted them in perpetuity in 1389. These little despots behaved as if they were independent. In September, 1497, Sanudo talks of a rumour that they were going to unite in a league with Urbino against the Pope.

Alexander knew that he could not act alone. Neither Venice, nor Florence, nor Milan would welcome a strong Power in Romagna. He had already created consternation in Venice and Florence. As we have seen, young Cardinal Juan had been sent North to join Louis as his legate. On the way he had sounded those Powers as to their willingness to assist in establishing Cesare in Ferrara. Such was the reward of the d'Este for their exemplary payment of their tribute. The news had the effect of making Ercole d'Este one of the most loyal partisans of the French in the peninsula. Without French help the Pope's proposed enterprise would have been impossible and

Cesare had been careful to secure it. The expedition had been decided at Milan.

The non-payment of tribute gave the Pope the excuse he needed. The various lords were declared deposed on that account. The Commune of Milan lent the Apostolic Chamber the sum of 45,000 ducats for raising men-at-arms, for which Cardinals Giuliano della Rovere and Francesco Borgia went bail. For Giuliano, feeling that his nephew, the Prefettino, was secure at Sinigaglia, since he was betrothed to Angela Borgia, was loyally supporting the Pope. Cesare, as Captain-General of the Church, received the money. In order to checkmate any Italian opposition, Cesare undertook this, his first *impresa*, as lieutenant of the French king, who was acting in accordance with the terms stipulated with the Pope and reducing his unruly vassals to obedience.

He left Milan on November 9th, two days after Louis had set out thence on his way back to France. Yves d'Alègre was in command of the expedition. His cavalry consisted of 1800 men, and Cesare, with his 100 French lances, nominally served under him. The Bailly de Dijon was at the head of 4000 Swiss and Gascon infantry and the French supplied the excellent artillery. This formidable force was in the Pope's pay. The Italian troops were enrolled during the campaign by Ercole Bentivoglio and Achille Tiberti of Cesena, the one town remaining in the power of the Popes, which was their headquarters.

It was also thought wise to begin by attacking the king's enemies, the Sforza. Cesare was given permission to pass through Bologna, where he was entertained in the Bentivoglio palace, after being welcomed and escorted thither by two sons of the house, at a splendid banquet. His army was encamped outside the town and he rejoined it for the night, after giving his hosts a horse, a helmet and a mace. Imola was his objective.

This campaign thus brought together two of the outstanding characters of the time in Italy, Caterina Sforza and Cesare Borgia, characters that appeal to the imagination of the reader to-day as forcibly as they did to that of their contemporaries. Caterina is for all time the incarnation of the *virago*, the dominating, fighting heroine of the Renaissance. The word then had no unpleasant associations, as Ariosto's heroines show. And unquestionably Caterina was a woman to the core. Her charm and her beauty, for the preservation of which we still have her recipes, were only enhanced by her fighting spirit as displayed in her strong jaw and her commanding hooked nose. Her vitality was exuberant. When she came to Rome as the bride of Girolamo Riario the familiarity with which this beautiful girl of fifteen was treated by her amorous old father-in-law, Sixtus IV, caused no little scandal. At a later date Giangiacomo Trivulzio, the famous condottiere who took Milan for Louis XII, wondered how anyone so attractive could have remained virtuous. She was the illegitimate daughter of Giangaleazzo Sforza of Milan and of the wife of a Landriani. Proud though she was of her Sforza blood, of which she showed herself a true scion, she was equally attached to her mother, a married woman of the middle classes, and to a sister, Stella, by a different father. Ultimately, they both lived with her at Forlì, where she may have been glad of the company of her only available relations amid a host of enemies and doubtful or interested friends.

The match with Riario merely cemented an old tie, for Sixtus owed his red hat and in no small measure the tiara itself to the Sforza. Though at heart she despised her worthless, vulgar, cowardly, blaspheming husband, she made him a good wife and bore him a child regularly every year. One thing they had in common, a devouring ambition, but she was far the better man of the two. Thus it was she who seized the Castel S. Angelo, girt with a sword, on the death of Sixtus IV, though she was, as in most of the crises of her life, far gone in the family way at the time. She is then described as " wise, brave, tall, well-knit, with a lovely face, talking little ".

When they settled at Forlì, where she was often treated cruelly and brutally by Riario, she helped him loyally in putting down the many conspiracies which the dispossessed Ordelaffi or the discontented nobles who were always ready to make trouble in these half-civilized, ill-governed little lordships of Romagna were continually hatching. They were encouraged by Lorenzo dei Medici, who had not forgotten the conspiracy of the Pazzi, and also by Innocent VIII, who would have liked to oust the Riario in order to make room for his own nephew. Caterina was genuinely religious and a good and grateful friend. It cut her to the quick when she found families whom she had trusted and benefited turning against her. Her character and energy enabled her to maintain her hold when Girolamo was murdered. Her historic answer, when, by a trick, she had got into the strong Rocca of Forlì, to the conspirators who hoped to terrify her into surrender by threatening to murder her children, gives us her measure as a force. She was pregnant at the time and, with a gesture that would appeal to her rough subjects, she bade them do their worst, as she was able to replace them. She punished her husband's murderers, but not with the savage cruelty she displayed at a later date when her lover Feo, whom she had secretly married, met the same fate. She then spared neither age nor sex. Her son Ottaviano, for whom she was acting as regent, was imprisoned. He, too, had joined the conspiracy, for Feo had once boxed his ears in his mother's presence.

Cardinal Rodrigo Borgia had stood godfather to Ottaviano. He had always been a good friend to the Riario and to her. How could he fail to succumb to her charm? And she was delighted at his election. He had frequently visited her at the Palazzo Riario when she was a bride in Rome, and when later she sent a special envoy to ask for a bishopric for one of her sons, he had received him with the utmost graciousness. This was in 1499. The first of the many questions he asked about her was whether she had kept her looks. In 1498 he had suggested Lucrezia as a husband for Ottaviano, before turning to Naples, but she had refused the offer as firmly as Federigo had rejected Cesare.

Her treatment by the French and her relations at Milan had decided her to turn to Florence. This was but natural, as her third husband was Giovanni dei Medici, of the younger branch, who was hand-in-glove with Charles VIII and had been sent to Forlì as Florentine ambassador after the expulsion of his enemy, Piero dei Medici. He was said to be the best-looking man in Florence, a worthy successor to Feo in the affections of the temperamental Caterina. She thus became the mother of the great condottiere, Giovanni delle Bande Nere, from whom the Grand Dukes of Florence descended. Her other sons preferred a life of peace, possibly because they had generally led such very active existences before coming into the world. But the turbulent Giovanni showed himself a son of his mother from childhood, a true scion of the great clan of condottieri, and she doted on him.

Such a land was a good nurse of fighting men. Was not Attendolo Sforza, founder of the family, a Romagnol? Caterina herself had superintended the training of the mercenaries with whom she supplied her friends in Milan and Florence. She did her best to prepare to meet the coming storm, which she foresaw, but she was left to meet it alone.

Tiberti, reputed to have been a lover of Caterina, was sent on with a small force to summon Imola.

The Imolesi had no intention of sacrificing themselves for their masterful lady, still less for Ottaviano. The Riario were no better loved than the other tyrants. Dionigi Naldi, a condottiere of repute, who commanded a regiment of the best soldiers of Romagna, with whom he had been fighting for Il Moro, had superseded Landriani, the aged husband of Caterina's mother, in command of the castle. He undertook to hold out to the end. Vitellozzo Vitelli, an old comrade of his who was serving under Cesare, appealed to him in vain. Little effect was produced upon the castle till a weak spot in the defence was pointed out, whereupon a breach was soon made by the French guns. Naldi promised to surrender, if no help came within three days. He and the garrison then marched out with all the honours of war. There is some reason for suspecting that Naldi treacherously played into the hands of Cesare. He afterwards became one of his most trusted captains. Cardinal Juan Borgia, now Legate for Romagna, arrived on December 17th, and the town took the oath. Two days later Cesare entered Forlì, which had also surrendered, to the disgust of Caterina, who was preparing to hold out till death in the Rocca.

Cesare entered Forlì in pouring rain and his troops, especially the Gascons, behaved as one would expect foreign troops to do in their billets. He did his best to bring them to heel, making special efforts to protect the nuns. Indeed, he showed a tact and patience in listening to complaints and a sympathetic charm in soothing the ruffled tempers of his injured subjects which won him the admiration of his enemies and showed that he had already decided upon the methods he would adopt in his new dominions. He soon made himself as loved as the Riario were hated. Some years after his death the Anziani of Forlì put it on record that they blushed to remember the oppression of the tyrants and blessed the memory of the Duca who, like a Minister of Divine Justice, abolished the worst taxes with his Cæsarean liberality.

On his way to Forlì he had passed by Faenza, where he was welcomed by the Venetian commissioner and young Astorre Manfredi, who, in spite of his position between Imola and Forlì, considered that he was safe under the wing of Venice. Caterina had broken off his engagement with her daughter, and he wrote that, however much the two cities may have suffered during the siege, they must rejoice at escaping from her tyranny.

Caterina had sent her children, including Ottaviano, as well as her valuables to places of safety. She now turned her guns upon her rebellious city, but her subjects suffered far worse at the hands of the Duca's soldiery, whose doings are likened by an eye-witness to the pains of hell. Everywhere in Italy the French made themselves hated, none more so than the Gascons, and the two thousand camp followers, women, priests, sutlers and the like behaved, if possible, worse than they.

Cesare admired Caterina's pluck, as he had done that of Naldi, and on December 26th, before beginning the bombardment, he rode out to try to induce her to surrender. He had no wish to waste time upon a siege, if he could help it. He wore his armour and the black velvet cap with the white plumes which was soon to be so familiar in Romagna. A herald and a trumpet accompanied his escort. She refused his offer, but she let him escort her to the drawbridge. She had given orders that it was to be lifted the moment he set foot upon it, but the men were too hasty and began to raise it before he was on it and her trick failed. No one would have appreciated the lady's attempted kidnapping, which was of a piece with all we know of her, more than Cesare.

The Rocca, immensely strong, was separated from the citadel, also strongly fortified, by a ditch, which was in its turn well protected. By January 12th the Rocca had been sufficiently battered for an assault and a terrific struggle ensued. It lasted all day and cost 400 lives, but it was successful, largely owing to the confusion, incapacity and treachery in the ranks of the besieged. Machiavelli ascribes the defeat to the Rocca, which was a source of weakness rather than strength, and Woodward, whose description of these campaigns is admirable, gives the reasons. Caterina urged on her men herself, clad in full armour and sword in hand. She could ply it vigorously on occasion. As a last resort she ordered the magazines and stores to be fired, but the confusion that ensued did more harm to herself than to the enemy. The white flag was treacherously hoisted without her orders by a captain of her own. The besieged received little mercy from the French and other mercenaries.

There are various accounts of Caterina's capture. The most probable is that one of the Bailly de Dijon's men came upon her with her women as he was wandering through the ruins and was rewarded with 5000 ducats for his prize. Cesare did not enter the Rocca till all resistance was at an end. With him was d'Alègre. The two of them escorted Caterina over the ruins with a few of her women.

Cesare was bitterly disappointed at not finding the children. Without them in his hands he had no security. There was not a spark of chivalrous feeling for a woman in his nature. Caterina was lodged in the same house with him at Forlì, and he is said to have treated her with the greatest brutality, compelling her to yield to him by force. Whatever their faults, the French belonged to the generation of Bayard and loyally obeyed their code of honour. The Romagnol chronicler, Bernardi, who cannot speak too strongly of their conduct in billets, notes with astonishment the reverence with which these Frenchmen, more especially the leaders, heard Mass on their bended knees, with their arms crossed. In character and moral force they were far superior to their Italian contemporaries. It was against their code of honour to keep a lady prisoner, quite apart from the fact that they were lost in admiration at the heroic courage of Caterina Sforza, and that this was increased by her beauty and charm.

The Swiss mutinied for higher pay, declaring that they had done all they were hired to do, and the Bailly with them insisted on his prisoner being given back to him. Not till d'Alègre arrived was order restored. The Bailly was induced to give up Caterina on condition that she was to be held as the prisoner of the King of France, and the Swiss were satisfied. At one time Valentino had talked of leaving these rebellious mercenaries to the tender mercies of the people of Forlì.

The capture of Forlì was saddened by the death of the Legate, Cardinal Juan Borgia. He was ill of fever at Urbino when he received the news, and died after a few days' illness, owing perhaps to his eagerness to hasten off to rejoin his cousin. From the first there were rumours that he had been poisoned, which shows how feeling was growing against the Borgias. Sanudo says that Cesare was jealous of the Pope's affection for him. A more absurd and baseless charge it would be difficult to imagine. The cousins worked well together and had been intimate from early youth, and Juan had succeeded Cesare in the archbishopric of Valencia. As they had not met for nearly three weeks, the death must in any case have been due to the wonderful slow poison.

Cesare was now preparing to attack Pesaro, the town of his late brother-in-law, Giovanni Sforza, which is on the coast, to the south-east of Cesena. He made Don Ramiro de Lorqua, his Spanish steward, his Vice-Governor at Forlì, where he also appointed suitable magistrates. On January 23rd, 1500, he left with d'Alègre at the rear of his army. Between them rode Caterina Sforza on a grey jennet, clad in her usual dress of black satin " in the Turkish style ", with a veil over the head. Her eyes were moist as she passed the gate.

Three days later news reached Cesare which caused him to call a halt. Ludovico Sforza was making a bid for the recovery of his Duchy. Their overbearing conduct had quickly made the French unpopular in Milan, as it did everywhere in Italy. Sforza came on at the head of 500 men-at-arms and 8000 Swiss, raised with the help of the Emperor Maximilian. The French commander, Trivulzio, who was hopelessly out-numbered, was forced to recall d'Alègre's contingent from the Romagna. In their retreat these mercenaries, especially the Swiss and Gascons, shocked even that age, as French historians admit, by their barbarous treatment of the inhabitants, plundering the country as ruthlessly as an enemy and abandoning the outraged women they did not carry off to die in the snow of the bleak Romagna winter. Cesare, who always did his best to protect his own subjects against his soldiery, was powerless.

Il Moro was betrayed by his own Switzers at Novara on April 10th. He ended his days a prisoner at Loches in the Touraine, where his name may still be seen, cut by his own hands on the wall of his dungeon. The man deserved his fate more richly than most for the many betrayals that mark his slippery career. Cardinal Ascanio Sforza was delivered into the hands of Louis by the Venetians and also imprisoned in France.

Cesare had already left Cesena, where the French were. There was now nothing for him to do but to swallow his disappointment, since it was out of the question to think of carrying on the campaign with-out his allies. He decided to return to Rome, after securing his conquests, to raise troops and money for another *impresa*.

Here we may mention an attempt to poison the Pope by means of a poisoned letter made by a citizen of Forlì who, when arrested, admitted the fact and said that he was quite ready to lay down his life, if, by killing Alexander, he could save his native town and its mistress. The plot, to which Caterina may possibly have been privy, was quite in accordance with the ideas of the time. The man was arrested in November in the previous year.

CHAPTER X

THE year 1500 was a Jubilee year and Alexander prepared to make the most of such an opportunity. The old Jubilee door at St Peter's having been bricked up according to custom, could not be located. Hence Alexander had a new one cut and ordered that it should be bricked up in such a way that it could in future be recognized without difficulty. Burchard describes the opening of it with full ceremony by the Pope on Christmas Eve, when the New Year still began in Rome. To facilitate the movements of the great crowds that would visit St Peter's, Alexander had a new road built to it from the Castel S. Angelo, the Via Alessandrina, now the Borgo Nuovo. This he opened on the same day. He it was who had, in earlier days, greatly strengthened the fortifications of the Castel S. Angelo, making it a thoroughly up-to-date fortress. He had also improved the covered way that led to it from the Vatican.

It was in this Jubilee year that the Pope restored the practice of ringing the Angelus bell throughout Christendom.

The Jubilee was a great success. Burchard tells us that as many as 200,000 people knelt to receive the Easter blessing in the Piazza S. Pietro—" orbis in urbe ", the world in Rome, as people said. Thirty thousand eight hundred foreigners died in Rome between Christmas and Easter, and many more must have perished on the way thither. This proves the numbers of the pilgrims and the risks they were willing to run at a time when the hardships of even a comparatively short journey were a severe test for a wealthy prince or princess. Plague was then endemic in Rome, and there was an inevitable increase of it at such a time. Among the pilgrims was Elisabetta Gonzaga, Duchess of Urbino, who came incognita and remained only a few days. Her brother, the Marquis of Mantua, was much perturbed at her putting herself into the power of the Borgia, whose designs upon Urbino were already suspected. She left before Easter. On January 1st the Pope was carried to S. Angelo expressly to watch Lucrezia ride with her husband and a brilliant company of both sexes, escorted by Don Rodrigo Borgia–Lançol, the Pope's grand-nephew, who commanded the Papal Guard, to the Lateran, where she was to pray. The sight must have set the pilgrims wondering, especially those from the North. The husband of Giulia Farnese was of the company.

The offerings that poured in from the faithful of all nations gladdened the Pope's heart, for they helped to finance Cesare's campaign, the expenses of which were heavy. Cesare was always lavish. He himself sent to Florence to demand the sums that had been collected in the churches there for the Jubilee for his own use.

To the Pope the return of his son as a conqueror of a couple of small towns, captured only by French help, was the great event of the year. His entry took place on February 26th, when the Cardinals Monreale and Farnese met him, bareheaded, with the ambassadors at the Porta del Popolo. Cesare wore the black velvet doublet in the Spanish style which he generally affected, with the Order of St Michel round his neck. Squillace and Bisceglie rode in front of the hero. The Pope gave no audiences that day. He laughed and cried hysterically when he heard that his son was approaching.

At last the procession crossed the bridge to the Castel S. Angelo, where the two standards were floating in the air, and wound down the new Via Alessandrina, to the Vatican. Here the Pope was waiting in a state of feverish excitement with five cardinals round him on the loggia. The official reception took place in the Camera del Papagallo. Valentino dropped on his knees before the Pope and kissed his hands and feet. His father raised him up, took him in his arms, and kissed him affectionately upon the mouth. His son thanked him in a few words of Spanish for all the favours he had showered upon him. The Pope replied in the same tongue, which Burchard did not know sufficiently well to be able to understand what was said.

The day following a pageant of the Triumph of Cæsar started from the Piazza Navona on eleven cars and went through the city to the Vatican, where His Holiness was so pleased that he made it pass before him twice. Next day began the Carnival races, which were witnessed by enormous crowds, since it was the year of Jubilee. The Pope enjoyed them as much as anyone, watching them as they finished on the Piazza S. Pietro. The Jews ran first. On Sunday came the race of the *barberi*, the bare-backed horses, when the first and third were mares. That day a couple of bulls escaped from the festivities on Monte Testaccio and swam the Tiber, creating great excitement. On March 2nd the old men ran and the Oaks was held for the mares—an unusual event, this. Was it instituted by Alexander? On March 3rd were the races for the donkeys and the buffaloes. It was a lively carnival, even for Rome. Burchard duly records these races, but it is clear that he never quite approves of them. In this, as in so much else, he is the Northerner in a strange country.

We are not told that Caterina Sforza was in the procession. Cesare would hardly have ventured to make a show of a prisoner of King Louis. Tragic indeed was her return to Rome. She who had lived there, the bride of the Pope's son, was now the prisoner of his successor, who had then been a rising young cardinal at her feet. She was imprisoned in the Belvedere, in the Vatican grounds, well treated, but guarded by twenty soldiers. When she endeavoured to escape she was transferred to the Castel S. Angelo and her confinement became much more rigorous.

The courtesy with which Valentino treated his former brethren, the cardinals, when he paid them his official visit, was much appreciated. He was next invested with the vicariates of the Riario and shortly afterwards issued a proclamation confirming the liberties of Imola, promising to restore such of them as had been violated, and also to protect his new subjects and govern them justly. To his credit be it said, he kept this promise. On March 29th the Pope conferred upon him the Golden Rose and he stepped into his brother's shoes as Captain-General and Gonfalonier of the Church.

An astrologer had warned the Pope to be careful, as the Jubilee year might prove fatal to him. On June 29th during a violent storm a chimney on the Vatican was blown down. Three persons were killed in the room above the audience chamber, where the Pope was seated in his canopied official chair, and a beam was driven through the ceiling upon it. The two men in the room with him escaped, as they had gone to shut the windows. Seeing the Pope's chair apparently crushed, they thought he must be dead, for he made no sign. Fortunately for him, however, the nails fastening the beam to the wall held and prevented it from falling upon him; indeed, it acted as a buffer to keep off the debris. He was only stunned and had two wounds on his forehead. He was helped from the room in a fainting condition, but was not seriously injured. The news that he had

PIAZZA DI S. PIETRO IN THE TIME OF SIXTUS V

been killed spread like wild-fire and many excellent people, who saw in his death the hand of Providence, were doubtless surprised at his recovery, but at least the accident might be put down as a warning. On Corpus Domini, June 18th, he had had one of his fainting fits, as we have seen, which obliged him to sit through Mass without his mitre.

On St John's Day Cesare gave the Romans an exhibition of his strength, skill and courage in the bull-ring, which had been built on the Piazza S. Pietro for the occasion, and greatly distinguished himself, killing five bulls with a spear. According to Capello he once beheaded a bull with a single stroke of his sword, " a feat which seemed great to the Romans ".

His next performance awakened very different feelings. On July 15, an hour after sunset, the Duke of Bisceglie had just left the stairs from the Vatican, when he was set upon by a gang of cut-throats under the *loggia* whence the Pope habitually gave the blessing, and badly wounded in the head, the arm and the leg. The ruffians left him for dead and fled to the cover of a troop of forty horse, with whom they made off by the Porta Portese. These men would have prevented Bisceglie from escaping in that direction. The courage of his gentlemen-in-waiting, who defended him vigorously, alone saved his life. More armed men barred his way to the house in S. Maria in Porticu, where he lived with Lucrezia and whither he was returning, so he took refuge in the Vatican. Lucrezia burst into passionate grief on seeing him, for she really loved him and his wounds were dangerous. She and Sancia, with Gioffrè and a lady of Lucrezia's suite, now the Pope's favourite, says Capello, who found them with him, had just been nursing Alexander. Lucrezia and his sister took complete charge of Bisceglie. They knew what Valentino's vengeance meant. Such was their fear of poison that they did all the cooking themselves, and for the same reason doctors were sent from Naples. The Pope, who had not yet recovered, placed a guard of sixteen men over the Duke. Valentino, as Gonfalonier of the Church, issued an order prohibiting the carrying of arms between S. Angelo and the Vatican.

From the first there was a general belief that Valentino was responsible. The day after the attempt the Duchess of Urbino was told by her agent that everyone suspected him, while the Florentine ambassador said that it was known that the crime was committed among the Borgias, " because in that palace there is so much hatred, old and new, so much envy and jealousy, political and other, that scandals are bound to occur." Sanudo says it was believed to be the work of the murderer of the Duke of Gandia, which is noncommittal. Cesare was almost certainly guilty. His fury at the murder having been bungled can be imagined. Don Alfonso is reported to have suspected him and to have said so. Valentino visited him once only during his illness, when he said, according to Capello : " What was not done at dinner will be done at supper." When the ambassador mentioned this to the Pope, he answered : " The Duke denies that he wounded him, but if he had done so, he deserved it."

Bisceglie was recovering rapidly, but on August 18th, to quote Burchard, " since Don Alfonso refused to die of his wounds, he was strangled in bed an hour after sunset." The story goes that Valentino burst into the sick-room, turned everybody out of it and ordered the chief of his myrmidons, Don Michelotto Corella, who had probably been in charge of the unsuccessful attempt, to strangle him. This is the first time we meet Michelotto. Under Julius II he is said to have confessed under torture that the Pope had given orders for the murder, but Alexander was then dead and he would never have betrayed his master. In a way this is a confirmation of Cesare's guilt. Possibly the Duca told him that such were the Pope's orders.

The women rushed to the Pope for help, but it was too late. The doctors and a hunchback servant of Don Alfonso were imprisoned and proceedings were begun against them, but they were quickly released.

There can be no real doubt as to the main facts. Burchard could not say more and even ambassadors had to be careful. Capello gives as the motive for the murder that Don Alfonso had shot at his brother-in-law in the garden of the Vatican with a cross-bow. Sanudo's diary enables us to follow the gossip of the day in Rome. One rumour was that Don Alfonso had plotted with the Colonna to attack the Orsini and that his letters had been intercepted. Hence the Orsini had planned the original attempt. Bisceglie's tutor, Brandolinus, who says that the shooting story is absurd, believed that Valentino meant to checkmate once for all the Pope's instinctive sympathy for Spain and the Aragonese in Naples and drive him into the arms of France. Don Alfonso was now useless as a political asset and Cesare may have thought that Lucrezia's hand might be disposed of to greater advantage. There was also his bitter grudge against Federigo for his insulting refusal of the hand of Donna Carlotta. Don Alfonso must long have realized his position. Valentino was the last man to leave him in the dark upon the matter, when it suited his interests to speak. He may well have let him see that he despised him ; they probably quarrelled, exchanging the highly flavoured abuse that was then usual in ecclesiastical circles at the headquarters of Christendom. Valentino knew that he had nothing to fear from the Pope, though matters might conceivably have gone differently had Alexander been well. But he never committed a crime in a fit of passion. All his actions were carefully calculated to serve his own ends and carefully planned. This was the first and the last time he bungled.

The murder of Don Alfonso, in the heart of the

Jubilee year, made a great sensation in Rome. It did much to poison public opinion against the Borgias, more especially against Cesare. Now it was that people began to speak of him more openly as the murderer of his brother. The Borgia legend may be said to have taken shape in the Jubilee year. Lucrezia's genuine grief awakened universal sympathy. She was only twenty; this was the one man whom she appears to have loved as sincerely as her rather shallow character allowed. She now retired to Nepi, a typical Etruscan hill town, where the strong castle had been built by Rodrigo when cardinal, " in the hope," says Burchard, " of finding some comfort or distraction for her grief." She had an escort of six hundred cavalry. In such circumstances both the Pope and Cesare would find her tear-stained face irksome, and in any case custom required a period of strict mourning. Her letters thence are signed " La Infelicissima ". She was still there in November.

In spite of all that had happened Alexander went in solemn procession on August 25th, escorted by Valentino, to S. Maria del Popolo to attend a Te Deum in honour of his recovery. He offered a handsome gilt cup to the Virgin, to whom he considered he owed his escape, containing 300 gold ducats. These the Cardinal of Siena emptied upon the altar for all to see, " and I do not think the Pope was displeased," remarks Burchard, who notes that he had a beard, not having been shaved since his accident. On one occasion Burchard ventured to remonstrate with a Borgia cardinal because his hair was two inches too long, but in vain.

Plague had broken out in Rome in July and two of the Pope's servants had died of it, but he refused, as usual, to take any precautions, for he considered himself immune, since he had had a sharp attack in his youth. This was the year in which Capello gave his oft-quoted description of him : " The Pope is seventy :

he grows younger every day : troubles never last over night with him. He is naturally cheerful, doing everything that is to his advantage, and his one thought is the advancement of his children."

Meanwhile Cesare was master in Rome. The Pope's accident had filled him with anxiety for the future, and he appealed to the Venetian ambassador for help, in case of his death. Capello replied characteristically : " You are wise : without the Pope your schemes could not endure for four days." Venice now thought it advisable to countenance him and in October he was made a Gentleman of Venice, to the unbounded satisfaction of the Pope. After the manner of the princelings of Romagna when in trouble, Giovanni Sforza had offered to give Pesaro into the hands of the Serenissima, but Venice declined the dangerous gift.

Louis was ready to help Valentino, as before. On August 23rd a masked horseman rode out of Rome to meet Villeneuve, the new French ambassador. On unmasking he proved to be Valentino, who had a long talk with his old friend. Cesare, however, had no desire to remain in complete dependence upon his allies. He was busy collecting an army of his own and securing the services of good condottieri. Giampolo Baglioni, now lord of Perugia, undertook to supply him with a contingent of infantry and Paolo Orsini joined him. More important was Vitellozzo Vitelli, lord of Città di Castello, a gunner of note, who was given charge of the artillery, consisting of 21 pieces. Mercenaries were also being enrolled and drilled in Rome. Cesare paid his troops better than any other commander, says Branca Tedaldini, " but no one could ever speak to him save the Signori, or Michelotto : these Romans of ours never spoke to him."

Money was, as usual, short. " He is truly royal, even prodigal," reports Capello, and this displeased the Pope. It was proposed to create a dozen new cardinals, who could be made to pay well for their hats. Cesare canvassed the Sacred College in person, to persuade them to support the scheme. The price ranged from 25,000 gold ducats, paid by the Bishop of Catania, to 5000 ducats, and the total receipts amounted to 120,000 ducats. There were two Borgias, Francesco, the son of Calixtus III, Bishop of Cosenza, who was much in the confidence of Lucrezia and had buried Don Alfonso, and young Pedro Borgia–Lançol, the new Archbishop of Valencia, as well as Valentino's brother-in-law, Amédée d'Albret. Six of them were Spaniards. Valentino entertained them all at dinner, when they are said to have handed over the sums stipulated.

CHAPTER XI

THE SECOND CAMPAIGN IN ROMAGNA
(1500–1501)

WHEN Cesare left Rome on October 2nd he was in command of an army which is said by Alvisi to have consisted of 10,000 men. The 4000 infantry were the pick of his troops. There were 700 men-at-arms and 200 light cavalry. The conduct of the Spaniards on the way through Umbria, which they treated like a conquered country, roused the fury of the Italians, especially of Baglioni's Perugians.

Cesena had already declared for the Duca and Pandolfo Malatesta had ceded Rimini on favourable terms. Giovanni Sforza talked of resisting, but by October 11th the pople were already shouting, Duca! Duca! in the streets. In any case the Rocca of Pesaro could not have held out for long, and Sforza can hardly be blamed for not running the risk of falling into the power of his ex-brother-in-law. He fled to Mantua, where he boasted that he could retake the place with 300 men, who, fortunately, were not forthcoming. The town threw open its gates and the commander of the Rocca, seeing that there was no hope of relief, came to terms before Cesare had appeared upon the scene.

His subjects were able to appreciate the qualities of their new master as soon as he entered his territory at Fano. He treated their rights, their persons and their property with the utmost respect, say the local writers, and was merciless in his discipline with his men. Not till October 27th was he at Pesaro, which he entered with the display he knew so well how to affect, in spite of the torrents of rain. He rode at the head of his bodyguard, which was commanded by Michelotto, dressed in his favourite Spanish black, wearing a coat of mail and a broad-brimmed black hat with white plumes. Here also the people took kindly to him. Sforza's rule had been no more gentle than that of the other princelings. The Duca did his best to protect the town from his troops, even from the Spaniards. The Borgia arms, quartered with those of Sforza, were on the palace to remind him of Lucrezia.

Here he was met by an exiled subject of Sforza, the eminent jurist Pandolfo Collenuccio, who had been sent from Ferrara to bring the congratulations of Ercole d'Este. Valentino welcomed him with great courtesy, sending him a present of wine and of sweets by de Lorqua. On the morrow he excused the delay in receiving him by his health—he was troubled with an abscess—and by all he had to do. He appears to have suffered from depression, or from a premonition of a violent death about this time. During the previous campaign, according to Cataneo, he had said that he knew that he was in danger of dying in battle, and that was why he liked to enjoy himself. He again talked about an early death in 1501. Possibly his health may explain this, as well as the hours he kept. He went to bed at four or five in the morning, rising at eight in the evening, when he sat down immediately to table and began to do business.

" He is held to be a man of spirit, sound and liberal, and is said to set store by men of worth. Ruthless in vengeance, everyone says he is a man of fine temper, athirst for greatness and fame. He seems to be more eager to win states than to organize them." It is natural that he should be more eager to win states than to organize them. He knew only too well that he must conquer his kingdom while his father was still alive: time enough to organize it later. Machiavelli was

136

told that one of his favourite ways of securing what he had won was to humour his subjects. Thus at Rimini, which he entered on October 30th, he at once recalled the exiles and tried to bring about a peaceful reconciliation. We read of his hanging a Gascon and a Piedmontese there with a placard on their chests recording that they were punished for looting. All supplies were paid for.

Cesare's success, his luck, as contemporaries put it, was causing no little anxiety to his neighbours, notably to the Florentines, who were not in a position to put up a real defence. If the French alliance was the chief source of his strength, the limitations it imposed upon him were a great comfort to the neighbouring Italian states. He owed the favourable neutrality of Venice, which had her hands full with the Turks, to the fact that she could not afford to break with France. On the other hand, it was Louis XII who refused to allow him to interfere in Tuscany or to attack the Bentivoglio in Bologna.

Faenza, between Imola and Forlì, was the next town that lay in his path. Here alone was he to meet with a whole-hearted resistance from the inhabitants, who were sincerely attached to their young lord, the handsome, attractive Astorre Manfredi. Venice at first promised to support him, but he soon saw that he would have to stand alone. Astorre thought of following the example of the other vicars and retiring, so as to allow Faenza to accept the highly favourable terms offered by Cesare and avoid the dangers of a siege, the end of which could hardly be doubtful. But his people would not hear of it. The women worked with the men in preparing to resist to the death, and when the time came they took part in the fighting.

By November 17th Valentino had appeared, and the Rocca was bombarded vigorously, the guns of Pesaro being brought into play. His troops, however, rushed to the assault prematurely, in spite of their commander's efforts to restrain them, and suffered severely. Some of them, including Onorio Savelli, a good artillery officer, were killed by the guns of the besiegers. This set-back put new heart into Faenza. The season was late for a siege, the Romagna winter was bitter and wood and provisions almost impossible to procure. The result was that the Duca had to go into winter quarters. Baglioni absolutely refused to remain and went back to Perugia. His men retaliated upon the Spaniards by murdering them whenever they found a chance. Valentino retired to Forlì, highly dissatisfied, after posting men at various points to blockade Faenza as effectively as possible. The besieged managed to lay in large quantities of supplies, as the neighbouring states were delighted at this, the first check to the Papal troops. The excommunication, which invariably accompanied Alexander's bull of deprivation, was no more observed in Faenza than elsewhere. The Council of the Anziani refused to consider terms, repeating their decision to resist to the last.

The Duke's winter quarters and his Christmas at Cesena, which he made his capital, were long remembered. Then it was that his subjects came to know and love him. No one could unbend more graciously when he chose, no one was fonder of a masquerade or a pageant. The gloomy Malatesta palace never saw a more brilliant Christmas. The people were even allowed to enter the room where their lord was reposing on his bed in his ducal cloak and insignia of office. He made his suite join him in taking part in all the amusements. At Christmas and in carnival he not only tilted at the ring, but joined in the village sports. He himself could hold his own in sheer strength with any of these hardy Romagnols, breaking a bar of iron or a horse-shoe or a new rope as easily as the best of them. As he said openly that he preferred such sports to the tourney, it is not surprising that he won his way to the hearts of these primitive peasants. No native-born Italian prince would have shown such condescension. Few, if any, had the strength, and few would have dared to mix so freely and familiarly with their subjects. On one occasion he insisted on a member of his staff giving his brocaded doublet to a peasant who had beaten him in a wrestling match.

Cesare visited other towns. Thus the early part of carnival was spent at Imola, where, on the last day of February, he was the hero of a great bull-fight, the first to be held in Romagna. Here, by the way, he also built a pious institution, La Valentina, the chapel of which still exists.

By these methods he really got on terms with his subjects and won their respect and affection as, when they compared his ways with the kind of treatment they had hitherto experienced, he well deserved to do. These were the days that made the cry of Duca! Duca! short though his rule was, live long in their memory. As we shall see, he did his best to establish a rule of law and order.

Other of his carnival amusements were less popular, at least with the more staid of his subjects. He delighted in going round with a band of his young officers and boon companions and playing all sorts of pranks. He would sally forth masked with a couple of them and splash respectable citizens with mud and naturally the women were looked upon as fair game.

In addition to the condottieri he had with him some young Italians of good birth who were on his staff, a Santacroce, a Farnese, a Mancini and a Savelli, as well as his cousin, Francesco Loris, Bishop of Elna, his secretary, Agapito, Juan de Castelar, Bishop of Trani, and his doctor, Gaspare Torrella. Torrella was Bishop of Santa Justa, for physicians, at least those attached to the Vatican, were often churchmen and bishops. He was also a Spaniard, like not a few of Valentino's companions. To him he dedicated his

Dialogus de dolore, and in the course of his dedication he maintains that his patron surpassed the justice of Brutus, the constancy of Decius, the continence of Scipio, the loyalty of Regulus and the magnanimity of Paulus Æmilius. It is hardly surprising that he bids us see in him one who is an ornament to his age.

Valentino's taste for literature seems to have been genuine. From early days he followed the fashion of a cardinal in having gifted young scholars and men of letters, which usually meant the same thing, in his train. In 1497 it was the able young Brescian, Carlo Valgulio, the teacher of Politian himself. To Valentino he dedicated his translations from Cleomedes' work on the world, which had its influence on Copernicus, who was at Bologna in 1496. A dedication to a cardinal so prominent would help him to fame. Nature, he declared, had surpassed herself in giving Cesare, to house his virtues, a body of surpassing beauty, dignity and easy grace, while on his character she had bestowed moderation, a seemly gravity and above all else royal generosity. This Cæsarian generosity is mentioned more than once. Capello, who did not love the Borgias, speaks of it, adding that, if he lives, he will be one of the first captains in Italy.

Valentino had several men of letters with him in Romagna, some of whom were to figure later in the *Cortegiano* of Baldassare Castiglione. They are barely names to us, since they wrote in Latin, men like Hieronimo Porzio, who dedicated his *Ad Bovem Borgia* to Cesare. Porzio, however, belonged rather to Alexander's court and was not with him on his campaigns. The best of Valentino's poets was Serafino Cimino of Aquila, the divine Aquilano, as he was called, who was something of an improvisatore and welcome in every court of Italy ; at least he was a poet of remarkable facility, such as one finds more readily in the South. He sang to his lute and the originality of his tunes made his sonnets universally popular.

He used to say that he would rather enjoy wide applause while alive than the fame of Dante or Petrarch after his death. Some of the subjects for his sonnets he admits to have been given him by Valentino, notably the sonnet likening his lady to a hydra with seven heads. These are the last ten lines. " She has seven heads and I will name them to you ; her glance, her smile replete with grace, her brow, her feet, her hands, her mouth, her breast ; and one and all they bite, they destroy and devour. Cut off a head and seven more spring up, disdain, despair, living death, suspicion, jealousy, doubt, fear. In this alone have they a different fate : the hydra, as I have heard, dies of fire, while she grows in strength from my flame." The conceit is certainly original. It may explain the device of seven snakes on one of Cesare's crests.

While on the subject of Valentino's taste in poetry we will give a few verses from his favourite love-song, quoted by Woodward from a collection of fourteen " Canzoni Musicali " current in Florence about 1406.

> Donna, contra a la mia voglia
>   mi convien da te partire ;
>   e non creder per fuggire
>   del tuo amore mai mi spoglia.
>
> La memoria sarà meco
>   de la tua dolze sembianza ;
>   l'alma mia resterà teco
>   a maggior testimonanza :
>   questo corpo sol m' avanza
>   che già sento arder con doglia.
>   Donna, contra a la mia voglia, ec.
>
> E s' avviene che 'n andando
>   resti alquanto per la via,
>   el mio cor ti raccomando
>   che ti diei per l' alma mia :
>   sai che 'nfamia ti saria
>   var (iar ?) come che foglia.
>   Donna, contra, ec.

141

I give a prose version. " Lady, sore against my will must I leave thee. Think not that in flying thee I escape my love. The memory of thy fair semblance will dwell with me ; my soul will remain with thee for a greater proof; this body alone is left me and already I feel it burn with pain. Lady, sore against my will, etc. And if it chance that, in going, it lingers awhile by the way, I commend my heart to thee, that I gave thee for my soul ; thou knowest that 'twould be infamous for thee to be unstable as a leaf. Lady, sore against, etc."

Aquilano died before he was thirty-five and was buried in S. Maria del Popolo, then the fashionable church. The poems in which his death is mourned testify to the high opinion held of him by his contemporaries.

Then there were the Latin poets, Francesco Sperulo of Camerino and Pier Justulo of Spoleto. They both belonged to the Academy of Pomponius Letus and both celebrated Cesare's achievements, but Justolo, who wrote three Latin poems chronicling his deeds, may be called his poet laureate. Thus he talks of " the unwearying strength of his limbs, those mighty arms, the sublime glory of his noble neck, the marvellous breadth of his chest, such as we see in the gleaming marble of the statues of Hercules, and the star-like eyes." Capello describes Cesare at twenty-seven as tall, with a magnificent body, better than King Ferrantino of Naples. There were other poets with Cesare. Their names are given by Alvisi, to whom I owe most of this account of his companions.[1]

Agapito Gherardino da Amelia, his loyal secretary, was, of course, there. His importance was considerable, greater, probably, or at least as great as that of Michelotto or Ramiro de Lorqua. His name appears on most of the documents of Cesare's dukedom, for he wrote the court style of the day to perfection. He

[1] Alvisi : *Cesare Borgia*, p. 98.

often acted as his proxy in taking over towns or making agreements. Quiet and retiring, he was never so happy as when he could slip away from Rome to his farm by the Tiber. Justolo praises his Roman simplicity.

Pinturicchio is the Borgia painter *par excellence*, and his work in the Borgia apartments, the magnificent addition Alexander made to the Vatican in continuation of the traditions of his predecessors, is the artistic glory of his reign. Doubts have been thrown upon the identity of some of the family portraits in these frescoes, but there can have been none about those in the garden court of the Castel S. Angelo which have disappeared. The castle owes its present form to Alexander and it was in the course of his alterations that the colossal bust of Hadrian was found there. Several of these frescoes illustrated the visit of Charles VIII, and were a glorification of the Pope. The king was there shown kneeling before him, serving at the Mass and holding his stole in the procession to St Paul's Without the Walls. There was also his departure for Naples with Cesare and Djem.

Pinturicchio had retired to Perugia, where he was living with his large family upon the property given him by Alexander. When Valentino passed through the town in 1500 the great painter asked him to let him have a certain water-tank which would make all the difference to his farm. He at once granted the request, saying that he had always loved the artist " for his virtues and had newly called him to his service ". Next year he pensioned him in the hope of being able to employ him again, but in 1502 the Cardinal of Siena, soon to be Pope Pius III, engaged him to paint the great frescoes in the Piccolomini Library in the cathedral of his native Siena, which illustrate the life of his uncle, Pius II.

Pier Torrigiano, the sculptor, also served in

Romagna. Benvenuto Cellini hated him for having broken the nose of the hero of his idolatry, the divine Michelangelo, in a quarrel when they were students in Florence, but he admitted that he was very handsome, full of dash, more like a great soldier than a sculptor, especially in his extravagant gestures and his loud voice. He had a trick of knitting his eyebrows that would have frightened anyone from anything. Torrigiano had already served under Vitellozzo's brother, Paolo Vitelli, against Pisa. Paolo had been executed, quite justly, by the Florentines for treachery and Vitelozzo had joined Valentino partly because he hoped to find a way of avenging his brother's death.

Formidable though he was in other ways, Michelangelo had not the making of a soldier in him. Cesare had in all probability met him. He had come to Rome in 1496 and been employed by Cardinal Riario, the brother-in-law of Caterina Sforza. The cardinal had the passion for antiques that had bitten most men of education at a time when they were being continually disinterred by the picks of the men engaged in the demolition of old Rome and the building of the new. He took the young sculptor round his collection, when he recognized a Cupid of his own. He had sold it to a dealer, from whom Riario had bought it as a genuine antique at a handsome figure. Raffaele Riario, who prided himself upon his taste, was disgusted at having been thus deceived, and gladly sold the statue to Cesare Borgia. It was Riario who engaged Bramante, soon after he came to Rome in 1499, to build him the noble Renaissance palace now known as the Cancelleria, probably the finest palace in Rome, which was begun before the death of Alexander. Michelangelo left Rome before the end of 1500, not to return till the days of Julius II. Patron and artist were a well-matched pair, with not a little of the heroic, even the elemental, about them.

The greatest and most interesting of Valentino's men was Leonardo da Vinci, who appeared in the camp before Faenza in the spring of 1501. After the fall of Ludovico il Moro, who had employed him in all manner of ways, he went to Florence, but as there seemed small chance of profitable employment there, he left and offered his services to Valentino, whose Cæsarian liberality made him an attractive master. Local tradition, as Alvisi records, assigns several works to him. He probably designed the canal from Cesena, and Porto Cesenatico, said to be the best harbour on the coast after Ancona, is certainly a product of his engineering skill. We shall come across him again.

An interesting company they make, a company such as one would hardly expect to meet in the campaign which the Pope's son was conducting. It was not altogether the Cæsarian liberality that attracted these men. The personality of the leader had something to do with it, his reputation for luck not a little. Robert de la Marck had no illusions about him, but "à la guerre il était gentil compagnon", is his not unwilling tribute, "et hardi homme". He was a good soldier, a genial companion and a leader of strength and courage, who knew how to win the devotion of his subordinates.

One day, some time after 1517, Bandello went to visit Elisabetta Gonzaga, who was ill, and found her with her inseparable companion, Emilia Pia, known to all readers of the *Cortegiano*. "The conversation turned upon the tyranny and cruelty exercised by Cesare Borgia in Romagna and the Marches long ago. As we spoke of these things, the poor Duchess could scarcely restrain her tears, remembering the cruelty of Borgia to one of her ladies, whom he surprised and captured on her wedding journey, slaying her attendants before her eyes. And many more things were said of the enormities committed by the said

145

Cesare Borgia, Duca Valentino, who not only killed his foes and strangers, but slew his own brother."[1]

The carrying off of Dorotea Caracciolo in February, 1501, out of which Bembo made a tale, created great stir at the time, and gave the Venetian orators plenty to do. Caracciolo, a member of the well-known Neapolitan family who was in Venetian employ, had gone to fetch his wife from Urbino, when his escort was attacked by some twenty horsemen near Cervia, in Venetian territory, several of them being wounded, and his wife carried off. The men were Spaniards. This rape gave the Venetians an excellent chance to make trouble for Cesare with Louis XII. Yves d'Alègre and M. de Trans had no liking for his high-handed ways with women and protested to him in person in the name of the King of France. Valentino denied all complicity, but said that Captain Diego de Ramirez, in the service of Guidobaldo of Urbino, was in love with Dorotea, that she was his mistress and that they had spent carnival together at Urbino. He had not yet succeeded in finding Ramirez. For himself, he had no lack of women; he did not need to carry them off by violence. Yves d'Alègre was convinced, or at least felt bound to appear to be.

Caracciolo was in despair and Venice did everything possible to help him. " The action is wicked, horrible, detestable," said the Pope to the Venetian ambassador. " I could not devise a punishment severe enough for one who has offended God and man by such a deed. If it is the Duke, he must have lost his senses."

The King of France was equally severe, saying to the Venetian envoy that, if he had two sons and one of them had been guilty of such a crime, he would have condemned him to death.

One thing was discovered. In December, 1502, Dorotea left Imola for Cesena on the same day as the Duca. The Serenissima refused Caracciolo leave to go

[1] Cartwright, *Is. d'Este*, II, p. 145.

in search of her, doubtless from fear of political complications, till after Alexander's death. He had heard
that she was at Forlì, where Cesare kept her guarded
by a trusty Mantuan till he should once more go
North. Whether he found her there we do not know,
but in January, 1504, she was brought to Rome,
when she wrote a letter to the Doge, thanking him
for the trouble he had taken to procure her freedom.
In all probability she had caught Cesare's fancy while
she was mistress of Ramirez, who had been obliged
to give her up, and he had taken care with his usual
efficiency that her whereabouts was not discovered.
It is possible that she was a not unwilling victim.
Similar deeds of violence, especially in time of war,
were too common at that time to excite much comment except in quite exceptional circumstances.

Meanwhile, Faenza was still holding out. Louis,
knowing that he could not do without the Pope's
aid in Naples, sent a useful contingent of 300 lances
to help Valentino under the command of his old
friend, Yves d'Alègre. Two attempts to surprise the
town failed, and it was not till April that Cesare,
who found the question of supplies a serious problem,
was able to move. After an outwork had been captured and fortified against the defenders, a powerful
bombardment was kept up for three hours. The
defenders used every device, from burning pitch to
falconets at close range, but on the next day the bombardment was maintained for seven hours—a great
feat for those times. Though the largest gun blew up,
killing Achille Tiberti of Cesena and its crew, it was
clear that further resistance was useless, and the
Anziani began to think of surrender. "They have
saved the honour of Italy by their defence," wrote
Isabella d'Este, only too pleased to see the hated
Borgia checked, to her husband, whom Valentino
had invited to witness the assaults. Valentino said
openly that, with an army of men like the defenders

of Faenza, he would undertake the conquest of Italy.

He was ready, as always in the Romagna, to offer the best of terms, gladly sparing the town the humiliation of having troops billeted upon it. Astorre Manfredi, like the rest, was granted full liberty to go where he pleased, while all property was to be spared. He, too, was *biondo e bello*, with a touch of melancholy about him that might seem to foreshadow his fate. In an evil moment this handsome young soldier decided to join Cesare's staff, as Dionigi Naldi had done before him, charmed by the manner of his late enemy and by the well-deserved compliments he knew so well how to pay, and also, no doubt, pleased at the prospect of making one of so goodly a company.

On June 26th, 1501, he entered the Castel S. Angelo, just as Caterina Sforza was leaving it. A year later, on June 9th, Burchard records that he was found strangled in the Tiber with a cannon ball round his neck, " a young man of about eighteen, so handsome and strong that it would be hard to find his match among a thousand of his coevals ". The story of Cesare and even the Pope outraging him, referred to by Guicciardini, is so absurd that it is hardly worth mentioning. Such a charge was never brought against the Borgias by any of their enemies, not even by Sannazzaro, during their lifetime. They were altogether normal in their sexual instincts.

There is nothing strange in Cesare wishing to make away with Astorre. He was the one lord of the Romagna who was dangerous owing to his popularity in Faenza, his youth, courage and looks. Probably, too, he was the only one who had not raised up a host of enemies by his oppression and his cruelty. Such political murders were not unknown in Italy at that time, but it helped to increase the ill-feeling against the Borgias. Later on Valentino made his tutor, Giovanni Vera, Archbishop of Salerno, now a cardinal,

Vice-Governor of Faenza. At least he kept his old friends and knew how to value and reward them.

Cesare was determined to get hold of the little enclave of Bolognese territory, centring round Castel Bolognese, to the west of Imola, which lay within the natural boundaries of the state he meant to acquire. He went to work with his usual swiftness and silence, sending Vitellozzo to attack it before the Bentivoglio were aware that he meant to move. He had tried in vain to induce them to cede it to him voluntarily and negotiations were not entirely suspended. Cesare's strength was such that all hope of resistance was out of the question. By the end of April the terms of the settlement were already arranged and Castel Bolognese was in his hands. Bentivoglio also undertook to grant him a *condotta* of 100 lances with three horses for each man for three years for use on any expedition he liked. Cesare had carried all before him, but Giovanni Bentivoglio gained a point which was afterwards to be of the utmost importance. Paolo Orsini and Vitellozzo were to guarantee the treaty. Cesare agreed to everything, but with the sweeping reservation that he did so subject to Alexander's confirmation. In any case, he was well aware that the King of France would never have allowed him to make further inroads on the possessions of the Bentivoglio.

To no one was Valentino's success more alarming than to the Florentines, who were seriously weakened by the unending struggle with Pisa. Their Government was far from strong and their territory ran unprotected along the borders of this new state, being within a short walk of Forlì. They were fully alive to the character of their neighbour, " the only lord in arms in Italy," as they wrote to Machiavelli, " the son of the Pope, who is a great friend of the King, lord of Romagna, and favoured by Heaven and by fortune."

The Pope was afraid that Cesare might do something against the Florentines, thus running the risk of offending Louis, and wrote expressly commanding him to come back to Rome without interfering with them. The Orsini, however, were insistent and Vitellozzo fell upon his knees, imploring him with tears in his eyes to march back through Tuscany. He promised to do no damage, but only to demand a little satisfaction from the Florentines for keeping in prison the chancellor of his brother, Paolo. The fact that d'Alègre was returning to Lombardy with his 300 lances freed Cesare from all fear of involving Louis in complications; indeed, there is reason to think that he acted with the connivance of the king. Moreover, the best way to Piombino, upon which he had designs, lay through Tuscany.

The exiled Medici were filled with high hopes of a speedy return. Cardinal Giovanni had joined Cesare, but he wisely declined his company. Piero, whose wife was an Orsini, with whom the Medici were naturally hand-in-glove, had also come from Rome. Valentino, however, who had no intention of attempting anything so foolish and no wish to make the Orsini too powerful, refused to see him.

But the Duca had made up his mind to compel the Florentines to allow him to march through their territory and to accept his terms. When he threatened to enter the Val d'Arno, adopting the methods he had employed against the Bentivoglio, commissioners were sent, who immediately agreed to his proposals. The Florentines became his allies and granted him a *condotta* of 36,000 ducats a year on his undertaking to supply them with 300 lances, 3 horses to each lance, as was then usual, for three years, to be used in any undertaking they might desire. These troops might even form part of their promised contingent for the French expedition against Naples. The Florentine authorities had not the slightest intention of observing any of these terms. Their object was to get this formidable army, with Vitellozzo and the Orsini and a possibility of the Medici in the background, out of the way as soon as possible at any cost. Cesare, however, lingered, demanding a quarter of his year's pay in advance and half the Florentine artillery for use against Piombino. The Florentines refused the money, as not in the treaty, and put him off with various excuses for the guns. Realizing that the game was up, and fearing trouble with Louis, he stayed long enough to send Vitellozzo to Pisa for artillery, which was gladly lent. Then he marched, like so many tourists, by Empoli, S. Gimignano and grim, frowning Volterra to the coast. The Papal fleet of a dozen galleys was sent to help him. He was thus able to capture the castle of Elba and blockade Piombino, poor though the Pisan guns proved to be. Its lord, Giacomo d'Appiano, fled and appealed to Genoa, Florence and the King of France himself. Instead of help he received the sound advice to accept the terms offered, which he did.

Before the surrender of Piombino, Cesare, styling himself Duke of Romagna, was back in Rome, ready to join the French on their way South to attack Naples in accordance with the terms of their partition treaty with Spain. He had returned almost secretly. There was no official welcome. Yves d'Alègre came first with the French advance-guard, then the Commander-in-Chief, Stuart d'Aubigny, who was given a cordial welcome and received with all the splendour of the Papal court in the Camera del Papagallo by Alexander, "though he was a Spaniard and a bad Frenchman", shrewdly observes the French chronicler. Did he feel that the Pope was never quite at home with the lilies of France, or was he thinking of his treatment of Charles VIII ? Rome was spared the presence of the troops, who were camped outside. But there was a great review of the 12,000 foot and

2000 horse by the Pope, who blessed them from the *loggia* of the Castel S. Angelo as they marched over the bridge. Alexander was surrounded by his court with Cesare, the Gonfalonier of the Church, at his side. With them marched his best force, 4000 infantry, many of them Spaniards, in their red and yellow uniforms. On June 25th the partition treaty was proclaimed in full Consistory by the French and Spanish ambassadors, and the Pope pronounced the deposition of Federigo on the ground that he had intrigued with the Turk. The expedition was declared to be the preliminary to a great crusade against the enemy of Christendom. The Turk was then as useful as the threat of a Council in the give and take of Vatican politics.

On June 26th Caterina Sforza left the Castel S. Angelo. Yves d'Alègre was highly indignant to find a woman, who was the acknowledged prisoner of his master, still confined in the castle on his return to Rome, and we may be sure that it is no mere coincidence that her liberation was effected so soon after the coming of the French, who doubtless let Valentino know pretty clearly what they thought. Such conduct was not expected from a French duke and a member of the Order of Saint Michel. Yves d'Alègre and his comrades regarded her as a heroine. Her sturdy resistance had increased their glory. Had she not been under French protection, she might well have shared the fate of Astorre Manfredi, though the Riario had too many enemies to be as dangerous. Her imprisonment was rigorous, and the Borgias may have hoped that it would prove too rigorous for a woman to endure. She afterwards said that, if she could write all, she would astonish the world.

The iniquitous partition treaty took Federigo almost completely by surprise, for hitherto the Spaniards had posed as his friends. The Neapolitans made their stand in the strong town of Capua, where they had the support of their faithful allies, the Colonna. When on July 24th the gates were thrown open by treachery, the sack that followed was so awful that the name of Cesare Borgia is still execrated in Capua. His presence was enough to bring all the blame upon the Borgia, though S. Severino was in command and therefore responsible. But Cesare was the more prominent figure of the two. The men were slaughtered without mercy, four thousand persons losing their lives. Women threw themselves from the walls or into the river to escape being outraged. Cesare is accused by Guicciardini, who was not a contemporary, of having chosen forty of the best-looking, but even Guicciardini does not say for his own use. Federigo's fate was sealed and he accepted the chivalrous offer of a pension and the dukedom of Anjou from Louis, scorning the promises of the Spaniards who had betrayed him.

Not only did the King of France write Valentino a warm letter of thanks for his services, but Ferdinand the Catholic made him Duca d'Andria, though by this time he had little affection for the Borgia. He also received comfortable additions to his revenues from both monarchs.

The fall of the Aragonese dynasty meant the ruin of the Colonna. The knowledge of this may have contributed to induce the Pope to accept the treaty. He at once began to seize their castles. Two days after the fall of Capua he went to Castelgandolfo and the neighbouring *castelli romani* to visit his new acquisitions. He spent the day rowing about the lake after dining. The people shouted "Borgia! Borgia!" and let off their guns. He delighted in such excursions and always tried to make one if anything had occurred to ruffle him.

It was for this trip that he took a step which may be regarded as the crowning point in the secularization of the Papacy. Cynical disregard of all that his great office meant could hardly be carried further. During his absence he left the entire control of the Vatican and of all ordinary business—but not, be it observed, the affairs of the Church—in the hands of his nineteen-year-old daughter, who occupied his rooms and was to open his letters. She was to turn to the Cardinal of Lisbon or some other cardinal for advice. When she sent for Lisbon on one occasion, seeing that it was a matter of no importance, he reminded her jokingly that in Consistory the Pope always had the Vice-Chancellor or another cardinal as secretary. There must be someone to take down what was said. She answered that she knew quite well how to write. " Where is your pen? " asked Lisbon, whereupon she laughed. " I was not consulted upon this matter," adds Burchard. She represented her father again for about a week at the end of September and then again in October. Unfortunately Portigliotti's story that, when a wealthy Papal chamberlain died during her reign, she said she ought to have his money, won't hold water, as he did not die till December ; but she did actually ask for the money on account of her approaching wedding and it was granted her, but the grant was quickly withdrawn as it proved to be illegal. Her knowledge of the ins and outs of the patronage work of the Vatican was probably unrivalled.

Burchard records two incidents in the year 1501 which throw light both upon the Pope's character and upon the times. At Easter his fool, Gabrieletto, followed him as he left the place of benediction, pretending to preach in Latin and Spanish as they went to the vestry and singing in falsetto. The Pope congratulated him on his performance. This kind of thing may shock us to-day, but fools were then privileged persons, though of course a really devout Pope would not have allowed it. At Pentecost, while the Pope sat facing the altar, a number of priests and friars bowed down to the ground as they filed by and kissed it in Turkish fashion. Burchard, thinking it not right, intervened. "The Pope was annoyed at my interfering and desired that I should let them kiss the ground, which I did." It is quite possible that the Pope's action was due to a momentary irritation at the officiousness of his Master of the Ceremonies rather than to personal vanity at the homage.

Alexander's shameless greed for money, which was used largely for the advancement of his children, has played no small part in blackening his character. He exercised his right to set aside the wills and claim the fortunes of dead cardinals and other Vatican officials to the utmost limits. Such cases are continually cropping up in Burchard, and they not unnaturally gave rise to the belief that he poisoned his cardinals when they were rich enough for it to be worth while— fattening them till they were ready for slaughter. This is a matter about which we shall have more to say later.

In June of this year, 1501, for instance, the Pope sent the Governor of Rome to a monastery where he had heard that Ascanio Sforza had deposited twelve silver statues of the Apostles which he had had made for his private altar with other goods he had been unable to take with him when he fled from Rome. Burchard learnt that the carters were engaged for four hours in bringing the property to the Vatican.

In March, 1498, when the Cardinal of Genoa, Fregoso, died, Alexander had his property carefully guarded, sending his *cameriere segreto* to make an inventory of the silver and confiscating everything. In May, 1501, Cardinal Zeno died at Padua, leaving over 100,000 ducats to Venice for a crusade against the Turks. The Pope refused to allow the will and demanded the money. Venice, however, was, as always, independent in her attitude towards Papal claims and declined to give it up. Alexander threatened interdicts and even a crusade, but in vain, and he had to be content with two coffers each containing 20,000 ducats which had been hidden in a convent at Ancona.

Not that Alexander was altogether indifferent to the Turkish danger; he was, indeed, far less indifferent than the other Christian Powers, except those in the danger zone. When the advance became a threat to Venice, he proclaimed a crusade into which even the preaching of the fiery Cardinal Peraudi could not breathe life. The cardinals were taxed ten per cent of their incomes to provide funds and the Papal galleys joined those of Venice and obtained some small successes about 1501. But the despatches of the Venetian envoy show that a crusade had a very small place in the Pope's heart compared with Valentino's campaigns in Romagna and a far smaller share in the contributions from the Papal coffers.

CHAPTER XII

LUCREZIA MARRIES DON ALFONSO D'ESTE (1501)

THE idea of a marriage between Lucrezia Borgia and
Alfonso d'Este, heir to the Duchy of Ferrara, now a
childless widower of twenty-four, appears to have
originated with the Pope, or at least the first moves
were made by him. Valentino, however, was behind
him, seeing that the match would turn out largely to
his advantage ; indeed, it was chiefly on that account
that it was suggested. The close alliance of the
d'Este with France put all idea of expelling them
from Ferrara out of the question, but an alliance
with a house of such standing and so highly respected
would greatly strengthen Cesare's position in the
Romagna and secure him against possible attacks by
Venice.

Alfonso at first refused to entertain the idea for a
moment. He was proposing to marry the widow
of the Duc d'Angoulême, a daughter of the royal
house of France, and the thought of taking in her
stead a woman of Lucrezia's reputation, the daughter
of the Pope, when Federigo had refused to give
his daughter to her brother, filled him with disgust. The little group of courts with which the
d'Este were allied had a unique position in North
Italy, cloaking the cruelty and the vices of the time
with a culture and charm that would have made
them memorable even without Baldassare Castiglione's
Cortegiano. The feelings of Alfonso's sister, the clever,
intriguing, dominating Isabella, Marchesa of Mantua,
or of her intimate friend and sister-in-law, Elisabetta

Gonzaga, Duchess of Urbino, at the prospect of having to welcome the Pope's daughter among them as an equal, can be imagined. Ercole of Ferrara himself, though age and responsibility and the realization of his own position forced him to take a longer view of the situation, was no less outraged and rejected the offer politely, but firmly.

But Alexander knew what he was about. He can hardly have expected the d'Este to jump at the bait, but he was so convinced of his ultimate success that, with his habitual eager, exuberant optimism, he spoke of the match as already settled in full Consistory as early as May, 1501. His close confederate, his datary, Cardinal Ferrari of Modena, had been in Ercole's service. Not only did he urge the advantages of the friendship of the Pope and of Cesare at Ferrara, but he set to work to win the support of France. Louis at first strongly objected to the match. He had no wish to increase Cesare's power at the expense of the proposed French marriage. But his need of the Pope's help in Naples and in allowing his army to march through his states was too pressing for him to dare to risk offending him. Rohan also favoured the project, as he hoped to have Cesare's support when the time came for the election of a successor to Alexander.

Louis soon changed his mind. He even refused his consent to the French marriage. The Borgias lost no time in pressing their advantage. But Louis sympathized with the feelings of his victim. He urged Ercole to raise his terms as high as possible. He also advised him to show no haste in the matter, but let the negotiations drag on as long as possible, till he himself reached Lombardy in the autumn. He told the Ferrarese ambassador that he thought it a pity that Ercole consented, as he could not know with whom he would be allied in the event of the Pope's death. They both hoped that Alexander's early demise might get them out of their difficulty. This much we learn from the despatches given by Gregorovius.

In fact the marriage was regarded with widespread disapproval, notably by Venice, always at loggerheads with Ferrara, and by the Emperor Maximilian who was deeply concerned and urged Ercole to refuse consent. Neither he, nor his wife, Bianca Sforza, a bitter enemy of the Borgias, wished to see any increase in the power of Cesare or of France.

No one felt more strongly on the subject than the bridegroom. The most callous of men must have hesitated before the scandals which clung to the name of the twenty-year-old daughter of the Pope, already twice married. They had been faithfully transmitted to Ferrara by its representatives in Rome. There was the illegitimate child and the terrible rumours of incest to be faced. Whether true or not, a prince of an old and proud house like the d'Este would never, in ordinary circumstances, have dreamt of marrying a woman about whom the lampoons of Sannazaro and others could be written. He would have been afraid of being the laughing-stock of Italy.

The satires on the Borgias were becoming more and more frequent and virulent. The writing of these libellous epigrams, generally in Latin elegiacs, which brought every conceivable charge against the victims, as often as not without the slightest foundation, was by then a favourite amusement among wits and scholars. Burchard includes a number of them in his diary. In August, 1501, we first read of a lampoon, a prophecy of the Pope's death in elegiacs, being fastened to Pasquin, the statue which the Cardinal of Naples (Carafa) had just placed in front of his palace ; but it did not become the regular place for displaying pasquinades till the days of Julius II.

To these attacks Alexander was completely indifferent. In December of this year appeared a ferocious diatribe against the Pope, the famous Letter to Silvio

Savelli, which is given in full by Burchard. It is supposed to be written to Silvio Savelli, one of the exiled barons of the Colonna party who had taken refuge at the court of the Emperor. The writer urges him to noise abroad the true state of Rome and the monstrous crimes and vices that are committed by the Borgias. Alexander is a second Mahomet, surpassing the original in the harm he does to such faith and religion as still remains by his foul crimes. These are the days of Antichrist. No greater enemy of God, Christ and religion can be imagined. Every conceivable vice and crime is openly committed in the palace of the Pontiff, where everything is for sale, even divorce or the repudiation of a wife. It would be an endless task to record the murders and plunderings, the adulteries and the incests that are committed there. Bisceglie and Perotto are mentioned, but not Gandia, be it observed, among the numbers who are said to have been killed or wounded or thrown into the Tiber. This piece of invective is too violent and couched in too general terms to carry conviction.

The Pope had this letter read to him and listened to it with interest. Later on he received Silvio Savelli with his usual affability when he returned to Rome. But his reputation has not gained by his callousness. It would have been better for him had he done something to check this licence which thrived on the impunity it enjoyed. But the fact that such things could be said of the Pope is in itself a sufficient condemnation.

Cesare had none of his father's easy-going good nature. He was sensitive to these attacks. " The Duke is a good-hearted man, but he cannot endure an insult," said the Pope to the envoy from Ferrara. " I have often told him that Rome is a free city where everyone is at liberty to write and say exactly what he pleases. Plenty of things are said about me, but I take no notice." The Duke answered, " That may be all very well for Rome, but I will make such people sorry for what they say."

And he was as good as his word. Stung possibly by the letter to Savelli, which was eagerly passed from hand to hand and from mouth to mouth, he made an example in that very month. Hearing that a masked man had spoken insultingly of him, he had him seized and his hand and the tip of his tongue cut off. The hand with the tip of the tongue fastened to it was hung up as a warning for a couple of days. We also read of a man being punished for making observations upon the very fragile reputation of the Princess of Squillace.

An incident recorded by Burchard brings out the Pope's moral cynicism which played straight into the hands of his detractors. In the year of Jubilee a Cardinal's major-domo came in great excitement to the Papal chapel to complain that his daughter had been carried off violently from church by her *fiancé*. His Holiness shocked both the father and his Master of the Ceremonies by smiling at the story, though he took care that she should be rescued by his troops and restored to her home.

It is not surprising that it was only after a struggle that Alfonso could be induced to accept Lucrezia for his wife. Indeed, it is said that Ercole actually announced that, if his son refused, he would marry the lady himself. But he did not forget the advice of King Louis. His demands were staggering, even for a father so *carnale* as Alexander, who had offered the handsome dowry of 100,000 ducats. Ercole wanted double the sum, the remission of the tribute paid by Ferrara to the Papacy and a number of minor concessions and benefices for his relatives and friends. The remission of the tribute would, the Pope knew, meet with strenuous opposition from the cardinals, who would feel it their duty to protest against such an alienation of the rights of the Church to further the

private interests of the Pope. But the advantages of
the match were so great both for Lucrezia and for her
brother that the Pope did not hesitate long.

Lucrezia probably had too much of her father in
her to feel any humiliation at the reluctance to accept
her hand. Marriage was a matter of business ; indeed,
it could by this time be little else to her, and she must,
young as she was, have long understood and accepted
the doubtful position she occupied in the eyes of the
world. She was well aware what a triumph it would
be for her to win the heir to the Duchy of Ferrara,
and she was quite ready to make the necessary sacri-
fices. From the first she used all her influence to
induce Alexander to accept Ercole's hard terms.
The Duke saw that she was his most valuable ally.
A correspondence began between them which ended
by inspiring him with a sincere esteem for his future
daughter-in-law's capabilities. By August the Pope
had given his consent. On August 26th the contract
was drawn up and signed in the Vatican. It was
immediately despatched to Ferrara, where, on
September 1st, the marriage *ad verba* was celebrated
in the Castle of Belfiore.

The same day Ercole wrote to Lucrezia a letter in
which he said that he had hitherto loved her for her
virtues and also out of regard for the Pope and for
her brother Cesare, but henceforth he loved her more
than a daughter. He wrote hardly less warmly to
the Pope, who had just made his son, Cardinal Ippolito, Arch-priest of St Peter's.[1] The tone of his
letter to the Marquis of Mantua is rather different :

" We informed Your Excellency that we had
recently decided to consent to consider the conditions
proposed for an alliance with His Holiness, by taking
the Most Illustrious lady, Lucrezia Borgia, sister of

---

[1] Gregorovius, *Lucrezia Borgia*, Chap. xx. Gregorovius is,
indeed, fundamental for the story of Lucrezia at this time.

the most beloved Duke of Romagna and of Valence, as the wife of our first-born, Don Alfonso. This we were induced to do largely by the exhortations of His Most Christian Majesty; always, however, on the condition that we should agree with His Holiness upon all the points affecting the marriage itself. The matter has been under discussion and now His Holiness and ourselves have reached an understanding; and the Most Christian King has continued to press us to conclude the marriage through the French ambassadors and the Procurators of His Holiness. And this morning it has been announced. . . .

FERRARA. *September 2nd,* 1501."

Knowing how Gonzaga, and still more the Marchesana Isabella, his own daughter, would feel on hearing of the betrothal, Ercole is careful to stress the part played by the King of France in bringing about the match.

When the news of the signing of the contract reached Rome, the guns on the Castel S. Angelo were fired continuously till dusk. The Pope's delight was unbounded. On the next day, September 5th, Lucrezia rode to S. Maria del Popolo, between the French and Spanish ambassadors, escorted by 300 horsemen and four bishops and preceded by grooms and by her buffoons in masquerade costumes, to offer up thanks to the Virgin. After the ceremony, following custom, she gave the rich dress she was wearing to one of her fools, who ran about the streets in it, shouting, " Long live the most illustrious Duchess of Ferrara ! Viva il Papa Alessandro ! "

The excited Pope, who was by this time quite unable to feel that there was anything incongruous with his great office in such a display of parental enthusiasm, summoned a special Consistory for the occasion and treated the cardinals to an enthusiastic eulogy of the House of Este. Duke Ercole was the greatest, the wisest prince in Italy and Alfonso better-looking and stronger than his own son, Cesare. His first wife had been a sister-in-law of the Emperor, and much more in the same strain. The great bell of the Capitol was rung till after nightfall, fires were lit on the Castel S. Angelo and elsewhere, and Rome was illuminated. Following the Spanish custom Donna Lucrezia, being a widow, had been eating from earthenware or majolica. Now she once more used silver plate, like a married woman.[1]

The gaiety in the Vatican, where there was dancing and gambling till well into the small hours every night, tired everyone but the Pope, who could not weary of watching the dancing. Cesare, who had been made Duke of Romagna soon after his return, was now back in Rome, and Alexander insisted on Lucrezia and he dancing every night. The Duke was growing more and more chary of granting audiences, but he did the Ferrarese ambassadors the honour of receiving them, when he was, indeed, fully dressed, but in his bed. This is how he had received the people of Cesena. These two special envoys had arrived on the 15th, for Ercole had no intention of sending for the bride till he had made sure of the whole of his pound of flesh. The Pope was continually calling upon them to admire his daughter's beauty. One evening, as he watched her with a proud smile, he said that he hoped they had noticed that she was not lame. All this was telling upon the bride. The envoys noticed that she was not looking too well and seemed tired. Yet she refused to take care of herself and continued to carry on business and grant audiences as usual. Fortunately the Pope went for a short trip to Nepi, so that she was able to have a little rest.

No one was more untiring in pressing on the negotiations than Lucrezia. His ambassadors told Ercole that already she seemed an excellent Ferrarese.

[1] Luzio and Renier, *I. d'Este e I Borgia*, p. 69.

Her agent was Calixtus' son, the Cardinal of Cosenza. Whenever she saw the ambassadors, she asked them when the escort was coming for her. Her eagerness and her eye for business impressed her future father-in-law more and more favourably and, according to Gregorovius, she wrote him gushing letters. She turned pale, say the ambassadors, and seemed deeply concerned when she heard that he was ill, remarking that she wished that she could nurse him with her own hands. When shortly after this the Pope became unwell with a bad cold and ear-ache, he sent for the ambassadors and told them that, though his face was tied up and he had lost a tooth, he would take Ercole, were he in Rome, on a boar hunt, adding that he had at last given up the bad habit of leaving the Vatican before daybreak and returning after nightfall. Alexander knew well enough that, if there were any possibility of his dying, Ercole would put off the marriage indefinitely. Both these illnesses must have alarmed Lucrezia and increased her eagerness for the arrival of the escort.

On October 31st, 1501, according to Burchard, occurred the dinner to the fifty courtesans, which was the crowning point in the debauchery at the Vatican under the Borgias. On that day Valentino entertained in his rooms fifty of the more decent courtesans of Rome at supper. After supper they ran about first clothed, then naked with some servants and some others who were present. Then candles were placed upon the floor and chestnuts thrown among them. These the women picked up, crawling upon their hands and knees among the candles, while the Pope, the Duke and his sister, who were present, looked on.[1]

[1] Burchard goes on, "Tandem exposita dona ultima, diploides de serico, paria caligarum, bireta et alia pro illis qui pluries dictas meretrices carnaliter agnoscerent; que fuerunt ibidem in aula publice carnaliter tractate arbitrio presentium, dona distributa victoribus."

The next day, being All Saints' Day, the Pope did not attend Mass and Burchard could not have access to him.

Then, on November 11th, a couple of female mules came to St Peter's Square with loads of wood. Some Vatican servants ran up, cut off the loads and drove them into a smaller court within the palace. Four horses were then driven out to them and fought for them, making a great uproar. The Pope and Lucrezia looked on from a window, enjoying the scene thoroughly and laughing heartily.

The story of the courtesans appears in Matarazzo of Perugia, in Sanudo and in a despatch of the Florentine ambassador. Indeed, it is clear that it at once became the common gossip of Rome. That Cesare should give such an entertainment and that the Pope should enjoy it is by no means improbable, but I can hardly think that they would have allowed Lucrezia to be present when the Ferrarese envoys were actually in Rome to arrange the conditions of her marriage. Yet, if we accept Burchard as among the best authorities we have, we cannot reject him in a case like this, or hold that he took the story from the Letter to Silvio Savelli. It is true that by now people were ready to believe almost anything of the Borgias, especially in Rome. Even Burchard is not altogether exempt from the prevailing hysteria, if we may so call it. Had Alexander not been Pope, there would be nothing extraordinary in such an evening's amusement at this time, and we must remember that in such matters he habitually behaved like a secular prince. When we realize that " The Decameron " was then the favourite reading of nuns, a girl brought up as Lucrezia had been, in surroundings that had a good deal of the demi-monde about them, might in ordinary circumstances have been present at such a scene and even amused by it. She had been twice married and was almost certainly the mother of an illegitimate child. But, if she had been present, it is difficult to believe that the fact would not have been reported to Ferrara.

Again, would there be anything extraordinary in Alexander and his daughter being amused by the incident of the mules had he not been Pope? If we substitute Alfonso d'Aragona and his daughter, Sancia, the story would be perfectly intelligible. The jokes and the masks of the Carnival were not particularly refined, but Alexander was not the only Pope who enjoyed them, with or without his daughter.

The choice of the suite of the future Duchess called forth a long letter from the ambassadors. Ercole wanted her to be escorted by a cardinal, but even Alexander felt that this would be rather too much to ask of a member of the Sacred College. However, he promised to try to arrange for the Cardinal of Salerno, Legate of the Marches, to meet her in Romagna and celebrate the nuptial Mass, if his health allowed. This letter also shows the Pope giving way to one of his characteristic tirades against Cesare. They are a proof of the fear in which he went of his formidable son and to which Capello alludes. He was very much put out when he heard that the envoys had failed to obtain an audience of Valentino. The deputation from Rimini had been in Rome for two months, he told them, without being able to speak to him. For Cesare night was day and day night, a habit which may have been the result of his ill-health. " He deeply regrets this way of life and doubts whether he will be able to keep what he has won with such methods."

Then the Pope went on to praise Lucrezia, saying that she was tactful, readily granted audiences and knew how to make herself agreeable when necessary. He assured his visitors that she governed the Duchy of Spoleto to the general satisfaction. If she were called upon to negotiate with His Holiness himself, he was

167

sure that she would best him. " I think that His Holiness said what he did rather with the idea of praising her (and, in our opinion, she deserves his praise) than of running down the Duke, though there is good ground for holding the contrary view."

Still the escort did not arrive. Ercole insisted that the dowry should be paid at the moment his envoys reached Rome through the Venetian and other banks, or they would start back without the bride. Pledges must be forthcoming for the other concessions and he must have the bull for the remission of the tribute. Such demands were not likely to please the Pope. He began to be afraid that the Emperor was succeeding in his plan of preventing Ercole from sending the escort at all. Ercole was too good a man of business not to have informed Alexander of Maximilian's bitter hostility to the match. The Pope flew into a passion, heaped abuse upon the ambassadors and called Ercole, not unfairly, a beggarly shopkeeper. However, by September 15th the bull reducing the *census* to 1000 gold ducats was ready and arrangements had been made for the payment of the dowry of 100,000 ducats in time. There could be no possible further pretext for delay.

Now, too, the territories of which Lucrezia held the lordship were distributed among the two Borgia infants. She would vacate them on going to Ferrara. Sermoneta, which had been taken from the Colonna, was made the capital of the duchy conferred upon the infant Rodrigo d'Aragona. The King of Spain also granted him the rank of his father, so that he became Duke of Bisceglie and Sermoneta. The rest of the property went to the much discussed Roman infant, Giovanni Borgia, who became Duke of Nepi. It is interesting to remember that Giovanni's daughter, Lucrezia, was grandmother of the Pamphili Pope, Innocent X, who was ruled absolutely by the masterful Donna Olimpia.

168

Lucrezia's marriage and the festivities held in her
honour are among the best known events of their
kind in the Italian Renaissance, so full are the descriptions of them preserved in contemporary letters.
The Marchesana Isabella had opposed the match
from the first and, though she fully realized that she
would have to make the best of it, she did not look
forward to the coming of a dangerous rival, the wife
of her own brother, whose purse was much longer
than her own, to dispute her claims to being the best
dressed woman in the most refined and cultured district in Italy. The long duel between the two dates
from these early days. For many years to come she
was insatiable in her curiosity to know every detail
of Lucrezia's toilet, and now she had a correspondent
in Rome, who signs himself El Prete, to tell her all
that she wanted to know. This priest, who might
have been in the employ of a fashionable *modiste*,
undertook to follow Lucrezia in her preparations for
her wedding like her shadow. He will describe the
size of her footprints. Where his eyes cannot penetrate
his nose will ; and he was as good as his word.

Ercole had reason to congratulate himself on the
bargain he had made. The inventory sent him with
obvious satisfaction by his agents in Rome, which is
eminently characteristic of the Italy of that day, went
far to justify the Pope's calling him a shopkeeper,
deeply though the word offended him. In addition
to the dowry, Lucrezia's jewels, linen, plate and
personal ornaments were valued at 100,000 ducats.
There was one dress costing over 15,000 ducats, 200
chemises, several valued at 100 ducats, each sleeve,
with its gold fringe and other ornaments, costing more
than 15 ducats. " In six months more gold has been
used and sold here and at Naples than in two ordinary
years." The towns of Pieve and Cento, with the
remission of the tribute, meant a further 100,000
ducats.

It is not surprising that, early in December, he sent a suite of 500 persons, headed by his son, Cardinal Ippolito, a worldly, vicious, handsome young man of two-and-twenty. With him were his brothers Don Ferrante and Don Sigismondo and other members of the family, the lords of Correggio and Mirandola, a Pio of Carpi, Annibale Bentivoglio of Bologna, and many other nobles of the highest birth. As they were entertained at the expense of the unfortunate towns through which they passed, they cost him nothing. The December weather took its toll and they had heavy ravages to repair after the last stage before making their entry by the Porta del Popolo on December 23rd, 1501. Nineteen cardinals came to welcome them, not one with fewer than 200 sumptuously equipped attendants. Valentino, splendidly mounted, was estimated to be worth, with his horse, 10,000 ducats, says Sanudo, " for you could see nothing but gold, pearls and other jewels." With him were 4000 troops, all in uniform. The receptions and introductions took two full hours. Cesare embraced Ippolito and rode with him to the Vatican. So heavy was the firing from the castle that the horses could hardly be induced to cross the Ponte S. Angelo. After paying their respects to the Pope, who had watched their approach from a window in the Vatican, they were entertained by Lucrezia herself. She met them at the top of the stairs on the arm of a gentleman of mature years and gave them refreshments and small presents of jewellery. El Prete's report cannot have been comforting to Isabella. He knew positively that the Cardinal Ippolito's eyes sparkled with pleasure, " she is a charming and a most gracious lady." Indeed, he warns Isabella that she will be a formidable rival. " I may tell you that the lady wears her hair quite simply, without curls, that she keeps her breast covered, as do all her ladies. She is improving every day, and is a lady of a very good brain and astute.

ALFONSO D'ESTE, BY TITIAN

You have to have your wits about you. Indeed, I consider her a very clever lady ; and this is not merely my opinion, but that of all here."[1]

The Duke's agent visited her on the evening of his arrival and his report is equally favourable. He found her wise and discreet, affectionate and good-hearted, while in her attitude towards her husband and her father-in-law she left nothing to be desired. Not only is she charming, graceful and of a becoming modesty, but she is a devout Catholic. She has sufficient beauty, which is much enhanced by her winning ways and manner, her grace and charm. " To sum up, she possesses such qualities, that there is neither right nor reason to suspect anything sinister from her "—quite the contrary.

This letter shows plainly the fears that were entertained at Ferrara. The mission consisted of men upon whom Lucrezia knew how to make a good impression. She would hardly have got off so easily had she been called upon to face a jury of her own sex.

El Prete writes that she is too busy to appear much, but he visited her on December 26th and found her by her bed. In a corner of the room were some twenty Roman women dressed in Roman style with the usual cloths on their heads. She danced very well and very gracefully with Don Ferrante. The ladies-in-waiting at Ferrara could well hold their own with those of Lucrezia. Angela Borgia–Lançol is charming. He has made her his favourite almost without realizing it. Nor was he alone in his choice, as Ferrara was to learn in due course.

The princes served at the Christmas Mass, where they were duly impressed by the majestic presence of the Pope as he celebrated. On December 30th the Ferrarese party came to fetch Lucrezia for the renewed wedding ceremony, which took place in the Camera Paolina in the Vatican, the Pope being on his throne

[1] Luzio and Renier, *I. d'Este*, etc., p. 75.

with his cardinals and Cesare in attendance. Once again he bade the Bishop of Adria shorten his address.

Then came the giving of the presents. Ercole was still the shopkeeper. Cardinal Ippolito was to present the jewels in a set form of words drawn up by Pozzi, so that, in case Lucrezia proved untrue to Alfonso, he need not be bound to the gift. Pozzi can assure him that the only gift to which he has pledged himself is the ring. This is another proof of the estimation in which Ercole held his future daughter-in-law. Among the jewels was a beautiful rope of Lucrezia's favourite pearls. When the first ambassador came from Ferrara, the Pope showed him à chest full of them and, running his hand through them, said that he wanted her to have more pearls and more beautiful pearls than any other princess in Italy. The Pope took this necklace in his hands and told Cardinal Ippolito that the grace with which he had presented it enhanced its value. Later Lucrezia and Cesare danced in the Camera del Papagallo and their proud father, seated on his throne, watched their performance with unfeigned delight. Then followed some lively comedies.

On New Year's Day there was a pageant of cars, celebrating the triumphs of Hercules and of Julius Cæsar and other classical subjects. In the evening Valentino danced admirably on the stage in the Camera del Papagallo in a Moresque. Last of all, at the Pope's request, Lucrezia danced with one of her maids of honour. The next day Cesare gave a remarkable display in the bull-ring, which he entered with eight companions all mounted, doubtless Spaniards, possibly professionals, armed with lances. He struck one of the bulls right between the horns and it fell dead amid wild enthusiasm. He next entered the ring on foot, dressed in gold brocade, with twelve companions, all armed with long lances. As the bull came at them, they all struck at it standing close together, quite suddenly. Eight bulls and two buffaloes were killed, the buffaloes putting up a poor fight. One man lost his life.

Lucrezia was to be accompanied by her faithful Cardinal of Cosenza and three bishops. Cesare, at his own expense, sent 200 horsemen with her, as well as musicians and buffoons to amuse her upon the journey. She retained her fondness for dwarfs and buffoons to the end of her life. After all, she was going through her brother's territory. There were 124 ladies in her train. Among the Pope's gifts was a French litter in which two people could sit side by side and 9000 ducats for the outfit of herself and her women.

Alexander also paid her the rather doubtful compliment of descanting at length upon her chastity and high moral standards to the ambassadors from Ferrara and they duly informed their master that she herself had said that the Pope should never have to blush for her conduct. Of this, they added, they felt assured, " for the more we see of her and study her life at close quarters, the higher is the opinion we have of her goodness, her chastity and her discretion. We have also observed that her life is not merely Christian, but devout." It looks as if they had had special instructions to enquire most particularly into the bride's way of life. A royal, or rather a ducal bride cannot often have started for her new home fortified with so damaging an array of certificates of good conduct.

CHAPTER XIII

LUCREZIA'S RECEPTION AT FERRARA (1502)

LUCREZIA left on January 6th, taking the precious bulls with her. At their parting Alexander said that he would do more for her when she was away from him than he had ever done for her in Rome. He followed her from window to window in the Vatican till her train disappeared from sight. Did he know instinctively that he would never see his daughter again ? Pozzi was not far wrong when he said that he loved her more than anyone else of his family. She was riding a white jennet with a gold bridle and wore a red silk dress trimmed with ermine and a plumed hat. El Prete faithfully describes all her costumes for his mistress with the care and detail of a dress expert, but I have not thought it necessary to try to follow him. The whole suite did not take the same route, as the cost of entertaining it would have been more than some of the towns could have afforded. Lucrezia's luggage required 150 mules and a number of carts. In recommending her to the care of her subjects at Nepi, Alexander describes her as his dear daughter in Jesus Christ. All along the route she was welcomed with triumphal arches and often with the elaborate mythological pageants of the day.

She went by easy stages, for it was the depth of winter, and a journey in January was a serious ordeal for a healthy man. Indeed, Ercole was soon warned that his daughter-in-law would not arrive as early as had been expected, for " the illustrious lady Lucrezia is of a delicate constitution and little accustomed to

174

riding; her ladies are even less so, and we realize that she would not like to reach Ferrara worn out and exhausted by the journey." The Pope gave express orders that she was to write to him with her own hand at every halting-place. She was especially well received in Spoleto and the places round, where she was well known, as she had been governor there.

They reached Urbino on January 18th, when Guido-baldo placed his beautiful palace at her disposal and welcomed her warmly, though he must have been anything but pleased at the match. His wife, Elisabetta Gonzaga, known to all readers of the *Cortegiano*, was Isabella of Mantua's bosom friend, so naturally she wished to do all she could for Lucrezia, quite apart from political reasons. She was dressed in black, as also was her lady, the delightful, witty Emilia Pia, of the *Cortegiano*. "Their mules approach, they touch hands and kiss," wrote El Prete. She accompanied Lucrezia some distance along the rough mountain road towards Pesaro. Here, in the town of her first husband, which now belonged to her brother, she was welcomed by a hundred children, dressed in Cesare's colours of red and yellow and shouting as they waved their olive branches, "Duca, Duca! Lucrezia, Lucrezia!" amid the genuine delight of her former subjects. But, though she allowed her women to dance with those of Pesaro, she herself spent the day she passed there in absolute seclusion, taking the opportunity of washing her head. Everywhere Cesare's subjects vied with one another to do her honour. At Imola she again washed her head, which she had not done for a week, as she was beginning to have headaches, and set about preparing her toilette for her entry into Ferrara.

At Bologna the Bentivoglio did her every honour. She was met at the frontier by all the sons of the House, with their haughty mother, Ginevra, while Giovanni, the head of the family, welcomed her two miles from the town. They gave a magnificent banquet followed by a ball. She must have been glad to dance again. On the day following they escorted her to the barge that was to convey her to the frontier of her future home. At the border town of Castel Bolognese Don Alfonso d'Este, duly masked, paid his bride a surprise visit. Obviously he was anxious to meet her again, for he had seen her many years ago, when she was a young girl, in Rome, before the ceremonies of her official reception. She received him with a charming mixture of grace and deference, Ercole was informed by his agents. As he stayed two hours, he cannot have been displeased. An interview so romantic was something quite out of the common in the princely courtships of the Renaissance. She at once wrote to the Pope, who was much gratified at the news. He sent for the Ferrarese ambassador to tell him so.

At Malalbergo, familiar to every reader of old books of Italian travel, on the Ferrara canal, occurred the meeting between Lucrezia Borgia and Isabella d'Este, Marchesana of Mantua, who was to act as hostess at the wedding ceremonies. With her was Elisabetta d'Urbino. Thus three of the most famous women of the Renaissance found themselves in each other's company for the first time. The detailed information we possess about them during the next few days makes that spacious time live again in their persons with an intimacy which we rarely have the opportunity of enjoying. The meeting must have caused Lucrezia many more qualms than that with her husband. She had to face her most dangerous rival on her chosen ground in the midst of her friends and relatives, and she felt and instinctively reacted against the " joyous fury " with which, as Isabella wrote to her husband, she embraced her. Isabella does not describe Lucrezia, as her husband had already seen her, but her obvious jealousy is a testimony to her charm.

Isabella had taken El Prete's advice to heart. She

spared neither pains, nor her credit, which was generally stretched to the breaking point, to hold her own with the hated *parvenue*, who had the coffers of the See of St Peter behind her. For once we will try to describe the clothes. Lucrezia wore a dress of wrought gold trimmed with crimson satin, with slashed sleeves in the Spanish style, a cloak turned up on one side with black satin and lined with sable, open at the throat and showing a worked chemise. Round her neck was a rope of large pearls, with a pendent ruby and a pearl. On her head there was no band, only a gold cap. Isabella wore a dress of green velvet ornamented with gold tassels, a cloak of black velvet lined with lynx, a gold fillet round her head and on her neck a gold chain set with diamonds. The Duchess of Urbino also wore a dress of black velvet covered with astrological signs in gold thread.

At Torre della Fossa Ercole and Alfonso were awaiting Lucrezia with the whole court. Here seventy-five mounted archers were drawn up along the canal in their livery of white and red. Lucrezia insisted on kissing Ercole's hand, though he tried to prevent her—here we see the daughter of the Pope—and he then kissed hers with the utmost gallantry. This is the point where the canal enters the Po and the whole party embarked on a roomy barge of state. Lucrezia was between the French and the Venetian ambassadors, the latter separating her from Isabella. Ercole and Alfonso were on deck, chatting and laughing at the antics of the two fools, who were singing Lucrezia's praise in Spanish verse.

The wedding party reached Casale amid a great deal of noise from the trumpets and the firing of guns. Here five carriages were presented to her, one covered with cloth of gold and drawn by four white horses, each worth 50 ducats ; another covered in red velvet, the others in purple satin, with horses of different colours. Here, too, she was met by twelve waiting-women of Ferrara and her chief lady-in-waiting. She spent the night at the palace of Ercole's illegitimate brother, where she was welcomed by a natural daughter of his. Would things have been arranged differently had she not herself been a bastard ?[1]

The festivities at Ferrara have remained famous even in the annals of the Renaissance. The bride's entry left nothing to be desired in splendour. First came the archers, then 80 trumpeters, six lent by the Duke of Romagna, dressed in cloth of gold, purple and white satin, followed by 24 pipers and tabourers. Then the nobles of Ferrara, who had among them 70 gold chains, none worth less than 500 ducats and some valued at 1200. At that time great importance was attached to gold chains. Next came the suite of the Duchess of Urbino, then the bridegroom with Annibale Bentivoglio. Don Alfonso was on a bay horse, caparisoned with purple velvet embossed with gold. He was dressed in grey velvet, covered with beaten gold, and was wearing a black velvet cap, with gold cords and white plumes. The Venetian ambassadors estimated the outfit of man and horse at 6000 ducats.

Next came Lucrezia's escort, twenty of them Spaniards dressed in black and gold, but there were only a dozen gold chains among them, and these could not compare with the chains of the gentlemen of Ferrara. Next came five bishops and after them the ambassadors, walking in pairs. The Venetians were in long scarlet mantles, the four Romans in long cloaks of cloth of gold lined with crimson satin. Behind these were six tabourers and the two Spanish fools in their parti-coloured costumes. At last the bride appeared, under a crimson baldacchino, carried by the Doctors of the University. In front of her was a great dapple-grey horse, a present from Ercole,

[1] The best descriptions of these festivities are in the letters of Isabella d'Este to her husband, given by d'Arco, in *Arch. Stor. Ital.*, App. 2.

caparisoned with crimson velvet, embroidered with gold. This she had ridden as far as the Ponte di Tedaldo, where it was so frightened by the firing that she would have been thrown if her grooms had not come to the rescue. Instead she mounted a roan mule, which was richly and splendidly caparisoned with velvet trappings embroidered all over with gold and fastened with small nails of beaten gold. She wore a dress of cloth of gold and very dark satin in alternate stripes, with flowing sleeves in the French style and a cloak of drawn gold, slashed at the side and, like the sleeves, lined with ermine. Her necklace of diamonds and rubies had belonged to the late Duchess, of blessed memory, Isabella's mother. On her head was a jewelled cap sent her by Ercole, together with the necklace, in Rome. She wore no fillet. With her were six of Don Alfonso's grooms with heavy gold chains round their necks. Beside her, outside the baldacchino, rode the French ambassador, whom she was said to have called to her and bidden take the place of honour as a token of the close relations in which both her father and her husband stood with his master. Behind her rode the Duchess of Urbino and Duke Ercole. Then came the bride's cousins, Hieronima Borgia, the wife of Fabio Orsini, the chief of her Roman ladies, followed by Adriana de Mila, who was treated with the utmost respect by everyone. The rest of the procession we can leave to the Marchesana and Sanudo, whose accounts are often so similar, even to the turns of phrase, that they might have been furnished by a news agency.

There were several triumphal arches, as well as the customary Latin poems of welcome and the mythological displays. Among these was a bevy of nymphs grouped round their queen, who was mounted upon a red bull, while satyrs danced about them. Isabella tells her husband that these things were not worth mentioning. On the Piazza, which still preserves almost intact its stern, forbidding medieval aspect, two tight-rope dancers slid down from the towers and made the bride pretty speeches. All the prisoners were then set free and the band began to play. The archers fought for the canopy, while after a long struggle with Ercole's men, those of Don Alfonso secured the mule. This was a regular custom. Caterina Sforza once redeemed a horse which was thus forfeit when she entered Forlì in state.

By this time Lucrezia had dismounted inside the great gate of the palace, flanked by the statues of Nicolò and Borso d'Este, and had been escorted up the marble staircase, at the top of which Isabella, in a splendid costume of cloth of gold embroidered with her favourite device of musical notes, was waiting to welcome her with an even larger dose of joyous fury in her heart. Like the Pope, Lucrezia appeared at her best on these occasions and, with her flowing golden hair, her frank glance, her gay, winning smile, she had already made her way to the hearts of many of her future subjects. Was the Marchesana responsible for the fact that the bride was welcomed only by the bastard princesses of the House of d'Este, the wife of Annibale Bentivoglio, a daughter of Ercole, and three daughters of Don Sigismondo, all married to men of position ? In the Sala Grande, where the bridal pair were seated on thrones, there was a great reception of the nobles of Ferrara, who were presented to the bride. A number of Latin poems, Epithalamia and the like, were recited. In one of these Helen is said to be ugly in comparison with Lucrezia. Ariosto, then a young man of twenty-seven, unknown to fame, was among those who provided a Latin poem for the great event.

Now it is that we begin to get a definite impression of Lucrezia. On such an occasion there were bound to be a number of descriptions of the bride, as well as of the ceremony of her entry. Gregorovius gives several. "Seducente e veramente graziosa", had written Isabella's priest from Rome, and his words may be said to set the note. The Marchesa di Cotrone, one of Isabella's ladies-in-waiting, wrote to the Marquis of Mantua that the bride's beauty is nothing remarkable, "but she has a sweet expression (dolce ciera). In spite of the charms of several of the ladies, including that illustrious Madonna, the Duchess of Urbino, who is very handsome and a worthy sister of Your Excellency, my illustrious lady was universally declared, both by our people and by those who came with the Duchess, to carry off the palm of beauty. Indeed, had the bride foreseen this, she would have made her entry by torchlight." She adds with an emphasis that speaks volumes, that in beauty, noble appearance, grace and everything her mistress outshone them all.

Thus even in the camp of her enemy Lucrezia's sweet expression was admitted. Moreover, she was six years younger than Isabella. The men are much more enthusiastic. She is very beautiful in face, writes Zambotto, quoted by Gregorovius, "with lovely eyes, full of life and gaiety, with an upright figure, tactful, prudent, very intelligent, lively, pleasing, most gracious. The people here liked her so much that they are highly gratified at her coming, hoping for protection and good government from her ladyship." It was also hoped that the city would benefit greatly by the influence of the Pope, "who loves his daughter dearly", as he had shown in all he had done for her and for Ferrara. Cagnolo of Parma describes her as "of middle height, delicate in appearance, her face rather long, as also is her finely cut nose ; her hair golden, her eyes greyish, the mouth rather large, with brilliantly white teeth ; the throat smooth and white, yet becomingly full. Her whole being breathes laughing good-humour and gaiety."

There we have the secret of her charm, as of that of her father and her brother. This is certainly the Lucrezia painted by Pinturicchio, gentle, yielding, incapable of deep emotions, altogether lacking in the will of Cesare or even of Alexander. Gentle, tactful, with charming ways, full of grace and sparkle in her talk, wrote Alfonso's secretary in his Life of his master.

On February 3rd there was a ball at the palace, but such was the crowd that it was impossible to dance, Isabella tells her husband, though they managed to get through a couple of dances. The three women were seated upon a dais, but Isabella does not mention, like Cagnolo, that Lucrezia came down into the hall and danced several Roman and Spanish dances with her tambourine, which were much admired. Whenever she danced her two dwarfs went about the room wearing dresses she had given them, crying, in their squeaking voices, " Look at the great lady, how sweet and pretty she is and how well she dances."

The theatrical performances given by Ercole for the wedding have been described in every detail by Isabella and others. The stage was in the large hall of the Palazzo della Ragione, off the Piazza del Duomo, where thirteen tiers of seats had been built, the places for the women, who sat in the centre, being railed off from those for the men, who were at the sides. The room could hold 3000 spectators. First there was a parade of the 110 dresses to be worn in the five comedies, so that Ercole's guests might assure themselves that they were all new and would not be worn twice. In few things has the taste of our own age changed more from that of the Renaissance than in this admiration for lavish display. The producer appeared as Plautus and recited a summary of the plots ; then the guests took their seats in the hall and the *Epidicus* began. Obviously the greater part of the audience, especially the women, found the *Moresche* much the most interesting part of the performance.

They fall into place in the brilliant pageantry of the Renaissance of which they were a living part far more readily than these revivals of Latin comedies. The first two *Moresche* were military ballets in which the dancers, fully armed, fought in time to the music. Isabella found the music of the third so sad that she did not think it worth mentioning. A car entered drawn by a unicorn with a young girl in it, who liberated some prisoners. Four lute-players made the music. The fourth of these ballets was danced by ten niggers with lighted candles in their mouths. After the comedy there was a performance by tumblers and jugglers.

Isabella was obviously bored, jealous and annoyed at the part she had to play. She tells her husband that, were these shows the best in the world, she would find them dull without her baby boy and himself.

That was the marriage night, and Isabella sent her husband the usual details, though she admits that she had not seen anyone in a sufficiently authoritative position to be able to guarantee them. There was no lively bedding of the bride, nor had the company been to pay the couple the usual morning visit, " because, to put it plainly, this is a cold wedding." She goes on to say that she hopes that she and her ladies have managed to hold their own.

Next day Lucrezia did not appear till the afternoon. The Duke took his distinguished guests a tour of Ferrara, showing them, among other things, his artillery, which was Don Alfonso's special hobby, and a nun of Viterbo who received the stigmata on Fridays. Ercole was particularly proud of having her in Ferrara and his guests were duly impressed. About five the bride entered the hall with the ambassadors. There was dancing, then the *Bacchides*, which Isabella found terribly wearisome, was acted. Among the *Moresche* was a torch-dance, where the men appeared in flesh-coloured tights.

183

On the 5th Lucrezia washed her head and wrote letters, among them, we may be sure, a long one to the Pope. Isabella says that this delay was caused by her anxiety to outdo the Duchess of Urbino and herself. As it was Friday, there were no dances, and she found the play duller than ever, wishing herself back at home. The French ambassador with the Duchess of Urbino supped in Lucrezia's apartments, when the talk was lively and brilliant. Afterwards she invited him into her own room and talked to him for more than an hour in the presence of two of her ladies. She then took off her own scented gloves and gave them to him, a favour which he received with the utmost respect and gratification.

On Sunday there was a Mass, attended by the whole wedding party, in the cathedral. The Archbishop invested Don Alfonso with a cap and sword blessed by His Holiness, and sent by him as a present to his son-in-law. At the ball Lucrezia, in a violet dress covered with fish-scales of gold, danced a French dance with a lady-in-waiting. The *Miles Gloriosus* was given with the usual *Moresche*. On the morrow there was a duel between an Imolese and a Bolognese, which interested the Marchesana Isabella particularly, as the Imolese was in her service. To her great joy he won after a hard fight. Ercole stopped it before any blood was shed, except that of the horse of the Bolognese. The *Moresche* of that evening were the best of all, especially one in which appeared a band of Satyrs, the leader holding a silver ass's head with a chiming clock inside it. Peasants danced to its tune and then joined in a great hunt of wild beasts. A famous performer from Mantua played three lutes at once. The last *Moresche* represented the chief processes of farming, from ploughing to the harvest festival and a rustic dance to bagpipes. This was held to be the best of the ballets.

On the last day of Carnival the ambassadors

184

presented their gifts. The French ambassador gave the bride a gold rosary, the beads of which were scented with musk. Angela Borgia received a valuable gold chain. For Don Alfonso there was a shield adorned with a painting of the Magdalen. The ambassador actually reminded him that he had chosen a bride whose virtues rivalled those of the Magdalen, who deserved much because she had loved much ; Cagnolo puts it, believed much.

The strangest gift of all was that of the two Venetian ambassadors. Once again it brings out the enormous importance attached to appearance and display in this brilliant epoch of Italian history. Their robes, of crimson velvet lined with rare fur, had been specially made for them at the public expense. They had paraded in them in the Sala del Grande Consiglio, where 4000 persons of rank had assembled to inspect them, to say nothing of a far larger crowd in St Mark's Square. After a long speech in Latin and another in Italian to the bride the pair withdrew, and, in accordance with their instructions, sent in their magnificent robes as their gift. This strange present set everyone laughing, no one more merrily, we may be sure, than Lucrezia herself.

As an interlude in the play six viola players performed with the skill for which Ferrara was famous, and the bridegroom, who was himself an expert, took part with them. Such an accomplishment, though common in high places a couple of centuries later, was rare in a prince at that time. Clearly Alfonso was something more than a gunner. After the last of the *Moresche* a golden ball burst in the air and the four Virtues appeared and sang divinely. Isabella found the *Cassaria*, the last of the comedies, so immoral that she refused to allow her ladies to see it.

Isabella returned to Mantua as soon as possible and her first letter to her sister-in-law leaves no doubt upon the state of their relations.

" Illustrious Madam, The love which I feel for your ladyship and my desire to hear that you are continuing to enjoy the good health in which I left you encourage me to believe that you are no less anxious to hear from me ; and therefore, in the hope of pleasing you, I am writing to inform you that I reached home safe and sound on Monday and found my Most Illustrious Consort in the best of health. It remains for me to hear in return the news of your ladyship, so that I may enjoy it as that of a very dear sister. And though it may seem superfluous to offer you what is already yours, I desire to remind you once for all that you may dispose of my person and of all my possessions as if they were your own. . . ."

Lucrezia answers in the same stiff tone :

" Most Illustrious Madam, My sister-in-law and highly honoured sister, Though it ought to have been my duty to anticipate the proof of affection you have given me, I console myself willingly nevertheless for my negligence, because I hold myself all the more beholden to you. I cannot tell you with what joy and satisfaction I have heard of your safe arrival at Mantua. . . ."

Lucrezia must have been genuinely relieved at the departure of her sister-in-law, who hardly troubled to conceal her repugnance. In such an atmosphere she naturally froze, so far as one of her character could freeze, and her manner became cold and haughty. She felt the strain severely. But on February 18th Teodora Angellini, an old Este servant, wrote to Isabella that she will be glad to hear that she hopes that all will go well. The lady " is beginning to be herself again, showing that she possesses ability and the kindest of hearts." Another writes that she is endowed with great goodness and prudence, far more than was suggested. She treats her ladies with great kindness and consideration. This is the Lucrezia whom Ferrara soon learnt to love.[1]

[1] Luzio and Renier, *I. d'Este e i Borgia*, p. 83.

Once again we come across the curious huxter side of the Renaissance, a side that is the inevitable obverse of a life which found its fullest expression in display valued primarily for its costliness. Ercole was unfeignedly glad to see the backs of his expensive guests. But there still remained the two Borgia cousins and Adriana de Mila, which meant that there were 450 people and 350 horses on his hands. Alexander had done his best to induce Cesare's wife to come to the wedding and then visit him in Rome, and it was for her that they were lingering at Ferrara. But Charlotte steadily declined to come, making all manner of excuses. Even Louis' threat to take her daughter from her and send her to Italy had no effect. Finally her brother, Cardinal d'Albret, appeared in Ferrara and said that her health made the journey out of the question. Probably she was only too glad to have escaped from her brutal husband, nor had she any wish to appear in Italy in her rather equivocal position or to become involved in the web of Borgia family politics. Ercole complained to his ambassador in Rome that the wedding had already cost him 25,000 ducats. He added that he had dismissed Valentino's gentlemen twelve days after their arrival, as they did honour neither to His Holiness, nor to the Duke of Romagna. On the same day, February 14th, he wrote to the Pope a letter which must have warmed his paternal heart :

" Before the arrival of the Most Illustrious Duchess, our common daughter, it was my firm intention to love and honour her, as in duty bound, and never on any occasion to fail to show her my special affection. Now that her ladyship is here, such is the satisfaction she has given me by the virtues and worthy qualities I find in her, that I am not only confirmed in my feelings towards her, but my will and desire so to do have been greatly increased, all the more so now that I see that Your Holiness has, by a brief in your own hand, affectionately called this to my mind. Your Holiness may rest assured that my behaviour to the Duchess will be such that Your Blessedness will realise that I consider her Ladyship as the dearest possession I have in the world."

Ercole goes on to press the claims of Mons. Giovanni Luca for a red hat. Alexander, however, thought that he had done quite enough for his son-in-law for the present. But he continued to watch over his daughter. He it was who insisted that Ercole should allow her 12,000 ducats, instead of 6000, which was not excessive for one who aspired to be the best-dressed woman in Italy. He was quite satisfied when he heard that Don Alfonso continued to be an active husband, sleeping regularly with his wife, though he might go and amuse himself elsewhere by day, as young men will, " and it is good for them ", added His Holiness to the ambassador, speaking from long experience.

CHAPTER XIV

THE THIRD CAMPAIGN IN THE ROMAGNA
ADMINISTRATION (1502)

THE Duke of Romagna was now busy with preparations for his next expedition. In February the Pope
accompanied him on a visit to his latest conquest of
Piombino. The visit was official. With him went a
sella gestatoria and a gilt baldacchino, half a dozen
cardinals and as many singers from his choir and a
large suite. They visited Elba, where Cesare meant
to improve the port, as also that of Piombino.
Probably Leonardo da Vinci was with them. In any
case it is almost certain that he designed the new
fortifications there. His notes, which are in Paris,
show that he visited these towns. They contain his
observations on the route and the places he saw, which
he was in the habit of jotting down in the notebook
he carried at his belt. We find his sketch and his
remarks on the action of a couple of waves there,
always a favourite subject with him, for he was
endeavouring to discover a theory of the movement
of the waves. On his way back by Siena he described
the strange note of a bell he had heard. He also
noted that he must borrow an Archimedes as well
as another book from Vitellozzo Vitelli. About
September he was in Rome, where he painted the
beautiful head of the Virgin in S. Onofrio.[1]

One day all the prettiest girls and women came to
dance in the square at Piombino, while the Pope looked
on from a balcony in the palace. This was a special

[1] Alvisi, *C. Borgia*, pp. 244–5.

treat prepared for him by Cesare, who had them dressed in cloth of gold for the occasion. On the way back the galleys were overtaken by a violent storm. Alexander, who did not suffer from sea-sickness, sat calm and absolutely fearless on deck, crossing himself and exclaiming *Gesù* at the largest waves. He was continually asking the men to get him something to eat, but for a long time the storm was too violent. At last they fried him some fish. Many of the cardinals were too ill to travel when they landed at Civita Vecchia, but the Pope came on to Rome at once " looking remarkably well and in excellent spirits ", says the Florentine ambassador. Burchard tells us that many of his suite ate meat the whole time, though it was Lent—not the Pope himself, be it observed. Many devout persons doubtless imagined that such conduct was the cause of the storm.

In June Cardinal d'Albret, Cesare's brother-in-law, and the invaluable Papal Secretary, Troches, left Rome with two pretty courtesans, Thomasina and Magdalena, for Savona. Their object, according to Burchard, was to entice Giuliano della Rovere, who was then at his native town, on board and carry him off to Rome, so that he could not give trouble by pleading for his relatives with Louis. The plot does not sound very probable. In any case it failed.

In July died the Cardinal of Modena, Giambattista Ferrari, the Pope's datary, " to the great satisfaction of the whole court ", writes Giustinian, who had just succeeded Capello as Venetian ambassador. His despatches are most important for the rest of Alexander's life. The Letter to Savelli calls Modena " the minister of the Pope's crimes, the seller of benefices for the sating of his avarice, placed, like Cerberus, at the gates of Hell, barking at all." His death afforded a splendid target for epigrammatists, and Burchard's collection shows that they did not miss the opportunity. This is perhaps the best : " Here lies Battista who, in

SUPPOSED PORTRAIT OF CESARE BORGIA, BY RAPHAEL

his efforts to fatten the bull, lost body, wealth, soul."[1]

The cardinal had declined to make a will. The Pope himself went to his palace to superintend the drawing up of the inventory of his property. Such a windfall was precious with Cesare clamouring ceaselessly for money. Cash to the value of 1500 ducats was found. From the first his secretary and favourite, Sebastiano Pinzòn, was said to have poisoned him by Alexander's orders. He certainly was given some of his benefices and even some money, a concession so rare when a cardinal died in the days of the Borgia pope that it not unnaturally increased the suspicions of foul play. On November 20th, 1504, under Julius II, he was deprived of all his benefices in his absence as guilty of having poisoned his master. Useful though he was to him, it is possible that Alexander, and still more Cesare, felt that his money would be still more useful and therefore decided to put him out of the way.

Valentino left Rome in June. There had been trouble about money, but the Pope, as always, had given way to his masterful son. Giustinian found the Pope so wrapped up in his expedition that he could think of nothing else. Only those who were as interested in the *impresa* as himself could obtain an audience. Before Cesare left, as we have seen, he had Astorre Manfredi put to death and thrown into the Tiber. Don Ramiro de Lorqua had acted as his viceroy during his absence, ruling with an iron hand. Complications had, however, arisen owing to the action of some of his captains. Vitellozzo, intent upon avenging his brother's death, had induced Arezzo and the neighbouring district of the Val di Chiana to revolt from Florence. On June 7th Arezzo rose with shouts of " Marzocco, Marzocco ! Medici, Medici ! " and

[1] Hic situs est Baptista, Bovem qui reddere pinguem
Dum studet, amisit corpus, opes, animam.

admitted Vitellozzo. The Florentines made no effort
to recover the town and Vitellozzo easily occupied
the whole region. He was joined later by Baglioni
of Perugia who, with all his house, had gone to
welcome Lucrezia on her wedding journey. It is
difficult to believe that Valentino had no knowledge
of what was preparing. In any case he cannot have
been sorry, as the Florentines had never paid him a
farthing of the promised money for the *condotta*.
The Pope denied all knowledge of the movement
and when, a little later, the Pisans offered Valentino
the lordship of their city—they were, of course, at
war with Florence—Alexander truthfully declared
that neither he nor Cesare would listen to such a
proposal. They had no desire to risk offending
Louis and the Florentines had taken the precaution of
placing themselves under French protection, undertaking to pay a subsidy of 40,000 ducats for three years
for a *condotta* of 2400 cavalry in case of need. War
had already broken out between France and Spain.
The partition treaty had inevitably led to trouble in
Naples and Louis himself would soon be in Milan,
so they could afford to wait.

Valentino reached Spoleto on June 15th, but he
made no attempt to interfere with Vitellozzo. Camerino was his ostensible goal: obviously it must form
part of his new state. The tyrant, Varano, had had
every opportunity of putting his town into a good
state of defence. Valentino now urged Guidobaldo
d'Urbino to send 1000 men to Vitellozzo in order to
help hold the Florentines in check. Guidobaldo,
who had no desire to become embroiled with Louis,
replied that, unless the Pope sent him a brief, bidding
him do so as Captain-General of the Church, he must
decline, but he offered to let Vitellozzo recruit in
his duchy and to contribute 1000 ducats towards the
cost. The sum should have produced 500 men.
He also sent Valentino a fine horse and promised to

procure all the supplies demanded by the Bishop of Elna, Cesare's cousin, Francesco Loriz, who was in charge of the commissariat. Guidobaldo cannot have felt altogether comfortable, in spite of the Duca's assurances of brotherly feelings.

Valentino was quickly assembling his forces. He issued a proclamation in accordance with his new decree, summoning a man from each household to his standard. This was one of the few unpopular measures he introduced. Rumours soon reached Guidobaldo that troops were advancing through his territories from two quarters. So complete was the surprise that the Duca's men had taken the strong fortress of Cagli without a struggle. True to his methods, Valentino struck with the utmost swiftness and without the slightest warning. In order to lull all suspicion he had told Guidobaldo that he should advance upon Camerino by way of Cagli, adding that, of all the princes of Italy, there was not one who was a dearer brother to him.

Guidobaldo was dining out in Urbino when the news reached him at midnight. With three archers and young Francesco Maria della Rovere, the Prefettino of Sinigaglia, nephew of both himself and of Vincula, who was soon to be adopted as his heir, he made for the impregnable fortress of S. Leo, but found the way barred. We cannot follow the details of his adventurous flight, which ended in his doubling back right across Cesare's territory to Ravenna, where he was safe under Venetian protection, and going thence to Mantua. His wife was visiting the Marchesana Isabella. A martyr to gout, he arrived in a state of complete exhaustion, with nothing but his doublet and shirt.

Valentino entered the town, lance in rest, as a conqueror, a few hours after Guidobaldo had left. In accordance with their Duke's orders the citizens surrendered without a struggle, for Guidobaldo did not wish Urbino to suffer. Cesare took up his abode in the palace, where his sister had been hospitably entertained a few months previously.

The surprise of Urbino was regarded as one of Cesare's most brilliant achievements by admirers of *virtù*, like Machiavelli. It had the *Cæsariana celeritas* of his great namesake. He was in Urbino before news had arrived that he had started. He marched sixty miles in twenty-four hours with 2000 men " without eating or drinking." Surprise was everything in that hostile and difficult country. A single serious check might have ruined all.

The only justification for this raid, apart from its success, was that Guidobaldo was secretly helping the lord of Camerino and there is no doubt that Varano was counting upon his assistance, whether justifiably or not. The Pope was delighted, praising Valentino's magnanimity, a sure sign that he was well aware that " il gran tradimento ", as Guidobaldo's friends called it, was the reverse of magnanimous. The treachery was no worse than Ferdinand and Gonsalvo de Cordova had used towards Federigo of Naples. When he spoke of him, says Giustinian, he could not conceal his feelings and was so puffed up with his good luck " that he thinks that God cannot harm him and that every other enterprise will now be easy for him." Like Cesare, he was dying to get Guidobaldo into his clutches " and treat him as he treated the poor boy from Faenza."

This brilliant stroke only increased the hatred against the Borgias. The Montefeltri were among the most respected, cultivated and popular rulers in Italy and their overthrow by the Pope's bastard, who was as treacherous as he was able and successful, following hard upon the marriage of Lucrezia, roused universal indignation which was increased by fear. Even Lucrezia openly expressed disgust. El Prete writes to Isabella that she was really distressed, as was all her court. She told him that she would have given 50,000 ducats not to have heard the news.[1] Though Isabella of Mantua felt the deepest sympathy with her friends, she was too true a daughter of her age not to profit by their misfortune. Three days after Guidobaldo's arrival she wrote to her brother, Cardinal Ippolito, that she had no acquaintance with Valentino. She goes on, " My brother-in-law, the Duke of Urbino, had in his house a small antique marble Venus and also a Cupid, which the Most Illustrious Duke of Romagna once gave him. I am sure that these, with the other things, have come into the hands of the said Duke in the revolution at Urbino. As I have been at great pains to collect antiques for my boudoir, I should much like to have them. I do not consider the suggestion untimely, for I am told that His Excellency takes little pleasure in antiques and would therefore be glad to bestow them as favours upon others." (June 30th, 1502.) Cesare was delighted to have the chance of doing a good turn to a family of such influence who were to be his near neighbours. He sent off one of his chamberlains at once with the statues, telling Isabella, however, that the Cupid was not an antique, but the work of Michelangelo. Isabella wrote to her husband that, for a modern work, it was unrivalled. She firmly declined to return the statues to the Montefeltri when their luck changed. Cesare was not behaving like one who expected to stay. He packed off the library and the art collections of Urbino to his own capital, Cesena.

It was in Urbino that the Florentine envoy reached him. He had been sent at Valentino's request in the hope of coming to an understanding. This was Francesco Soderini, Bishop of Volterra. With him, acting as his secretary, was Niccolò Machiavelli, then aged thirty-three. News of the taking of Urbino had reached them on the way. The first interview

[1] Luzio and Renier, *Mantova ed Urbino*, p. 125.

195

between Valentino and the great thinker, to whom, more than to anyone else, he owes his fame, took place a little before midnight on June 24th. Cesare still followed his practice of turning night into day. The Urbino palace, soon to be the scene of the *Cortegiano*, was quite deserted, except for an occasional secretary or a gentleman of the guard. The door was carefully guarded. The two Florentines were met by Agapito and escorted by torchlight to the room where Cesare was at work with Don Ramiro de Lorqua, who had come over from Cesena to help his master.

The first two despatches are certainly from Machiavelli's pen. They leave no doubt as to the impression the surprise of Urbino had made upon him. " This lord is very splendid and magnificent, and has such spirit in arms that there is nothing great enough not to seem small to him. To win glory or to increase his power he never rests, nor does he know fatigue or danger. He is at his goal before you know that he has left his starting-point. He makes himself popular with his troops and he has got hold of the best men in Italy. These things, combined with his unfailing good fortune, make him victorious and dangerous."

The meeting may, without exaggeration, be called epoch-making. Here we have the Prince in embryo. Machiavelli had at last found a man, an Italian, who held his own with the best of the men of action of the day, one who might even be capable of delivering Italy from foreign domination. However disillusioned he became later, it was to the Valentino whom he had known in the Romagna that his imagination was always returning and whom he was to make the hero of his *Prince*.

Valentino went straight to the point. He complained of the Florentines not keeping the terms of the Campi agreement. He did not like their government, he could not trust it. They must change it and give him guarantees for the fulfilment of their promises : " otherwise you will very soon learn that I do not mean to go on like this. If you will not have me for a friend, you shall have me for an enemy." Having received instructions to temporize, Soderini could not satisfy him. He continued : " Do not imagine that I shall begin by doing you any service, for you have done the very opposite of deserving it. It is quite true that Vitellozzo is my man, but I swear to you that I knew nothing of the Arezzo business. So far from being sorry at what you have lost, I was glad and shall continue to be glad, if you go on in this way." " Make up your minds quickly," he added later. " I cannot keep my army here in this mountainous region. . . . There can be no half measures between you and me. You are either my friends or my enemies." He reminded them that Florence was too weak to face even Vitellozzo. He did not covet other people's possessions. He was not there to play the tyrant, but to crush tyrants.

This last remark is interesting. In his treatment of his own subjects Valentino was undoubtedly true to it. No one could be more ruthless when necessary, but Ugolini, the historian of Urbino, who was no friend of the Borgia, says that " the impartiality of history compels me to admit that Valentino's rule in the Duchy was unsullied by a single act of vengeance, just and mild."

When Soderini mentioned the King of France, he cut him short by saying that he had nothing to learn about French policy from anyone in Italy. Next day Giulio and Paolo Orsini came to visit Soderini and made it clear that they were far more dangerous enemies than the Duca. Valentino gave him four days in which to obtain an answer from home. So Machiavelli was sent back to Florence for instructions. The Florentines, however, especially the common people, were in no way alarmed. They had not forgotten how they had stood up successfully to Charles VIII of France with his 30,000 men. Why should they be afraid of a handful of tatterdemalions led by an unfrocked bastard son of a priest? Soderini, left alone, was continually asking to be recalled or to be provided with a colleague, for Valentino had inspired him with a wholesome terror and respect. He was more than a match for him in argument. However, Louis had no intention of letting Valentino increase his power more than he could help and he speedily prepared to protect the Florentines, though he both disliked and despised his allies. By July 7th he was at Asti and lost no time in giving them his support.

In July Camerino was captured. Varano had a strong Rocca and a considerable force, including some Colonna and other exiles, and had beaten the cavalry of the besiegers in the open. But the citizens had seen enough of Valentino's success and his methods to be anxious to come to an agreement with him quickly. While the aged Giulio Cesare Varano, formerly a condottiere of Venice, was trying to haggle about terms, the gates were thrown open. Seeing the uselessness of further resistance, he surrendered the Rocca unconditionally. His captors made him sleep in the stable with the mule on which they placed him. He died in prison, and two of his sons were executed in October. According to Olivieri, the diarist, the youngest, Piero, sought to return during the revolt of 1502, but was caught at Pesaro and strangled outside the church of S. Francesco. He was carried into the church. As he showed signs of life, some people endeavoured to revive him. A Spanish priest who was there called in the executioners to finish their work. This barbarous act, which helped to increase the bitter feeling against the Spaniards, was never forgotten by the rough Romagnol peasantry. The story is still current. Later, the priest was recognized in Cagli and torn to pieces by Guidobaldo's subjects.

There was great rejoicing in Rome over the fall of Camerino. Bells were rung, bonfires were lit and the city was illuminated. The Governor of Rome went about the streets all night with a large crowd, shouting, " Duca, Duca ! " as did the Papal Guards. The festivities lasted three days, for it had not been possible to celebrate the taking of Urbino, which, as Giustinian puts it, was not altogether without a touch of treachery. The Venetian noted the animus His Holiness showed against Varano in his next audience, when he could talk of nothing but Camerino. He was also suspiciously enthusiastic about " the honour of this duke of his, insisting that no man ever kept his word more truly than he and that he never breaks a promise." He went on to laud him to the skies, ending by pointing out how valuable an ally he might be to Venice. Giustinian assented, adding a few words of praise of his own, " the better to scratch his ear, knowing that this always gives him extraordinary pleasure."

Alexander could on occasion show himself most affectionate with the diplomatic corps. In an audience of July 22nd he appealed to the Spanish ambassador to testify to his good will towards Venice, and when he remained silent he put his hand under his chin and caressed his neck, saying, " You know how we desire to come to a good understanding with the Signoria of Venice." Indeed, Sigismondo dei Conti, in his character of the Pope after his death, considers that he was sometimes too polite and condescending for the dignity of his position.

Cesare had not forgotten his sister. She was unwell as her first confinement in Ferrara drew near. He wrote her the news of the fall of Camerino in the hope that it would cheer her up and begged her to tell him so, because, he added, her illness made it impossible for him to take delight in anything. He sent her not only Gaspare Torrella, but a famous doctor of Cesena.

The arrival of Louis made a great stir in Italy. When he reached Milan the swarm of enemies whom the dragon's teeth of Cesare's successes had raised against the Borgia hastened to meet him, hoping to do Valentino harm and recover their lost territories. Thither flocked the dispossessed Duke of Urbino and a Varano, the Bentivoglio, who could never feel safe in Bologna with so dangerous a neighbour, the outraged Florentines, the tactful, diplomatic Venetians, flushed with their success against the Turks, and the blustering Gonzaga of Mantua, free from the guiding hand of Isabella. There was an absurd rumour of a quarrel between himself and Valentino—*bastardo*, *figlio di prete* and the like—followed by a challenge. No wonder that " Machiavelli in Petticoats ", Isabella, was nervous, in spite of the Venus and the Cupid. Fearing that her husband might give vent to his hatred of Cesare, she told him that it was generally believed that Louis had an understanding with Valentino, and begged him to be careful what he said to the King about him. He should be circumspect, keep a good watch on his actions, his tongue, and his food, for she had the wholesome horror of poison of her day. There was everything to fear from a man who would plot against his own flesh and blood. " In politics men do not consider the interests of their friends, nor the quarrels that have formerly occurred between them." She certainly followed her own counsel in this respect. The letter has the affectionate charm that never fails her when she is writing to her husband. Indeed, the letters of the ladies of Mantua and Urbino are as good a proof as we have of the superiority of the culture of their courts when compared with those in less fortunate parts of Italy.

Louis, in any case, was not too pleased at the brilliant success of his vassal, as he showed by the energy with which he came to the help of the Florentines.

So alarming was the state of affairs that the Papal Secretary, Monsignor Troches, one of the most confidential of the Borgias' servants, who had been sent by Alexander to pay his respects to the King at Milan, turned aside in order to see Valentino on his way back to Rome and give him a word of warning, telling him he must leave the Florentines alone. Cesare at once sent off messages to Vitellozzo, bidding him quit Arezzo and even threatening, according to one account, to seize his own Città di Castello if he refused. He did not put this threat into execution, so that it was left for the French forces to restore their rebellious city to the Florentines.

However, he saw that something must be done to counteract the machinations of his enemies at Milan. As usual, he acted silently and swiftly. On July 25th he left Urbino in the dress of a Knight of St John of Jerusalem. Three days later he was at Ferrara, by the bedside of Lucrezia. Ercole despatched a messenger to tell Louis of his coming and the King bade Chaumont, the new Governor of Milan, send him fresh horses. At first he kept the news secret, but on August 5th he informed Giangiacomo Trivulzio in an audible whisper that His Excellency Cesare Borgia was at Ferrara, on his way. Chaumont then said that he had even better news, as the Duke was already nearing Milan.[1] Louis rode out to meet him with a small suite, threw his arms round his neck and kissed him several times, exclaiming, " Welcome, my cousin and good kinsman." He ordered his dinner himself and visited Cesare more than once in his room, even when he had put on his night-shirt to go to bed, and bade him use his clothes and horses as if they were his own.[2] Louis was clearly gratified at Valentino paying him his respects in person. Rohan was

[1] Bernardi, *Cronache forlivesi*, II, 13.
[2] Luzio, *Niccolò da Correggio*, *Giorn. Stor. Lett. Ital.* 21, p. 240.

no less cordial. He was as eager for Valentino's support at the next conclave as was the King for that of the Pope in the coming struggle for Naples with Spain.

The changed state of affairs is well reflected in the despatches of Giustinian. No one was more friendly than Gonzaga of Mantua, lately all eagerness to be entrusted with the task of driving Cesare from Romagna. The new friendship was cemented by the betrothal of Cesare's daughter, Louise, to the son of the Marquis. Isabella must have found this a bitter pill to swallow, but the advantages of the betrothal as an additional guarantee of security were obvious, and the death of the Pope might at any moment deliver her once and for all from the hated upstarts. Cesare accompanied Louis to Genoa, where he enjoyed the same favour, and back to Asti. At his departure he was escorted out of the town by a royal guard of honour.

On September 7th he was once more at Ferrara, where Lucrezia had been brought to bed of a daughter. She was dangerously ill. Don Alfonso hardly left her room. A secretary told Ercole that, but for the presence of her brother, who held her foot, it might have been impossible to bleed her. " Her ladyship chatted for a couple of hours with the Duke, who put her in good spirits and gave her courage." The Pope had sent his daughter his favourite physician, the Bishop of Venosa. Apart from other considerations, the death of Lucrezia would have been a serious political blow to Valentino. On her recovery Don Alfonso fulfilled a vow he had made and went on a pilgrimage to Loreto.

Cesare was soon back at Imola, where he was met by Cardinal Borgia, the Bishop of Elna, and Don Ramiro de Lorqua. His " excellent and well beloved engineer," as he styled Leonardo da Vinci in the commission he gave him, had completed his tour of the fortresses of the state. Alvisi enables us to follow his footsteps. On July 30th Leonardo was at Urbino, where, among other things, he drew a dovecot and a staircase; on August 1st at Pesaro, where he made drawings of some machines; on the 8th, at Rimini, he was struck by the music of the plashing of the water in a fountain; on the 11th, at Cesena, he drew a house and described a cart festooned with vines. On September 6th he was sketching the harbour at Cesenatico. From a Cesena diary we learn that the Duca, then at Imola, commissioned him to erect various buildings at Cesena, among them the Palazzo della Rota, or Court of Appeal, he was establishing, the University, and a fountain, as well as to restore the harbour at Cesenatico.

Valentino was already busy organizing his state. In nothing did he show greater wisdom than in the choice of Antonio dal Monte San Savino, whom he placed at the head of the administrative and judicial system with the title of Presidente di Romagna. There is not a discordant note in the praise of dal Monte. Machiavelli calls him " uomo dottissimo e di ottima vita ". Cardinal Monreale also helped in the work of administration. Don Ramiro de Lorqua, the ruthlessness of whose methods as governor is described by Alvisi, was henceforth employed only as a soldier.

Perhaps the most interesting of the Duca's reforms was the raising of his militia. There was no better fighting stock in the peninsula than the Romagnol peasantry and Cesare was anxious to be independent of mercenaries and of outside help. His decree that each house should give him a man ensured there being ample material. From Fano alone he obtained 1200 recruits. At Imola he himself superintended the training of two regiments, each of 500 men, armed with the pike and dressed in his colours of red and yellow. The militia was under the charge of Don Michele Corella. This experiment made a lasting impression upon Machiavelli, who saw at once that it was only by raising an army of her own nationals that Italy could hope to deliver herself from the yoke of the foreigner. Valentino was the first Italian ruler of the day who ventured to trust his subjects sufficiently to arm them and use them to fight for him.

He made a point of choosing Romagnols by preference to act as governors in his towns. All those whom he appointed in Urbino were from the Romagna. He was also quite ready to take former enemies into his service. One of his physicians, Niccolò Massini, had fought against him. He did his best to lighten taxation, whenever possible. Since he had the Vatican purse behind him, he could afford to be more lenient in his taxes than other rulers. As we have seen, he made strenuous efforts to protect his own subjects against his foreign mercenaries. He also scrupulously respected the rights of the various towns and often granted them special privileges, as in the case of Sinigaglia. Serravalle, at the foot of the lofty hill upon which stands San Marino, obtained complete freedom from that city as a reward for its fidelity to the Duke.

One of the most successful of the institutions he introduced was the Rota, a court of criminal appeal, modelled on that of Rome. Antonio dal Monte was its president. The opening of the first session (June 24th, 1503) was a great day for Cesena. A picture of the president and the lawyers seated on a high platform is said by Alvisi to be an early work of Raphael, who was a native of Urbino. There were various displays, ending with a triumphal car, upon which were Cæsar and Cleopatra—an odd combination for such an occasion—and a chorus of girls and boys who recited so well that Don Antonio and others listening were moved to tears. Mass was celebrated by the Bishop. On the return to the palace a solemn edict on the administration of justice was read amid salvoes of artillery.

CHAPTER XV

THE CONSPIRACY OF THE CONDOTTIERI

THE condottieri were in the worst of humours after leaving Arezzo. They complained that, while they had endeavoured to make Valentino king of Tuscany, he had not only refused, but put them in bad odour with Louis. The Duca had not wasted his time while in the North, and a definite treaty had been made between him and the King. The only clause of which we have certain knowledge is Louis' promise to lend Valentino 300 lances to help him to conquer Bologna and crush the Orsini, Baglioni and Vitellozzo. Thus he was ready to sacrifice his allies to secure the support of the Pope.

It was not long before Alexander began to show his hand. Whatever their faults, the Bolognese preferred the Bentivoglio to Papal rule, and when two sons of the House were summoned to Rome, guessing what would happen, they refused to let them go and showed that they were ready to resist to the utmost.

It appears also that Cardinal Orsini had received a warning at Milan, probably from Rohan, that the Pope was preparing to crush his family as he had crushed the Colonna. This was a step Alexander must take, if he were ever to be master in his own states. Cesare, "molto solitario e segreto", as Machiavelli put it, made no sign. Alexander, however, showed what was brewing by beginning, after his wont, to heap abuse upon the Orsini. When he ordered Giulio Orsino to attack Bologna, there could no longer be any doubt. The condottieri, who must all along have been feeling uneasy, realized that it was time to see that " they were not devoured one by one by the dragon ", as Giampolo Baglioni, the chief of the Magnificent House, expressed it.

The guarantee of the agreement between Valentino and the Bentivoglio in 1501 had established a bond of union between the rulers of Bologna and the condottieri. The troops of the latter were assembled at Todi, and here they held a meeting on September 25th, when they undertook not to attack Bologna, if ordered to do so. Five days later there was a more important meeting at La Magione, an estate belonging to Cardinal Orsini, by Lake Trasimene, near Perugia. The favour enjoyed by the Cardinal with the King of France gave him great weight. Those present were Paolo Orsini, the head of the clan, Francesco Orsini, Duca di Gravina, Franciotto Orsini, Giampaolo and Gentile Baglioni and Oliverotto da Fermo. Vitellozzo Vitelli, who was in a desperate state with *mal francese*, was carried in a litter. Guidobaldo d'Urbino and Pandolfo Petrucci were also represented. Ermete Bentivoglio joined them a little later. They undertook to put into the field an army of 10,000 men and to stand by one another. They realized that they must act before the arrival of the French. Baglioni, who saw that Perugia's turn would ultimately come, was the leader, but Valentino always maintained that Pandolfo Petrucci was the brain of the conspiracy.

The utter want of real cohesion or trust among the conspirators was plain from the first. Pandolfo Petrucci sent to tell the Duca that he would help no one to harm him, while Giulio Orsini came to a separate understanding with the Pope, and feeble, vacillating old Paolo Orsini offered to go to Imola in person to assure Valentino of the loyalty of the family. This kind of underhand dealing amounted to little more than prudent reinsurance in Cinquecento

Italy, but it rarely brought the parties concerned any advantage in time of trouble.

For us, as for his own future fame, the most important step taken by Valentino at this time was to ask the Florentines to send a representative to discuss with him their mutual interests. The revolt of the condottieri was a matter of no small moment to the Florentines, since Vitellozzo was their sworn enemy, thirsting for revenge at any cost, while the Orsini were hand in glove with the Medici. This was but natural, for Piero dei Medici, the head of the family, was the son of one Orsini and the husband of another, and was living in Rome, like his brother, Cardinal Giovanni.

The choice of the government fell upon Niccolò Machiavelli, Secretary of the Florentine Republic. His despatches are by far the most important documents we have for the events that followed, written as they were by a man of genius on the spot. To this mission we probably owe the Prince. Machiavelli had already had considerable experience. He had been sent as envoy to Caterina Sforza in 1499, when she had distinctly bested him. In the following year he had been chosen to go to Paris to discuss the Pisan question with Louis XII. So profoundly was he impressed by the little he had already seen of Valentino that he spoke highly of his political wisdom in the report he had just drawn up upon the best way to deal with the rebels of the Val di Chiana who had gone over to Vitellozzo.

Machiavelli's abilities were fully recognized by his official superiors, but he started sorely against his will. For one thing, he had just married; then the mission would be difficult. The object of Florence was, as usual, to temporize and above all to avoid paying Valentino a farthing as condottiere. Machiavelli was told to deal only in generalities. Such methods were peculiarly irritating to a man as downright as the

Duca. Machiavelli had too sincere an admiration for one who embodied the vigorous qualities which were painfully lacking in the rulers of Florence, whose defects he felt to be at the root of the present state of Italy, not to regret having to play such a game with a man who, by contrast, was to be the nearest approach to a hero he could then find in Italy.

Also, he was a poor man and it was impossible for him to live on his meagre salary, with the result that he was continually asking for money. He liked to keep up a decent appearance. One remembers the famous description of his putting on his best clothes when he retired to his study to spend the evening with the heroes of the ancient world in his later days, while he was writing his greatest works. Then he was by temperament a sedentary man and a scholar, who was never quite happy away from Florence, his friends and his books. We may judge of his tastes by the things he asked his friends to send him : velvet, a doublet, some cloth and a Plutarch. The Plutarch, Buonaccorsi tells him, is not to be found on sale in Florence ; it had to be ordered from Venice ; " and, frankly, you are a perfect nuisance to ask for so many things." We may be sure that it was Valentino who had turned his mind to the great men of Greece and Rome, with whom he wished to compare him by reading Plutarch. Such a man had no taste for the hardships of camp life in the Romagna winter. He was often unwell and always begging to be re-called, exaggerating his troubles in the hope of attaining his object.

Nor was information easy to come by. Thus, in apologizing for not having written for a week, he reminds the Signoria that the truth cannot be arrived at by guesswork. They must remember that they are dealing with a Prince " che si governa da se ", and that a man who wants to write something better than rubbish or moonshine must verify his facts.

"This takes time, and I try to use my time, not to waste it."

Yet it may well be that the very disadvantages of which he complains acted as an irritant, a stimulus to his genius, raising it to a higher power in his daily pictures of the remarkable drama of which he was the witness, and which, in spite of himself and of the circumstances of which he complained so loudly, soon became of absorbing interest to so keen a thinker and student of life and character.

Machiavelli reached Imola on October 7th, two days after the meeting at La Magione. It was late in the evening, but he was taken immediately, just as he was, to the Duca. Next day Cesare showed the envoy a letter from Louis to Chaumont, bidding him send Valentino the forces he needed, adding that this was a reply to a request for help against Bologna. How much more easily would he obtain it when defending himself against men who were the King's enemies. But he continued to press for a speedy declaration of friendship on the part of Florence, the moral value of which he fully realized, in the form of an effective *condotta*. This much a secretary, probably Agapito, gave Machiavelli to understand in a long talk. The Duca also said that the Cavaliere Orsini had been to see him three days ago and that Petrucci was continually writing and sending messages to say that he would never attack him. Words could not describe the demonstrative affection he showed him. But Machiavelli saw clearly that at bottom he was "full of fear", as, indeed, he himself admitted later.

Luck was on the side of the conspirators. Some loyal subjects of Guidobaldo succeeded in rushing a gate in the great fortress of S. Leo while repairs were being carried out, killing the garrison and capturing the place. Its fall made a great impression. Cagli, Gubbio and finally Urbino itself were carried by the loyal peasantry who hastened into the town, the citizens helping them turn the guns left in the Piazza against the Rocca, which soon surrendered.

Cesare did not hesitate. Seeing that he must for the moment abandon Urbino, he ordered all his troops in the Duchy to retire on Rimini. Michelotto, who was sent to see that the order was obeyed, did not carry it out to the letter. Accomplices in Pergola and Fossombrone, which had declared for Guidobaldo, admitted him and Ugo Moncada, who was later to rise to fame as a captain under Charles V, with his Spanish infantry. They behaved as only Spaniards could, sacking the towns without mercy. Women jumped into the river with their children in their arms to escape Don Michele and his men. Valentino said gaily to Machiavelli, " This year the stars do not seem to favour rebels." But the condottieri were advancing upon Urbino and the Orsini attacked the Spaniards, inflicting a sharp defeat upon them and taking Ugo de Moncada and other prisoners of distinction. This and the return of the old Duke to Urbino by way of Sinigaglia, where was his sister the Prefettessa, greatly encouraged the rebels. Bentivoglio and the Orsini now declared openly against the Pope.

Every advantage appeared to lie with the condottieri, but Machiavelli saw more clearly. They were mere captains, without a leader, too jealous and suspicious of one another to act together and quite without the ability to plan an effective campaign— " Una dieta di falliti ", an assembly of bankrupts, as Valentino called them. Instead of combining and attacking Cesare, says Guicciardini, they sat and looked at one another.

Valentino lost neither head nor heart. His enemies, he said, had chosen their time badly. " The presence of the King of France in Italy and the fact that His Holiness is still alive are two things that keep a fire burning under him which it would require more water than they could find to put out." (October

CESARE BORGIA, PAINTER UNKNOWN
THE BEST AUTHENTICATED PORTRAIT

8th.) On October 20th he spoke scornfully of the *falliti*. The more he knew of them, the less he thought of them. He did not want to boast, " but Vitellozzo, with all his reputation, I never remember to have seen do anything worthy of a man of spirit. He makes his *mal francese* his excuse." The Duca could speak from experience. " All he can do is to lay waste unprotected country, robbing people who dare not stand up to him, and commit such-like acts of treachery." He had betrayed him when he was his soldier and taking his money. And he continued long in the same strain, speaking very quietly, without displaying the slightest emotion. He would never trust them again. Every day Petrucci sent to assure him of his friendship, but he knew him now. " Look how they behave. They plot together, they write me nice letters, to-day Signor Pagolo is coming to see me, to-morrow the cardinal, and so they go on playing with me. . . . For my part, I temporize, I listen to all they have to say and I bide my time."

Nor did Machiavelli think they could now do him much harm. " In this court," he writes, " things that are to be kept silent are never mentioned. An admirable secrecy is preserved about them." This is how he sums up the situation on October 27th. " On the one hand is this Signore, full of dash, lucky and sanguine, supported by a Pope and a King, who has been wronged by them not in a state he meant to acquire, but in one he had already acquired ; while we see them jealous of their states and afraid of his greatness before they injured him, and now far more so, since they have done him this wrong. Nor do we see how he will be able to forgive the injury or they to put aside their fear." He acutely observes that the only hope of an understanding is that they should all unite in attacking a third party.

Meanwhile Guidobaldo had returned to Urbino, being escorted into his capital by the Bishop in full canonicals amid the rejoicing inhabitants in defiance of the interdict. Oliverotto da Fermo helped Gian Maria Varano to recover Camerino and Baglioni kept Michelotto shut up in Pesaro. In fact, the condottieri were busy frittering away their chances on trifling undertakings which could have no bearing upon the main issue. Valentino did nothing, biding his time.

These events greatly distressed the Pope. He delivered an angry tirade against the Orsini in Consistory, when he also read extracts from letters of Louis and Rohan, promising him all possible help against traitors. The strain of keeping Valentino supplied with money was severe. By December he had had over 60,000 ducats. Giustinian received endless blandishments from His Holiness in the course of which he recommended Cesare to Venice as her devoted son and continued to urge the need of a close alliance between Rome and the Most Serene Republic. The following speech (December 2nd) is particularly interesting : " It will not be long before we die, because at our age Nature demands it, and we have to consider the state in which we leave Italy, for above all things we must leave a pledge behind us. You who are immortal (because your Signoria never dies) . . . ought to be more careful than others. . . . Do you know what people say about you ? They say that you are too cautious and that you want to see too far ahead."

Alexander also had his family troubles. He had been obliged to shut up Sancia in the Castel S. Angelo, no one could tell why. She spent her time at the window or on the balconies, often shouting down to passing Spanish acquaintances in the crowd. Nor was Squillace making a favourable impression. He was always the feeblest of the Borgias. He was now going about Rome with his troop of a hundred men and making a fool of himself with his incapacity either to equip or handle them. His attempt to drill them before the Pope, who insisted on watching, was a lamentable fiasco.[1]

Valentino showed his hand clearly in the long talk Machiavelli had with a confidential secretary, doubtless Agapito, who spoke quite openly. Valentino knew the Pope might die at any moment. In addition to the King of France and his troops, he wanted to be on good terms with neighbours like Florence, Bologna, Mantua and Ferrara. For Mantua there was the betrothal of Cesare's daughter and the red hat for the Marchese's brother, the 40,000 ducats paid for which would provide the child's dowry. Florence had two weak spots, Pisa and Vitellozzo. The capture of Pisa and the elimination of Vitellozzo would be great advantages. Cesare would spare some of the Orsini, because, on the death of the Pope, he must have some friends, but Vitellozzo was a poisonous snake. The Duca would not listen to a word upon that subject. He even hinted that the King of France might compel Florence to grant a *condotta*. Machiavelli agreed and added, speaking for himself, that His Excellency the Duke must not be judged like other lords, who have nothing but their coaches, by the state he kept. He must be regarded as a new Power in Italy, with whom it would be better to enter into a league, a friendship, than to hire him with a *condotta*. (Despatch, November 8th.)

It was not long before Valentino saw a rift in the clouds. His Fabian policy was justified. The chief towns in Romagna remained loyal, thus rewarding him for his good government and the consideration he had shown them. By the end of the month the French troops were arriving. Ferrara sent him 600 men. On October 25th the foolish talkative Paolo Orsini— "un cervello di non grande levatura," says Ugolini, —who was known as Madonna Paolo in Urbino, came to Imola disguised as a groom to propose terms.

[1] Guistinian, I, 207.

He was dismissed with handsome promises and no less handsome presents. Cardinal Orsini also submitted a plan for an agreement to the Pope, from which it is plain that he had no more sense than Paolo. The Duca was, among other things, to surrender three fortified towns, the Kings of France and Spain were to guarantee the treaty, and the Pope was to make five cardinals to be chosen by the condottieri. No wonder His Holiness flew into a passion.

The blind stupidity with which the condottieri walked into the trap laid for them caused universal amazement. Machiavelli relates (October 29th) that, in talking over the proposed agreement with Agapito, Valentino had laughed and said that it was only something to hold them at bay with. "From the Duke's language I have always gathered that he wanted to gain time till he was quite ready. Nor can I believe that the others do not also realize this; hence I am astounded." Two days later Agapito said that the merest child must laugh at such terms, extorted after such injuries.

By mid-November Cesare had come to an agreement with Paolo, whom he had flattered to the top of his bent. Cesare pardoned his captains and took them back into his service, but only one of them was to have the command at a time. He was to recover Camerino and the Duchy of Urbino, except S. Leo and two other fortified towns, where Guidobaldo might take up his residence. Separate terms were to be made between the Pope and Bentivoglio.

Paolo hastened off, highly satisfied with himself, to Cartocetto, a village not far from Fano, where the condottieri were assembled. Even the popular poets of the day, to say nothing of the shrewd peasantry and the soldiery, saw the madness of trusting a man like Cesare after having betrayed him. They gathered in the Church of S. Maria. Outside waited Gorvalan, the Spanish captain whom Cesare had sent with Paolo to bring him the result of the discussion. The men of the condottieri vented their disgust at the folly of their leaders and their hatred of the Spaniards upon him as he stood there, calm and impassive, under their abuse. Baglioni alone refused to consider the terms for a moment. He urged his comrades to remember with whom they were dealing. If they were not quite mad they must see that their only hope lay in their arms. But the voluble Paolo Orsini—Pagolo, as the name was then often written—carried the day. The basilisk had lured them by his soft whistling, says Machiavelli in the *Decennali.* Vitellozzo hesitated long. The strength of the Orsini faction and his own state of health may have helped to weaken his resolve, added to the undoubted strain of fatalism there was in him. He ended by giving way and was followed by Oliverotto, who had learnt soldiering first under his brother, Giovanni Vitelli, and then under himself. Baglioni was adamant. As he left the church he shouted that Paolo was the undoing of them all. If the Duca wanted him, he must come and fetch him, with arms in his hands, in Perugia.

Judging by the facts, by Valentino's words and by the talk of his chief men, Machiavelli argued that things boded ill for the captains, especially for Vitellozzo, " the traitor who has stabbed us and thinks he can heal the wounds with words." Vitellozzo, who guessed as much, wrote Cesare an abject letter, saying that, given an opportunity, he knew that he could justify his conduct. Cesare received these overtures with an ominous silence.

Bentivoglio, who was a friend of Louis and a man who could help Cesare, obtained much better terms. His treaty with Alexander was guaranteed by France, Florence and Ferrara. The Pope promised to respect his rights in Bologna, while he gave Cesare troops and a *condotta* of 12,000 ducats for five years. Bentivoglio thus obtained a respite, Valentino men and money.

Any misgivings Paolo Orsini may have felt were allayed by Cesare sending him to Urbino with Don Antonio dal Monte San Savino, now his right-hand man in all civil matters : the Duke of Urbino knew better than to stay and Cesare gladly gave him a safe-conduct. Many of his subjects begged him to fight, notably the women of Valbona, who offered their gold and silver ornaments. No reprisals were made by Valentino or his officials. Guidobaldo was impotent and Cesare wanted him to become a priest, leaving his wife free to marry again. He promised to compensate him.[1] There was talk of making him a cardinal. Alexander denied that he would do so and praised Elisabetta to Giustinian for remaining loyal to her husband. But it is difficult to believe that he would not have jumped at such a chance of securing Valentino's rights to Urbino, had Guidobaldo been willing. The Pope's denial is almost a proof of it.

The Pope was pressing Giustinian more and more earnestly to bring about an alliance with Venice. He saw only too clearly how things stood. The jealousy between France and Spain alone saved Italy, he said, nor could Venice hope to escape. " We are old and must think of our children and our one hope lies in the Serenissima. For the love of God, let us unite and provide for the safety of Italy." He spoke, says the ambassador, as if from his heart. But Giustinian knew that, to serve Valentino, he would have turned against Venice before the ink of the treaty was dry, as, indeed, would almost every other Power in Italy at that time, had it been to their advantage to do so. " Every action, every thought of Alexander VI was planned to deceive men," says Machiavelli in the Prince. " And he always found a victim ready to his purpose. Never did anyone keep his word less, yet his deceptions always turned out

[1] Luzio and Renier, *Mantova ed Urbino*, p. 142.

to his advantage." Indeed, Machiavelli selects him as the outstanding example of successful deceit. Guicciardini hits off the difference between father and son with his usual neatness. " The Pope never did what he said, Valentino never said what he did."

The folly of the captains and above all of the Orsini caused no less astonishment in Rome. " Are they not like a pack of wretched bankrupts ? " exclaimed the Pope to Giustinian, echoing Cesare's phrase. " They distrust each other and admit that they are traitors in their terms, even the cardinal, who pretends to be our friend, though he makes it a condition that he is to be in Rome only when he wishes." The cardinal seemed to be more intimate with the Pope than ever, merely smiling at all warnings and answering that any differences that he had had with His Holiness had always been settled amicably.

Valentino left Imola on December 10th. Machiavelli followed him, but could not resist the temptation of lingering an extra day at Cesena " from love of the lodging ". Valentino's troops were scattered about Romagna and their stations were carefully changed, but the presence of so large a force produced something like a famine in this wild district and the inhabitants had a good deal to put up with. The country suffered severely, for, says Machiavelli, the French and other soldiery are not different in Romagna from what they were in Tuscany. Valentino found it difficult to provide food, but he did his best not to oppress his subjects, importing a quantity of grain from Venice. He showed himself, as always, as considerate and affable as possible on the march. He went out of his way to grant the *grazie* asked him by these, who were among the poorest of his subjects, even to releasing the husbands of some wretchedly poor women from gaol.

Christmas was spent at Cesena. The troops were not billeted in the town and he punished without mercy any act of oppression against the inhabitants. His force consisted of about 12,000 men. Naturally the size of the army set men talking. Machiavelli, however, was convinced that it could have no other object than to secure those who had treated the Duca so scurvily. His interest was keenly awakened.

On December 20th, to his amazement, Machiavelli, while on his way to headquarters, met a number of French officers, who, from their appearance and gestures, were clearly excited and angry. He learnt that they had been to take leave of the Duca, who was sending the whole contingent back to Lombardy, with the exception of two companies of fifty men. One of these belonged to his brother-in-law, d'Albret. This move caused great surprise. It set all men's ideas topsy-turvy, says Machiavelli, and everyone built his own little castle upon it. The arrival of a thousand Swiss mercenaries about the same time made it all the more puzzling. But the French were expensive, they treated the inhabitants badly and Cesare had no real authority over them, such as he had over hirelings like the Swiss. Woodward also suggests that he felt that they might not altogether approve of the brigand-like *coup* he was preparing and that he had no wish to increase the bad name he had already acquired among his adopted countrymen, with their exalted ideals of knightly conduct, by his treatment of Caterina Sforza.

As usual, he threw himself into all the festivities of the season. On December 22nd, the day when the French left, some of the principal inhabitants prepared a dance for him which he thoroughly enjoyed, leading the dances himself with his customary grace and skill. Late that night he sent for Don Ramiro de Lorqua and imprisoned him in the Rocca. Next day it was proclaimed throughout Romagna that he was imprisoned because of the many charges of fraud against him, fraud in which he persisted in

218

spite of all warnings and all the favours shown him. More especially he was charged with trafficking in grain and sending such quantities out of the country that it had been necessary to import. The charge did not take long to prove. Don Ramiro was beheaded on Christmas morning. His body was exposed on a mat in the square in front of the Rocca, dressed in all his decorations, throughout the day, the head being impaled on a pike. By it was a bloody block and a knife.

This execution of one of his most trusted adherents made a profound impression, as it was meant to do, and on no one more than on Machiavelli, who was thus given another example of the secrecy and swiftness with which his hero could strike. " This morning Don Ramiro was found in two pieces on the Piazza, where he still is, and all the people here have been able to see him. The reason for his death is not rightly known, beyond the fact that this Prince so willed it, who shows that he can make and unmake men at his will, according to their deserts." It is quite likely that he was executed on account of his cruelty. He was bitterly hated, not only by the inhabitants, but also by Cesare's Italians. It was said that, but for his cruel massacre, Urbino would not have revolted so easily. In the *Prince*, where Machiavelli may always be idealizing, he tells us that Cesare gave Don Ramiro full power to be as merciless as he chose in reducing his states to order and then, when he had served his purpose, sacrificed him to the hatred of his subjects. " The ferocious spectacle both astonished and satisfied the people there."

Other suggestions are that Don Ramiro had behaved with unbecoming familiarity towards Lucrezia when he entertained her on her wedding journey, but this does not sound very probable. There is more ground for believing that he was intriguing with the Orsini. If so, his end is quite intelligible.

The fate of Sinigaglia had long been sealed. Giustinian shows us the Pope spending the day counting out money for the Duca. " He sends the money very unwillingly, because he almost throws it away ; but he cannot refuse the Duca, who promises to do great things, though he can see no results. It is thought nearly certain here that the attack on Sinigaglia will take place and that it is being kept secret. The Pope is continually complaining and railing against the lady " (December 17th, 1502), that is to say, Guidobaldo's sister, the Prefettessa. As there was no hope of successful resistance, she had left Sinigaglia.

On December 26th Cesare started from Cesena and three days later was at loyal Fano, where he was met by Commissioners from Ancona. Here he learnt that the town of Sinigaglia had opened its gates of its own free will, but that the commander would surrender the Rocca only to himself in person. He replied on December 30th that he would be there on the morrow with his guns, in case there was trouble. He issued orders that the condottieri, who were to meet him there, should leave the town for his own troops, and quarter their men in the suburbs and the neighbouring villages. Oliverotto Euffreducci da Fermo remained in the suburbs, while Vitellozzo and the Orsini occupied the villages that stretched along the coast towards the River Esino, ten miles to the south of Sinigaglia. The captains had no idea of the strength of Valentino's army, as he was careful to march his men in small detachments by different roads. That evening he sent for eight of the most trusted men in his service and gave them special instructions.

Vitellozzo had come from Città di Castello very unwillingly. Clearly he had a premonition of his fate. Even his men, to say nothing of Baglioni, warned him not to trust Valentino. Still less willing was he to meet him with the other captains on the morning of the 31st. At last, however, he yielded to Paolo Orsini's persuasion and mounted a mule, for his horse was not ready. He was unarmed, wearing a black cape, lined with green. When he left his men he commended his family to them, as though it were for the last time.

The meeting took place about a mile from the town. Paolo Orsini rode up first. Valentino welcomed him in his most charming manner and asked eagerly after " his brother " Vitellozzo, whom he guessed to be a doubtful starter. Like the rest of the Vitelli, he was a soldier of some mark. The Orsini were a poor lot, and without Vitellozzo Valentino's plan would have failed. He knew that Vitellozzo would never forgive him for having forced him to leave Arezzo. Hence the effusive joy with which he received him was more genuine than it might have seemed. Valentino threw his arms round his neck, gave him a Judas kiss, and refused to hear of his dismounting. According to Machiavelli, Vitellozzo looked pale and troubled and anyone could see that he felt that he was doomed. The two other Orsini were also there. Not seeing Oliverotto, Valentino signalled to Michelotto with a glance to fetch him. He was in the Borgo, looking after his men. Michelotto told him to leave them in their billets and come with him to the Duke.

All the birds were now in the net. Cesare rode between Vitellozzo and Francesco Orsini. Each of the captains was, however, shadowed by one of Valentino's most trusted retainers. Vitellozzo grew more and more uneasy. As they approached the walls, he showed that he had no intention of walking into a trap. He turned round, intending to rejoin his escort which he had left by the river and go back to his own men. Paolo Orsini saved Cesare the necessity of showing his hand too soon by once again persuading him to stay where he was. But Vitellozzo told him that he had a presentiment that, if he went on, he would

meet his death, adding that, since the others were ready
to run the risk, he would face it with them. Valentino
was chatting with them in his most winning manner.

The River Misa flows round two sides of Sinigaglia,
with its narrow streets and tall, gaunt houses. An
artificial canal connects it with the sea round the
suburb, not directly under the walls, on the south.
Over this canal, leading to the suburb, was the bridge.
As soon as they had crossed it, the vanguard of cavalry
under Michelotto halted, faced round and lined the
road, thus securing the bridge. Through their ranks
marched a thousand Swiss and Gascon mercenaries,
followed by the Duca with his staff and his prisoners.
The rest of his troops followed. The gates were
closed behind them.

Michelotto, who knew the town, had chosen the
Palazzo Bernardino, a house with both a back and a
front entrance, for his master. On reaching it the
condottieri prepared to take their leave and return to
their men. But Cesare pressed them to come in, as
there were matters of importance he wished to talk
over with them. They did not like the look of things,
but it was too late to turn back now. The moment
they were seated Valentino said that he wanted to
leave the room for a moment. The door had hardly
closed behind him when a body of the Duca's men
entered and made them all prisoners. Valentino left
the house by the back door and ordered the officer
commanding the escorts of the condottieri to retire.
They were disarmed or cut down by his own men on
the way back. Other bodies of his troops arriving
from Fano disarmed the forces of the condottieri
quartered round Sinigaglia.

When Machiavelli reached Sinigaglia late that
evening the Duca's men were badly out of hand,
plundering and rioting unchecked. But before midnight Valentino rode into the narrow streets, and
by hanging a few of the plunderers, succeeded in

222

restoring order. Some Venetian merchants who complained to him that their goods had been pillaged received a stern answer. He reminded them that after making him a gentleman of Venice, the Serenissima had plotted against him. Already he was feeling more sure of himself.

Machiavelli wrote that he did not expect the captains would be alive in the morning, nor was he mistaken. Vitellozzo and Oliverotto were strangled that night, after the Spanish fashion, by Michelotto in the Palazzo Bernardino, where they had been taken. As was to be expected, there were many rumours about the way they met their death. Oliverotto is said to have broken down and Vitellozzo to have begged that the Pope would grant him a plenary indulgence. Paolo Orsini and the Duke of Gravina were spared for the moment.

That evening Valentino also sent for Machiavelli and, with the most cheerful air imaginable, expressed his joy at his success, saying that he had given him a hint of what was to happen the day before. He then spoke wisely and most affectionately of Florence. She should be pleased that he had made away with men who were bitter enemies of the King, of himself and of Florence, and he hoped she would send troops to help him against Città di Castello or Perugia. He even hoped that the Florentines would detain Guidobaldo d'Urbino, if he entered their territory, but to this Machiavelli demurred.

Next day, January 1st, 1503, as the Rocca had surrendered, Valentino left for Corinaldo. He now sent off a number of despatches to the Powers, justifying what he had done by saying that, when the French troops left, the condottieri had plotted against him and he had merely forestalled them. The Pope bore out this story, informing Giustinian that, before his execution, Ramiro de Lorqua had told Cesare that Vitellozzo had intended to kill him. It is, of course, possible that there was some plot, but Valentino was the last man to trust the condottieri again and he was anything but forgiving.

Indeed, if treachery can be justified, it was certainly justified in the case of the victims of the *bellissimo inganno*, the most beautiful stratagem, as Paolo Giovio, who was no friend of the Borgias, called it. The treachery and cruelty of these petty tyrants of Romagna was a byword and Oliverotto was among the worst of them. Machiavelli cites him as a classic instance of a man who has got possession of a state by crime. He had been brought up by an uncle in Fermo and treated with every kindness. When he had risen to be Vitellozzo's lieutenant, he returned there with a troop of horse lent him by his chief and was welcomed affectionately by this uncle. Then he gave a banquet to the leading inhabitants, among whom was his uncle. When they left the table, he gathered them into a smaller room, where he had them all butchered in cold blood by his own men. These were the means by which he established himself as Lord of Fermo, maintaining himself in power by the support of his adherents and by the terror inspired by his methods and the strength of his forces. He acted with the full concurrence of Vitellozzo, whose life would have been forfeit for his treachery in any state of the day, unless it had served the purpose of his commander to let him live.

The complete success of the *bellissimo inganno* made a profound impression upon the imagination of Valentino's contemporaries. His wife was horrified, but as a rule it aroused sincere admiration. Louis XII described it as a deed worthy of a Roman. Also it was another proof of the amazing good luck, as many thought it, of this " son of fortune " of the astrologers. No one admired the *inganno* more sincerely than Machiavelli, who saw that its success was due to efficiency, not to luck. Judged by the standard of the

time it was a master-stroke of *virtù*, a stroke calculated
to inspire fear as much as respect, carried out with
the swiftness and sureness that characterized all that
Valentino did. It may be said to mark the zenith of
his career. " He had an intuitive grasp of certain
ends to be attained, of certain modifications in the
civil life of peoples, necessary, inevitable, attainable
only in times when there is intelligence and thought
in plenty, but little belief," says Tommasini in his
admirable book on Machiavelli, " times when the
high and sure instinct that discriminates between
justice and injustice is degraded below the sordid and
unstable standard of what pays."

The Gonzagas were among the first to whom he
wrote and Isabella answered (January 15th, 1503):
" The successful progress of Your Excellency, of
which you have informed us in an affectionate letter,
has given us the pleasure and satisfaction which is
natural to the mutual affection and goodwill existing
between you and our Most Illustrious Consort and
ourself. So, in his name and ours, we congratulate
you on all the safety and prosperity that are yours ;
and we thank you for the news and for offering to keep
us informed of your success, in which we beg you
of your courtesy to persevere, because, loving you as
we do, we desire often to hear of your movements,
in order that we may wish you joy of your success
and of your rising fortunes. And because we think
that, after the toil and fatigue you have suffered in
these glorious enterprises, you may wish to indulge
in a little recreation, I thought I would send you a
hundred masks by my messenger Giovanni. . . . As
to business matters, there is nothing more to say until
we hear from Your Excellency about the security."

The last allusion is to the dowry of Louise and the
proposed match with Isabella's son. Cesare replied
from Acquapendente in a suitable letter on February
1st, addressing her as *Commare,* as he was godfather

225

to her son. The masks, the beauty and variety of
which he praises, could not have arrived at a more
suitable moment, as he was just off to Rome, after
finishing his campaign. The letter, like all those of
this time that are preserved, was written by Agapito
and countersigned by himself, " Compare et fratello
el Duca de Romagna," etc.[1]

Cesare was known to be fond of going masked,
partly, perhaps, because of the condition of his face.

Giustinian's despatches at this time are especially
interesting. They enable us to realize the general
uneasiness and nervousness that prevailed in Vatican
circles during the last days of 1502. The Pope was in a
state of unusual excitement. How much he knew we
cannot say, but he was irritated by Cesare's long stay
at Cesena. On learning that he was still there (December 23rd) he burst out angrily, " Al fio de putta,
bastardo ! " repeating the words three times quite
audibly and adding other remarks, probably quite as
uncomplimentary, in Spanish. He was very relieved
at the news of the flight of the Prefettessa from
Sinigaglia on Christmas Eve.

The size of Valentino's army caused widespread
alarm. Perugia and Siena were particularly nervous.
The news of the dismissal of the French brought
general relief, as it was now thought that he could not
have any important expedition in view.

Christmas went off as usual in Rome. The Pope was
much amused by a procession of thirty masks with
long noses " in formam priaporum " which paraded
before him in St Peter's Square, followed by a mask of
a cardinal with all the usual adjuncts of a member of
the Sacred College. We need not go away with the
idea that Alexander was the first pope to be amused
by this kind of thing. It shocked Burchard, but
then he was a Northerner. Alexander was most
attentive to Cardinal Orsini, whom he kept continually

[1] Both are in Gregorovius, *Luc. Borgia*, App. 10.

with him. On December 29th he was invited to supper at the Vatican, remaining till nearly daylight and sharing the usual amusements of the Pope. "There were women present, for without them there can now be no entertainment at the palace which gives any pleasure. Several hundred ducats were won and lost at play."

On December 31st His Holiness broke into another of his attacks upon Cesare, probably as a result of the nervous strain he was feeling. "This Duca must for ever be doing something new. He has too much spirit. We wish he was a little less extravagant. If he is here for carnival, he will be up to some mad prank or other and throw away some thousands of ducats over and above what we have spent." Turning irritably to the cardinals, he complained that the Duca had been spending over a thousand ducats a day. It was no use telling him to be more careful. Cardinal San Severino, who was then popular with Alexander, as was his brother, Fracassa, with Cesare, said that he should not be vexed, because His Excellency did not spend his money uselessly. He put him into the best of humours by saying that all the Court was longing for his return. Without him there would be no fun in carnival.

On New Year's Day the Pope was overjoyed at the news of the voluntary surrender of Sinigaglia, pretending that it was a complete surprise to him. Then he added ominously to the assembled cardinals and ambassadors that it was not in the Duke's nature to forgive an injury or to leave vengeance to others, and he mentioned Oliverotto, whom, he said, the Duke had sworn to hang with his own hands, if he could get hold of him. "When Our Lord had told the news, everyone, as usual, congratulated him and scratched his ears in different ways : he was delighted and, spreading out the fringes of his robe, began a long harangue upon the virtues and the magnanimity

227

of the Duke. Most of the cardinals, though they expressed their assent, looked at one another cautiously and shrugged their shoulders."

On January 4th Alexander gave Giustinian his version of the plot and the events at Sinigaglia, adding that the others were being kept prisoners " and, if they have been at fault, they also will be punished." He then announced that he had arrested Cardinal Orsini. Giustinian gathered that it was the Pope's intention to see that he died and also that he knew that he was lying in what he said about the plot revealed by Don Ramiro de Lorqua.

Cardinal Orsini had ridden to the Vatican to congratulate the Pope on the fall of Sinigaglia, the Governor of the City joining him, as if by chance, on the way. The Pope's Cardinal Secretary had refused to leave his rooms on the previous day from fear that, if the arrest failed, he might be accused of having revealed the secret. When Orsini entered the Camera del Papagallo he found a number of armed men there who instantly arrested him. His mule and the horses of his suite were taken to the Vatican stables. All his property, even the straw in the stables, was carried off. His mother, an old lady of eighty, was turned into the streets with nothing but the clothes she was wearing and a couple of maids with her. No one dared shelter her.

This arrest, followed by the imprisonment of two excellent priests, created something like a panic in Rome. The Bishop of Chiusi is said to have died of fright. The panic affected not only wealthy ecclesiastics, but gentlemen of property, many of whom fled from Rome. So great was the alarm that Alexander thought it advisable to send for the Conservatori and reassure them, bidding them go and have a merry carnival, in order to keep people cheerful and allay their fears. In this he was sincere, for he liked gaiety and it pleased him to see others enjoy themselves.

Cesare meanwhile was continuing his progress. On January 5th Vitellozzo's town, Città di Castello, sent to accept his rule. The rebels who had escaped had taken refuge with Baglioni at Perugia, but they fled on the approach of the forces of the Gonfalonier of the Church and on January 6th Perugia sent to offer its submission.

Machiavelli's last despatch is dated January 10th. He had already told the Signoria that he thought the executions would bring peace to both Tuscany and Romagna and that Valentino's later conquests were for the Church, as he meant to keep only Romagna for himself. Valentino then informed him that his final undertaking would be to turn Pandolfo Petrucci out of Siena. This he must do because, with his brain and money and position, he might prove a spark capable of starting a big fire. It would be easy to drive him from Siena, but he wanted to get him into his hands. " Hence the Pope is trying to lull him to sleep with briefs, explaining to him that all will be well if they have the same enemies, and meanwhile I go ahead with my army, and it is good to deceive those who have shown themselves masters in treachery." He had no intention of taking Siena " because the master of the shop, the King of France, would not be pleased." He was anxious that Florence should understand exactly what he meant to do. Now that he has disarmed his enemies, he meant also to have their brain, which belonged entirely to Pandolfo.

Not till the 18th were Paolo Orsini and Francesco, the Duke of Gravina, executed. The young Cavaliere Orsini was liberated. Alexander was trying to induce Louis to arrest Giangiordano, saying that he did not mean to leave a single Orsini alive. Gioffrè was sent to seize the Orsini property in the neighbourhood of Rome.

The Pope was setting his subjects an excellent

example by the thoroughness with which he enjoyed carnival. On February 21st he watched the usual races, then listened to some comedies, of which he was very fond, often having one performed in private. These, however, were " public and a number of cardinals were present, some in their robes, some masked ", with the company the Pope liked best, some of the girls sitting at the feet of His Holiness. He now forbade the mother of Cardinal Orsini to send food to her son. Later he was induced to withdraw the prohibition when he was given 2000 ducats and a lovely pearl worth the same amount, which the old lady sent him by a mistress of the cardinal, dressed in man's clothes, to whom he had given it. Meanwhile, however, it was generally believed that " he had drunk " and the belief was confirmed when he died on February 22nd. It is impossible to be certain of the cause of Cardinal Orsini's death. In any case, the Pope clearly meant him to die. He was elderly and in poor health ; Pastor says he was blind ; and a rigorous imprisonment could be an effective means of accomplishing this purpose. Soderini wrote to Florence that the cardinal was showing signs of madness and clearly believed that he had been poisoned. The Pope saw that he had a suitable funeral, in which all the Orsini in Rome took part, but Burchard says that he would have nothing to do with the arrangements, as he had no desire to know more than he ought. By the Pope's orders the doctors were summoned and issued a declaration that death was due to natural causes. Such was the end of the man who had done more than anyone except Ascanio Sforza to secure the tiara for the Borgia.

CHAPTER XVI

THE BORGIAS AS POISONERS
THE POPE'S DEATH (1503)

CESARE was by this time back in Rome. Giustinian, like everyone else, recognized him, with Cardinals d'Albret and Borgia, at some more comedies on the 27th, though they were masked and wished to remain incognito. The Pope had been pressing eagerly for his return. Realizing their danger, other barons had rallied round the Orsini. Gioffrè was incapable of dealing with such a situation, even if he had had sufficient men. The Orsini ventured to attack the Ponte Nomentana, causing such alarm in Rome that the Pope shut himself up in Castel S. Angelo. On the way South the conduct of Cesare's troops aroused general indignation, but, as they were not in his Duchy, he made no effort to restrain them. Cardinal Ippolito d'Este left Rome hastily, possibly warned by Sancia, who had no desire for trouble. He was afraid of Cesare's jealousy on account of his relations with the lady.

Once again there was a serious difference between father and son. The Pope wished him to besiege Bracciano, where was Giangiordano, the most formidable of the Orsini clan, against whom he was particularly bitter. Cesare left his presence in a passion. He declined to attack Giangiordano, who was not only a protégé of the King of France, but a member of the Order of St Michel. These were sworn not to war against one another. Nor would he attack Pitigliano, which belonged to the famous

condottiere of that name. He had no desire to risk
offending Venice, in whose service Pitigliano was.
But he laid vigorous siege to Caere, which tested his
siege-train to the utmost. It seems probable that
Leonardo da Vinci helped in devising some of the
machines used. Valentino took deep interest in them.
But after five weeks Louis, who was annoyed at
Cesare's continued success, intervened and terms were
arranged. The Cardinal's brother, Giulio Orsini,
who was in command, came to Rome with Cesare,
and was well received and honourably treated by the
Pope.

The state of affairs in Naples was causing the Borgias the gravest anxiety. The French were in a hopeless position, and it was clear that the Spaniards, led
by Gonsalvo, must inevitably become masters of the
kingdom. The Pope was always a Spaniard at heart,
and there was little doubt that he would be delighted
to turn against the French. He told the Bolognese
envoy that, if the French were going to look on while
the Italians did the fighting for them, " we shall
take steps to secure what we have gained, for we
see that the success of the Spaniards is the will of
God, and if God wills it so, we have no right to wish
otherwise." And he went on to abuse the French
and praise his own people.[1]

The King of France was also anxious and drawing
closer to the Florentines, whom he meant to protect
against any designs of Valentino. Indeed, it was
generally believed that the Pope was only waiting
for the fall of Gaeta to declare in favour of Spain.

Valentino, however, did not share these views.
He saw that it was not the Spaniards in Naples, but
the French in Lombardy who mattered to him.
In his anxiety to win the friendship of Venice he
arranged to see Giustinian, when he called at the
palace, coming forward to meet him with his usual

[1] Giustinian, June 23rd, 1503.

winning smile. The Pope once again frankly admitted that on his death all Valentino's hopes of retaining his conquests depended upon Venetian support. One cannot help suspecting that the interview may have been arranged by Alexander.

Valentino was preparing to support Louis, in accordance with his promises, on the new expedition he was planning against Naples. Among the troops he proposed to send were some of his Romagnol militia, of whom he was pardonably proud. In April the Pope watched 500 of them, " molto bella gente ", admits Giustinian, from the Vatican windows as they marched round St Peter's Square to the sound of the drum behind their flag, which bore Cesare's motto, " Aut Cæsar, aut nihil." They were dressed in jackets of his colours, red and yellow, in quarters, with " Cesare " on breast and back and their belts were made in the form of snakes. In this, as in all else, Valentino acted regardless of expense. It is not surprising that he had the reputation of being the most splendid captain of his day in Italy.

The difficulty of finding money for this army greatly troubled the Pope. In March eighty new posts were created at the Vatican, for which the recipients paid 760 ducats each. Michelotto was sent out to round up a number of so-called *marrani*, who could be fined, and in May nine more cardinals were made. Five of them were Spaniards, two of them being relatives of the Pope, while another was the lifelong friend of Cesare, Francisco Remolines. The Florentine Soderini, Bishop of Volterra, was also chosen. In all they paid from 120,000 to 130,000 ducats for their red hats.

On May 15th Monsignor Troches, the Pope's confidential secretary, disappeared from Rome. At first it was thought that he had been sent on a confidential mission, but he was captured in Corsica and brought back. Beltrando Costabili wrote to Ferrara that he had complained to the Pope because he was not among the new cardinals and when Alexander said Cesare had drawn up the list, he spoke bitterly against him. Alexander said he must be mad to use such language. If the Duke heard him, he would kill him. Whereupon Troches fled. : Whether the story is true or not, it shows the state of opinion in Rome. It is more probable that, being a partisan of Louis, he was suspected of betraying the Pope's Spanish proclivities. He was making for France when caught. Again, according to Costabili, Cesare had an hour's talk with him in his prison, then withdrew and was an unseen witness of his being strangled by Michelotto.

The Pope continued his usual life. He thoroughly enjoyed a trip to Caere with Cesare and was much impressed by the strength of the fortifications. Costabili notes that on April 17th everyone was struck by the strength of his voice when he sang Mass, and said he looked wonderfully well. Valentino continued to drill his men, and great alarm was felt about the destination of so large a force, especially in Florence. His methods had not changed. When some of his Albanians asked to be released from service, because of the captain he had placed over them, he raised no objections, but he sent men after them when they were outside Rome and put a couple of the ringleaders to death.

In April the Pope had another windfall in the death of Cardinal Mihiel, which was said to have brought him 150,000 ducats. Everything was seized and on the next day Giustinian was refused an audience, as His Holiness was spending a happy day counting his gains. From the first there were grave suspicions of poison. Indeed, this is the one cardinal whom it is fairly certain the Borgias did try to poison. Even those who are most sceptical about their crimes are bound to admit that the evidence is very damaging. In 1504, under Julius II, the Cardinal's secretary, Asquinio de

Colloredo, was tried and confessed, after torture, that he had administered the poison. He was executed on the Capitol and frequently interrupted the reading of his sentence by declaring that he had acted under orders from Alexander and Valentino. One thing is certain. If Mihiel was the only known victim, he was not the only person whom the Borgias attempted to poison, whether successfully or not.

As the Borgias owe not a little of their bad name to their reputation as poisoners—in popular imagination the words Borgia and poison are almost synonymous —this seems a good place to say something on the subject. The general impression seems to be that they never moved without a supply of their deadly *cantarella*. The legend arose in their lifetime. It was felt, quite naturally, that men so utterly without principle, and withal so able, as the Pope and his son, would stick at nothing. Whenever anyone was imprisoned or seriously ill whose death might benefit the Borgias there were instant rumours that "he had drunk". The indecent haste and thoroughness with which the Pope gutted the houses of deceased ecclesiastics, combined with the silence and ruthlessness of Valentino, tended to confirm the belief. Alexander was believed to fatten his cardinals with benefices and then, when they were in prime condition, to poison them in order to inherit their savings.

"They say that the dragon is made and formed by a big serpent devouring and eating a number of other serpents and snakes," says Brantôme with reference to Cesare and the condottieri; and one of his seals had seven snakes with open mouths above the arms.

The first mention of the white powder, the *cantarella*, as it was later called, of the Borgias is by Paolo Giovio, who wrote after the events.[1] In describing the death of Djem he says that Alexander was said to have given him a deadly powder, rather

[1] *Hist. Sui Temporis*, I, 27.

like sugar, of extraordinary whiteness, not unpleasant to the taste, which did not kill at once, but poisoned gradually and with which he was afterwards said to have put out of the way some rich senators (i.e. cardinals). Thus even Paolo Giovio does not go beyond suggesting it as a rumour. He tells us that Cardinal Orsini was killed with cantharides, which is the usual meaning of *cantarella*, but those who believe that the Borgia poison was a white powder, make it arsenic.

The belief in poison as a common cause of death was, as we have seen, very prevalent at this time. The slightest suspicion was sufficient to start the wildest rumours. But when we come to examine the evidence the most striking fact about these medieval poisons is their futility, the rareness of their success. We must turn to Venice if we wish to learn something about the official use of poisons. Full details are to be found in the archives. Horatio Brown has gone into the question in his paper on political assassination.[1] The Serenissima had a special cupboard for poisons which was destroyed by fire in 1514. A famous master in the art of poisoning, "nostro fidel Vilandrino", custodian of the herb-garden of the University of Padua, was chosen from among several others, whose names are given, and bidden supply some more with the receipts for brewing the concoctions. He sent a poisoned water, with which experiments were made upon a luckless Mustapha. When it did not produce the slightest effect and a second dose proved equally harmless, Vilandrino was dismissed. We also have an account of a scheme for poisoning the whole Turkish army, which was naturally an utter fiasco. The trouble with the poisons of those days was that they were generally so complicated and the ingredients so many that no ordinary stomach could retain them. There is an

[1] *Studies in Ven. Hist.*, Vol. I.

appalling prescription given by Brown. I imagine that the receipt for a *veleno a termine* given by Portigliotti from Caterina Sforza's well-known book of receipts of all kinds would prove equally ineffectual for the same reason. If the Borgias possessed a white powder, it may well have been arsenic, which was known at that time, and if they had the sense to give it in wise doses, whether as a rapid or a slow poison, they were certainly ahead of the time as poisoners. But there is no evidence that they did so, nor is there any evidence that the victims whose bodies were found in the Tiber had been previously poisoned; nor do I see why they should have troubled to poison them first. Doctors at the time had no means of diagnosing death by poison. The state of medical knowledge was such that poison and witchcraft were equally easy methods of explaining a mysterious death. Probably the Borgias did, on occasion, try poison, but the number of the cases in which they succeeded cannot have been very great. Statistics are sufficient to prove that they were not very successful, if they tried to murder the cardinals wholesale. Here is a list of cardinals under four Popes taken from Ciaconius :

	Created	Died	Years of Papacy.
Sixtus IV .	35	27	13
Innocent VIII	13	11	8
Alexander VI	34	27	11
Julius II .	27	36	19½

From this table it is clear that the number of deaths in the Sacred College under Alexander VI was slightly above the average for the four reigns as a whole, but not noticeably so ; and it is worth observing that the one cardinal whom the Borgias do seem, upon substantial evidence, to have succeeded in poisoning was so old and in such poor health that he could not have survived long.

There were many rumours about the future of

Valentino, who was preparing to return to Romagna. Some said that the Pope was trying to induce Spain to grant him the kingdom of Sicily, others that he had designs upon Tuscany. In his *Discorso del modo di trattare i popoli della Valdichiana*, Machiavelli had said that the Duca "having always thought little of the Venetians and even less of the Florentines . . . it is natural that he should strive to win for himself such a position in Italy that it will make his friendship worth having to another Power." He ends by expressing it as his opinion that he is aspiring to the sovereignty of Tuscany as being nearer and well suited to form a single kingdom with the other states in his possession.

The course of the Borgias was now nearly run. Roman fever, a form of malaria, was very prevalent and more fatal than usual in Rome, as elsewhere in Italy, that summer, which was exceptionally hot. Among the victims was Cardinal Monreale, Juan de Borja–Lançol, the Pope's nephew. Giustinian talks of the Pope's cheerful mien, of the fortune he will reap by the death, amounting to 100,000 ducats, and repeats the eternal gossip about his having been sent to join the others, after being nicely fattened.

Till a few years ago it was generally believed that the question of the death of Alexander VI had been definitely settled. He died of malaria, and the picturesque legend of his having been poisoned by drinking some wine with which he was intending to poison the wealthy Cardinal Adriano di Corneto was finally laid to rest. But the discovery that the "pernicious fever" of his day is caused by the bite of a mosquito has enabled Signor Portigliotti to give it new life, though his arguments do not strike me as convincing. In any case the evidence is not sufficient to make it possible to arrive at a definite conclusion.

Early in August the Pope and Cesare dined with Adriano Castellesi di Corneto, the Protonotory, one

of the newly-appointed cardinals, in his *vigna* on Monte
Mario. He was a scholar and a humanist. It was he
who was building the splendid palace in Alexander's
new street in the same style as the Cancelleria, which
some modern critics decline to allow to be by Bramante—the Palazzo Giraud–Torlonia, in the Borgo
Nuovo. The exact date of the dinner is uncertain.
It is usually given as the 5th, but Cattaneo wrote to
Mantua as early as the 4th that " the Pope is out of
sorts and has been bled. Considering the unhealthi-
ness of the season and his age, the doctors thought it
advisable. The Duke has fever and is vomiting."
It is possible that they were unwell before the dinner,
but this has never been suggested. We may therefore
have to date it as early as the 2nd or 3rd. Catteneo's
despatch has only recently been published by Luzio
and Renier, and it is certainly a small point in favour
of the poison theory. But he is merely repeating
gossip at second-hand and it is clear that the Pope was
not seriously ill, for on the 7th Giustinian had an
audience. He found him not very cheerful and he
began, " Domine Orator, all this illness in Rome and
the daily deaths have frightened us so that we are
inclined to take more care of our health than we used
to do." He went on to tell him that Cesare would
be leaving Rome on the morrow and swore, with his
hands at his breast, on the word of the Vicar of Christ,
that he had no sinister designs and that the Tuscans
had grieved him by sending for French protection,
which was quite unnecessary. On the 11th, the anniversary of his accession, Giustinian notes that His
Holiness was less cheerful than usual on such occasions,
looking depressed and troubled.

The day before he was taken ill he saw the body of
a near relative who commanded the Papal guard and
was very fat, carried out to burial, and said sadly that
it was a bad month for fat people. He had hardly
spoken when an owl flew down at his feet. " A bad

omen, a bad omen ", he exclaimed and retired to his bedchamber.

Next day matters became serious. Costabili tells Ercole d'Este that he hears from a good source that on Saturday (12th) His Holiness vomited a yellow fluid and had a high temperature. He records that nearly all the chief Vatican officials were ill, which was not surprising " considering the badness of the air there ".[1] The Duke was very ill with a double tertian, vomiting and with severe pains in the stomach. Giustinian adds that no one is allowed in or out of the Vatican and that it is given out that the Pope and the Duke are busy with preparations for the Duke's departure. He also refers the illness back to the dinner, which he dates on the 5th—and surely he is not likely to have been mistaken—adding that all the guests had been taken ill, beginning with Cardinal Adriano, who was very seriously affected.

On the 13th the Pope was bled. Rumour said that the amount of blood taken was 14 to 16 ounces, but the Venetian wisely accepts the lowest estimate of 10 ounces, which he finds an astonishing amount for an old man of 73. This drastic measure did not, however, allay the fever. The Pope spent the day watching some cardinals play cards. The Duke was worse. The Bishop of Venosa, the Pope's trusted physician, was sent for, and, with Maestro Scipio, was in attendance. The Bishop, who had himself been ill, was kept at the palace and forbidden to leave. The bleeding was particularly necessary, as there was danger of coma setting in. The Pope was also said to be troubled and worried about the Duke's health. On the 15th he was better and free from fever, or so it was said. But the fever soon returned and on the 17th Giustinian writes that the gravity of the illness was generally recognized. Those at the palace persisted in declaring that all was going well, but they

[1] Giustinian, II, 459.

were secretly removing their property. Costabili, who had been told that the Pope was suffering from a tertian fever, went to the palace on the 17th, as that should have been his good day, and received reassuring news from the Cardinal of Cosenza, but on the 18th he learnt that there had been no real improvement. On the 18th Maestro Scipio visited Giustinian, who was the doyen of the diplomatic corps, and told him that the Pope would not live another day. He also said that the cause of the trouble was apoplexy. The Duke was out of danger, free from fever and could get up when he liked. But we must remember that the doctors could not tell all that they knew. On that morning His Holiness had confessed and communicated and heard Mass in the presence of five cardinals. He said that he felt ill. About the hour of Vespers, after receiving extreme unction, he breathed his last. According to Burchard during his illness he never once asked for, or even mentioned, any of his children.

Few Popes can have been so little regretted as Alexander. Giustinian expressed the general feeling when he said that everyone hoped that this illness might be the end of the tribulation of Christendom. Burchard dressed the body, which he had carried to the Camera del Papagallo, as he describes in great detail. There was no one to watch it, or even to repeat the Office of the Dead over it. On the next day it was laid in state in St Peter's, as usual, being placed before the bars of the High Altar, behind a closed grill, from fear that it might be outraged. The face was already the colour of a very dark mulberry, the features swollen, the tongue twice its natural size, filling the whole of the mouth, which was open, a hideous sight, says Burchard. In this all witnesses agree. Giustinian calls it the ugliest, most monstrous and horrible human corpse ever seen (black as the devil, says another), without any appearance or form of a man. For very shame they kept it covered for a while.

That evening (19th) it was temporarily buried in the Capella delle Febbri, being carried thither by half a dozen porters. Burchard says they made fun of the Pope. Such ribaldry was a sure sign of nervousness. The coffin was too small. Helped by two carpenters, they forced his mitre off, covered the body with an old carpet and squeezed it in with their fists. There were no lights or candles, and no one paid the slightest attention to the dead Pope. Burchard is obviously glad to include what must have been one of the most bitter of the epigrams upon him.[1]

There is considerable evidence to show that something was wrong at the dinner given by Cardinal Adriano di Corneto, who was, by the way, Bishop of Bath and Wells. He was deprived of the purple for poisoning Alexander by Leo X. Remolines and at least two other cardinals were present and they were all ill. Paolo Giovio says that he was told by Cardinal Adriano that " when he had drunk the deadly cup, he was so heated by a sudden fire in his bowels that his brain became clouded and he lost his senses. He was made to plunge into a bath of icy cold water ", a favourite drastic cure at the time. Nor did he recover till his skin had peeled off.[2] The same violent remedy was tried with Cesare, with the same results, but it was long before his skin recovered.

Neither Giustinian nor Burchard suggest poison, and they were more likely to know than anyone else

---

[1] Sævitia, insidiæ, rabies, furor, ira, libido,
  Sanguinis atque auri spongia dira sitis,
 Sextus Alexander jaceo hic : jam libera gaude,
  Roma, tibi quoniam mors mea vita fuit.
 Sextus Alexander vastavit cædibus orbem,
  Tertius at reparat nomine reque Pius.
 Vendit Alexander cruces, altaria, Christum :
  Emerat ille prius, vendere jure potest.

[2] *Life of Gonsalvo*, p. 261.

then writing; nor can they be accused of any undue partiality towards the Borgias. The appearance of the corpse was enough to start the rumour among the populace. Peter Martyr, who was in Spain, Giovio and Guicciardini, who were not contemporaries, are our chief authorities for the story of the poisoning. There are slight variants, but this is the usual version, as told by Guicciardini. The Pope intended to poison Cardinal Adriano, possibly with other cardinals there present, for their wealth. Cesare sent on the poisoned wine with orders that it should be given to no one. The Pope arrived early, very thirsty, and asked for a drink. The butler, not being in the secret, thought that the wine was something special, reserved for the Pope's private use, and gave him a cup of it. Cesare arrived soon after and also had some. Yet elsewhere[1] Guicciardini admits that the story is nothing but a rumour, though a widely spread rumour. Sanudo's version is that Adriano di Corneto discovered what was in the wind and bribed the Pope's servant, who was to give the drink, with 10,000 ducats to serve it to the Pope instead of to himself. The story was too admirable a case of poetic justice not to have found general credence, but it will hardly bear looking into.

Had the Pope and his son been poisoned, they would both have been taken violently ill at once. There would have been no delay before the crisis. Fever does not usually accompany poisoning. Arsenic is held to have been the chief ingredient in the *cantarella* by Portigliotti, as by most if not all other authorities. Now it is a well-known fact that arsenic acts as a preservative of the body after death. The state of the body is important evidence for the presence of arsenic in any quantity. The rapid decay of Alexander's corpse, which was popularly regarded as a proof of poisoning, is, on the contrary, a convincing

---

[1] *Stor. Ital.*, VI, 33.

proof that he had not been poisoned by arsenic, that is, by the *cantarella*.

Our information about the symptoms is not sufficient to give a definite clue. None of it is first hand and we are expressly told that the Vatican staff had orders to hush up the truth and that the doctors were not allowed to leave the palace. Signor Portigliotti says that vomiting is not a symptom of malaria, but I am told by a doctor friend who saw a good deal of it in the war that it can go with malaria. It may be unusual for three or four people to be taken ill with malaria after the same dinner, but the fever was remarkably prevalent that season and obviously there were a number of mosquitoes about. Altogether I can see no reason to believe that malaria was not the cause of Alexander's death.

Portigliotti finds additional support for the poison theory in the fact that Cesare never spoke of the matter. But, in the first place, Cesare was not in the habit of talking ; he left that to his father. In the second place, we do not know what he said to the one or two people whom he trusted and who would, on that very account, not be likely to talk.

Finally, is it necessary to assume that all the guests were taken ill of the same complaint ? What little we know of the Pope's illness is strongly in favour of its being malaria. Apparently, however, Adriano, Remolines and Cesare became violently ill at once. Without resuscitating the old deliberate poison theory, it may well be that they were attacked by some form of ptomaine poisoning, or some other similar trouble caused by bad food. Anyone who has gone into the question of cooking at that time and, indeed, much later, with the wealth of sauces used by cooks to disguise the taste of food that was often tainted, must have asked himself whether the sudden deaths that not infrequently followed a feast were not due to something of the kind. In a hot and unhealthy August in Rome nothing is more likely.

The extraordinary rumours that speedily got about concerning the Pope's last illness, even among people of intelligence, may be gathered from the following letter from the Marquis of Mantua to his consort, Isabella (September 22nd, 1503):

"While ill he began to talk in such a manner that those who did not understand his meaning thought that he was wandering, though he was quite conscious while he spoke, saying: 'I will come, it is right; only wait a little longer.'" And it wås discovered by those in the secret that, after the death of Innocent, while in the Conclave, he made a pact with the Devil, purchasing the Papacy with his soul. "Among other conditions it was bargained that he was to live to enjoy the throne of St Peter for twelve years, as he did with the addition of four days. Some say they saw seven devils in the room when he was at the point of death. When he was dead, the body began to boil and the mouth to foam, like a cauldron on the fire, and so it continued to do as long as it was above ground. It also swelled up in an extraordinary manner, ceasing to have human shape, nor was there any difference between the length and the breadth of the corpse." And he proceeds to describe the ignoble character of the burial. "The dwarf wife of a lame cripple has a more honourable one in Mantua, and for his last reputation the most insulting epitaphs in the world are found posted up about him."

CHAPTER XVII

CESARE AND JULIUS II (1503–1504)

VALENTINO, still very weak, remained in his rooms, which are now famous as Raphael's Stanze. He had thought out everything, he told Machiavelli a month later, that might happen when the Pope died and made his plans accordingly, except that he never expected to be himself at the point of death at the time. We have no means of knowing what his plans were, but it has been suggested that he intended to secularize the Papacy. I cannot help thinking that he would have had too much sense to attempt anything of the kind, for in the long run France and Spain, backed by public opinion in Italy and the Christian world, would have proved too strong for him. But he might have secured his position in the Romagna, though this again is doubtful. With the death of the Pope he would have been useless to the King of France, who was getting jealous of his growing power. He had not had time to consolidate his position sufficiently to be able to withstand a combined attack by his neighbours and the lordlings whom he had dispossessed. Their fear and hatred of him were strong enough to make them sink their differences for the moment and unite against him. There was something in his inscrutable strength, his ability and thoroughness, his amazing good luck which made him feared more than any other man of his day by his contemporaries in Italy.

Michelotto was with him. He was sent to demand the keys of the Pope's treasury from the Papal Chamberlain, Casanova. Drawing his dagger, he threatened to throw him out of the window if they were refused. In this way he secured 100,000 ducats on August 18th, before the news of the Pope's death became known, besides jewels and altar plate, worth in all, according to Sanudo, some 300,000 ducats.

Friends were almost more necessary than money. The surviving Orsini, led by Giangiordano, seized their old castles, while the Colonna were making an even more formidable display. Valentino decided to come to terms with the latter, on the advice and with the help, it is said, of Agapito, who was himself an adherent of the Colonna. The little Duke of Sermoneta was to marry a Colonna and they were to support him in the Romagna. From the Orsini, even in those cynical times, Cesare could expect no mercy. On August 20th they attempted to make trouble, whereupon Michelotto set fire to their palaces on Monte Giordano. Silvio Savelli was there releasing all the Borgias' prisoners while the mob was venting its hatred on the Spaniards whenever possible. As Captain-General of the Church Cesare controlled the Borgo with an army of 12,000 men, but the commander of S. Angelo, though a Spanish nominee of the Borgias, remained loyal to the Church. Meanwhile the French army, commanded by Francesco Gonzaga, was at Viterbo, while Gonsalvo de Cordova was advancing North with his Spaniards, ready to meet all contingencies. Altogether the period of the Conclave threatened to be unusually stormy.

Cesare saw that his one hope lay in the election of a friendly Pope. His Spanish cardinals might have been his chaplains, such was their loyalty. Hence he was formidable, but he showed the utmost deference to the College. The Colonna now returned, led by Don Prospero, and reoccupied their palace. The Capitol was illuminated and bonfires were lit in their honour. They also promised obedience to the cardinals, But when the Orsini appeared, putting some of the Borgia party to death and burning over a hundred houses of Spaniards, the cardinals decided that, if there was to be peace, all armed forces must withdraw from Rome, as the laws of the Conclave demanded. Valentino did his best to evade the order, pleading his health in excuse and asking to be allowed to retire to the Castel S. Angelo, but in vain. On September 2nd he left Rome with his usual magnificence for Nepi. His men and his guns were as smart and well-equipped as ever. The litter in which he was carried was covered with crimson cloth. Behind it came his horse, caparisoned in black and gold, with his arms and the ducal crown, ridden by a page sumptuously attired. He was escorted by the ambassadors of Spain and the Empire and with him went Vannozza and Gioffrè. He declined to give Cardinal Cesarini, who was waiting at the gate, an interview.

Sancia was released from S. Angelo, where she had remained in safe keeping, and Don Prospero Colonna was entrusted with the duty of escorting her to Naples. He was bitterly chagrined to find that Valentino had deceived him by signing a treaty with France the day before leaving Rome, for he had been given to understand that he was now Spanish in sympathy.

But, in spite of the treaty with France, Valentino's state was beginning to fall to pieces. Guidobaldo was back in Urbino. His subjects came out in whole townships, with shouts of " Feltro, Feltro," to meet him, eager, if only to touch his hand. The Venetians were especially active, restoring Malatesta in Rimini and Giovanni Sforza in Pesaro, while Camerino and Piombino also returned to their former lords. The nephews of Vitellozzo, now back in Città di Castello, carried a golden calf in procession round the town. Venice dared not go too far, for neither France nor Florence wished to see her power extend further into the Marches. Romagna, however, remained loyal, thanks not a little to the popularity of Antonio dal

CARDINAL FARNESE, AFTERWARDS POPE PAUL III, BY RAPHAEL

Monte, who established himself at Cesena, and the energy of Naldi. The inhabitants as a whole had no wish to exchange the Duca's rule for that of their former lords.

Now that the city was comparatively safe, it was decided to hold the Conclave as usual in the Vatican. Valentino was less powerful. His dozen or so Spanish cardinals could prevent an election, if they held together, but in his absence they looked to Carvajal as their leader. The Spanish and French parties were strong enough to checkmate each other, and the Italians were determined not to have a foreign Pope. Spaniards still went in terror of their lives. Meanwhile Giuliano della Rovere had arrived. He told Giustinian that he was there to do his own business. He would not give his vote to Rohan, unless the Frenchman was strong enough to carry the election without him. He was a good Italian, and meant to choose a Pope who would be good for the Christian faith and the peace of Italy. Ascanio Sforza, too, had been released by Louis on condition that he voted for Rohan, but, though he kept his promise, he worked steadily for himself. When it became clear that none of the big men were quite strong enough—Ascanio was still Vincula's enemy—Rohan proposed the aged and infirm Piccolomini, who could not live long. He was elected, thanks largely to the Spanish cardinals.

Pius thus owed his election indirectly to Valentino, and he proved himself grateful. He supported him against Rovere and the others who wished to bring back the old tyrants to Romagna, telling Giustinian that it was God's will that they should be punished by a " tristo istrumento ". Pius admitted that he could not help pitying Valentino, though it was the last thing he had ever expected to do, now that he was being plotted against on all sides. He granted the request that he might be allowed to return to Rome, on the plea, urged by the Spanish cardinals, that he was not safe at Nepi and his health was bad. D'Alviano had approached Giustinian with a view to obtaining the permission of his employers, the Venetian Government, to attack him. Cesare had only some 650 men with him on his return, when he was welcomed back by Ascanio, Rohan, Sanseverino and d'Albret. A number of his troops had been sent to join the French. He returned to his palace of S. Clemente in the Borgo. Giustinian found him better than he had expected, though his face was still without skin and in a bad state. He was as sanguine as ever, talking haughtily, possibly bluffing, and saying that he would soon recover all that he had lost. A Papal bull confirmed him in his states and reappointed him Gonfalonier, as Pius had promised. His prospects in the Romagna were certainly brighter. Dionigi Naldi recovered Rimini and Cesena utterly defeated a force sent against it from Urbino. The Orsini sought a reconciliation.

But the respite was brief. The Pope was rapidly failing and his enemies were gaining power. His Spaniards were leaving him, including the best of them, Ugo de Moncada, who was later to win fame under Charles V. Trumpeters went about Rome summoning all good Spaniards to join Gonsalvo de Cordova, even in front of Valentino's Palazzo S. Clemente. Bartolomeo d'Alviano, raging like a mad dog, was watching every gate of the city. He and Giampolo Baglioni told Giustinian that they meant to have Cesare and hound him to death. They proposed to attack him in his palace. Realizing the danger he endeavoured to escape by the Porta Viridaria, but the Orsini were on the watch and were amply strong enough to head off his small force, two companies of which had deserted the moment he started. He took refuge in the Vatican, his troops being encamped on S. Peter's Square. This was on October 15th, just ten days after his return to Rome. On the urgent advice of his friends, for his enemies were threatening to besiege him in the Vatican, he made his way along the covered passage to S. Angelo with his two illegitimate children—Burchard says daughters—Lucrezia's son, Roderigo, and the *infans Romanus*. The Orsini talked of taking legal proceedings against him. His palace was sacked, but not before he had despatched his valuables to Cardinal d'Este at Ferrara. D'Alviano secured a couple of noble chargers. Valentino now sent for Michelotto as well as for the contingent which had joined the French under Taddeo della Volpe, a good soldier, who was always loyal to his master. When crossing the Ponte S. Angelo, della Volpe was attacked by a strong force of the Orsini, but he used his sword so effectively that he cut his way through to safety.

On October 18th Pius died. On the 27th Machiavelli came to Rome as special envoy. From the first the election of Giuliano della Rovere was a foregone conclusion. On October 28th Machiavelli gives the odds in his favour as thirty-two per cent. Then on October 29th Valentino left S. Angelo with his bevy of cardinals and met Vincula, now a man of sixty, in the Vatican. He solemnly undertook to confirm him in his post as Gonfalonier of the Church as well as in his possessions in Romagna. Valentino would have preferred Rohan, but there was now less chance than ever for a foreigner. On the 30th Machiavelli gave the odds as sixty per cent, much to his astonishment, as he could not believe that Valentino would be so foolish as to support the bitterest enemy of his house. Giustinian placed them as high as eighty-two per cent, no one else having more than six per cent. The simony was as shameless and open as in the days of Alexander VI, but no other method was then possible. It was not a question of hundreds, but of thousands, " to the great disgrace of our religion and an offence against the Lord God ", says Giustinian. "For now there is no difference between the Papacy and the Sultanate. It goes to the highest bidder." Vincula expressed his own feelings to the ambassador on the eve of the election. "You see the wretched state to which the carrion left by Pope Alexander has reduced us, due to the number of the cardinals. Necessity forces men to do what they hate doing when they depend upon others, but, once free, they act differently." "The Spanish cardinals do not mean to be poor when they leave the Conclave," says Costabili. Valentino saw that his only chance was to back the winner and when Rohan and Ascanio went over to him his election was assured. The Conclave began on October 31st. The window had not been closed to the outside world when Vincula was elected and proclaimed as Julius II on November 1st. It was the shortest Conclave ever known.

Julius began by treating Valentino well. He lodged him in the Belvedere with some forty of his immediate following and every evening he admitted him to his presence, when they chatted amicably together. There was a suggestion of Cesare's daughter, Louise, marrying the Prefettino of Sinigaglia, the Pope's own nephew. Machiavelli was astonished to see how his sanguine self-confidence carried Valentino away and to find him believing "that other people's words will be better kept than his own or that these marriage projects will hold." Valentino was probably trying to bluff, possibly also to deceive himself, by talking far more confidently than he felt. Giustinian saw that under it all he was full of fear and anxiety. From the first Julius had no intention of keeping his promises, which might well be considered as having been wrung from him by force, and Valentino was the last who could complain. On November 10th he told Giustinian that he did not mean to leave him a battlement in Romagna. "Though we have promised him something, we do not mean our promise to go beyond

the preservation of his life, his money and what he has
robbed, most of which has been dissipated. We intend
that his states shall return to the Church and we wish
to have the honour of recovering what our predecessors have wrongfully alienated."

Giustinian saw that the Pope was not to be trifled
with, but his warnings had no effect in Venice, which
persisted in her policy of conquest in Romagna, a
policy which was to end in her undoing by the League
of Cambrai, led by the Pope. It was Machiavelli
who told Julius of the rebellion of Imola and the
advance of the Venetians upon Faenza. The task was
not unpleasant, as Florence was anxious to sow dis-
cord between Venice and the Pope. He remarked
to some cardinals that His Holiness would soon be
nothing more than the chaplain of the Venetians. He
then broke the news to Valentino, who flew into a
passion, saying that, when Florence might have
saved his state for him, she had refused to do so. He
would hand over all that was left to Venice. Machiavelli might have replied effectively, but he thought it
wiser to try to calm him in order to escape from such
dangerous company as quickly as possible.

Valentino's position was, indeed, desperate, since it
depended upon the will of the sworn foe of his house,
and no one knew this better than himself. Hitherto
luck had always been on his side and, like many men
so favoured, he proved incapable of rising to the
occasion when it failed him. It is, indeed, difficult
to see what he could have done, for the initiative had
passed out of his hands. Moreover, his health was
bad and was not improved by the anxiety of his situation. The little court which was wont to look up to
his decisive, unquestioned leadership could not understand the change. His cardinal cousin, the Bishop of
Elna, said that " he seemed to have lost his senses,
because he did not know his own mind and was
confused and irresolute." Soderini found him

" changeable, irresolute and suspicious, unable to make up his mind ". Those who had often been snubbed by him doubtless enjoyed turning the tables. Giustinian who, as doyen of the diplomatic corps, had carried on the negotiations with him after Alexander's death on behalf of the College of Cardinals, now frequently refused to see him, from a desire not to increase his importance.

Julius was anxious above all things to check the progress of Venice in Romagna and prevent the return of the old lords, and in order to do so he was quite ready to avail himself of Valentino's popularity. With this object in view he sent special commissioners North, urging the Duke's subjects to remain loyal to him. This would give him great satisfaction, " for we love the Duke on account of his distinguished virtues and outstanding merits." Valentino had decided to take such men as he still had through Tuscany to his Duchy, or what still remained of it, and he therefore applied to Florence for a safe-conduct. Julius expressed his satisfaction when it was refused almost unanimously. Machiavelli wrote that it was clear that " he means to get rid of him without appearing to break his word. Hence he does not care a fig what others do to harm him."

Valentino, who was still in Rome, came round one day to see Machiavelli, very much out of temper. He treated him as an old acquaintance. He said that he had already sent off his men to Tuscany, and was going to start for Ostia. He could not wait. If the safe-conduct were refused, he would come to terms with Venice, or, if need be, with the Devil himself. He would use all his means—he was said to have 200,000 ducats at Genoa—and all his friends, once he was at Pisa, to do Florence all the harm he could. Machiavelli tried to calm him, promising to write to Florence. But he bade the Ten pay no heed to his letter and take the first opportunity of disarming his men. Shortly afterwards he left for Ostia, to the undisguised relief of the Papal court, though Giustinian regretted that the Pope had shown him such favour. Machiavelli even heard men laugh at Valentino. His secretary, Agapito, did not accompany him.

The Pope was much concerned when the Venetians seized Faenza and then Rimini. Machiavelli saw that this would either open the door of Italy to them or prove their ruin. Julius felt that it was time to throw off the mask and show himself in his true colours. Valentino had been given permission to hire five galleons to convey himself and his staff to Leghorn or Genoa, proceeding thence to Ferrara, while Don Michele took his men through Tuscany. The Pope immediately sent Cardinals Remolines and Soderini to Ostia, ordering him to give up the passwords that would place the fortresses in his hands. He refused. This was on the 22nd November, and three days later the Rocca of Faenza fell into the hands of Venice. Julius was so perturbed at the news that he could not sleep. " Since he is a prisoner," wrote Machiavelli of Valentino, " whether dead or alive (there was a rumour that he had been flung into the Tiber) you can act without giving him a further thought." On the 29th Valentino was brought back to Rome a prisoner, and on the same day, at the Pope's request, Michelotto, Taddeo della Volpe and the Duca's other officers were arrested in Tuscany. The men, like those with Cesare, were disarmed. The capture of Don Michele was a welcome piece of news for the Pope, who wanted him " in order to find out all the cruelties, robberies, murders, sacrileges and other crimes that have been committed against God and man for the last ten years in Rome ". He added, with his characteristic smile, that he should like to have a chat with him in the hope of learning a trick or two that might help him in ruling the Church.

Don Michele was tortured, but no information of

value was obtained from him. In spite of his black record, he suffered nothing worse than imprisonment. He owed the next step in his career to the admiration he had inspired in Machiavelli by his work in training the Romagnol militia. The most valuable lesson the Florentine Secretary learnt from Valentino was that, if Italy was to be free, she must depend on her own citizens for her soldiers. The organizing of a citizen army for Florence became the passion of his life. When he got his way Don Michele, on being released from his prison in the Tor di Nona in 1506, was, at his suggestion, made Captain of the Guard at Florence. But the Tuscans were not the Romagnols, nor was the Florentine state governed on the same lines as Valentino's Duchy. Though the mere presence of Don Michele was sufficient to strike terror into the most formidable breakers of the peace, the appointment does not appear to have been a great success.

Valentino was a prisoner in the apartments of Rohan, a cardinal whom Julius, with his French sympathies, always treated with the greatest respect. He had succeeded him as Legate to France, and also as Bishop of Avignon. The rooms were above those of the Pope himself. On December 2nd Cesare consented to reveal the passwords, but he wished for a guarantee that the castles would be restored, as the Pope had promised, and asked Rohan to countersign the promise. Rohan, who was anything but pleased to have such a guest on his hands, declined. Meanwhile, Julius had appointed his own governor in Romagna, and all loyal citizens had been ordered to hoist and obey the Papal flag. Imola defended itself desperately against the Duca's enemies, and when Antonio dal Monte read the Pope's proclamation to the assembled Cesenati, they had replied with loud shouts that they would be governed by the Duca. Since then, on the urgent recommendation of dal Monte, the town had returned to its allegiance to the Church, but Pedro

Ramires held the Rocca and refused to give it up so long as the Duca was a prisoner. Pedro de Oviedo was sent with the passwords. Forlì, dreading the return of the Riario, which the Cardinal of S. Giorgio, Raffaele Riario, was urgently pressing, had refused to admit him. When he made his way thence to Cesena through the deep winter snow Ramires told him that he regarded any Spaniard who brought such a message as a traitor and hung him from the battlements without allowing him time to confess.

The news threw Julius into one of his towering passions which were afterwards so much dreaded. His threats against Valentino, whom he considered, possibly rightly, to have given secret orders beforehand which had prevented the surrender, were so awful that they threw the whole Borgia clan into a panic. Remolines de Ilerda and Luis Borgia, Archbishop of Valencia, fled to Naples with the children. They were to ask Gonsalvo de Cordova for a safe-conduct for Cesare. Julius was for sending him to the Castel S. Angelo, but the Spanish cardinals persuaded him to confine him in the Borgia tower instead. Here he occupied the two rooms where Bisceglie had been strangled. Cattaneo wrote that he saw him shed tears while he was being taken to them. All his property was confiscated and the men whom he had plundered were encouraged to send in heavy bills for damages. Guidobaldo d'Urbino asked for 200,000 ducats, and Raffaele Riario for 50,000 for his nephews.

Guidobaldo was now in Rome, where the Pope showed him every kindness. He wished to recover his noble library, which he valued above all his possessions, and the other property carried off by Valentino. So when Valentino asked for an interview it was granted. Ugolini gives what purports to be an account by an eye-witness.[1] Valentino entered the presence of his successor in the command of the

[1] *Storia Duchi d'Urbino*, II, 523.

Papal forces hat in hand and made two bows, touching his knee to the ground. Owing to his gout, his former victim was reclining on a sofa at the end of the room. He rose, took off his hat, raised up his enemy and placed him beside him. Valentino humbly implored forgiveness for the past, " blaming his youth, the wicked counsels he had been given, the evil deeds and the thoroughly bad character of the Pope and others who had urged him to the enterprise, expatiating at length upon the Pope and cursing his soul ". It is not a pleasant picture, but it is quite in keeping with Valentino, who was as ready to fawn as to bully when it served his purpose. He promised to restore everything, except some tapestries of Troy, which he had given to Rohan, and some other things he no longer possessed. Guidobaldo's answer was as curt as it was courteous. Its tone left Valentino " pauroso assai e ben chiarito ", but he at once sent men to fetch the stolen goods.

Meanwhile he was visited by his old friends, among the most constant being Cardinal Giovanni Vera, his former tutor. His intimates continued as loyal as ever. Indeed, he is said to have remarked that he found no friends so loyal as those whom he had rewarded for their virtues. Taddeo della Volpe, a prisoner in Florence, refused absolutely to take service under the Republic, while the Duca's treasurer, Alessandro Francio, faithfully kept the 300,000 ducats he had deposited in Florence and Genoa. He was still weak and laughed at those who pretended to be afraid of him, seeing that his life was hardly worth an hour's purchase. He spent most of his time lying in bed, silently watching his suite play chess, the game being just enough to distract his thoughts. One remembers Alexander watching the cardinals play cards on his death-bed. Like many men of great physical strength, Cesare was indolent when not actually called upon to exert it. It was said that he knew but two positions, lying on his bed and bestriding a horse.

The victory of El Gran Capitán at the Garigliano on December 28th, where Piero dei Medici was drowned, proved as lucky for Valentino as the defeat of the Spaniards by the French might have done. His Spanish friends could now speak with assured authority, and the Spanish ambassador intervened on his behalf. The Pope realized his own helplessness in the Romagna, where he had no army to check the Venetians or recover the castles, and when Valentino offered to guarantee their surrender within forty days, on condition that he should be liberated, he consented. Meanwhile Valentino had been allowed to go to Ostia, after taking an affectionate leave of the Pope on February 14th, 1504, where he was placed in charge of Cardinal Carvajal. The castellans refused to surrender so long as the Duca was a prisoner. On March 10th it was agreed that, if Cesare arranged for the delivery of the fortresses and provided the 15,000 ducats demanded by the commander at Forlì, he should go free. On the 26th, when Cesena and Bertinoro had been given up and the commander at Forlì asked for hostages, Carvajal, not trusting the Pope, whom he suspected, not unreasonably, of having designs upon Valentino, let him go free. But he made him sign a document, sworn and sealed, by which he undertook never to serve against the Pope or any of his family.

Valentino rode out of Ostia on April 19th. A Spanish ship was waiting for him a few miles along the coast, and he reached Naples on the 28th. Cardinal Pedro Luis Borgia, who was Bishop of Sorrento, received him in his palace, where were also Cardinal Francisco Loris and the Prince of Squillace. Donna Sancia, now the mistress of Don Prospero Colonna, who was serving under Gonsalvo de Cordova, was living in her own palace, in which her husband was not allowed to set foot. After the imprisonment in

Castel S. Angelo her attitude is not altogether surprising. Here Cesare dined with her and did his best to bring about a reconciliation, but he had no more success than others who had tried, among them being Gonsalvo de Cordova himself and the Queen of Hungary. Only a man in Valentino's desperate condition could have failed to read the meaning of Gonsalvo's refusal to supply him with the forces for which he asked, or even to allow him to enter into possession of the estates he had been granted in the Kingdom. Gonsalvo knew better than to trust him. Queen Isabella was even more suspicious, for, like the widow of the Duke of Gandia, she was convinced that he had murdered his brother. However, he set about collecting a small force with which he meant to take ship to Pisa, where he would be welcome, and make his way thence to Romagna. He often visited Gonsalvo, talking openly of his plans, and Gonsalvo appears to have helped him with his preparations, or at least to have done nothing to hinder them. But Pandolfini, the Florentine ambassador, guessed that he was merely playing with him till he received instructionsfrom Spain.

On May 26th Valentino went to bid farewell to Gonsalvo, now Duca di Terranova, in the Castel Nuovo, where he was staying. "Late at night he passed from his room to take his leave of the Gran Capitán, before retiring to rest, seeing that he had to rise betimes in the morning. The Duke said to Pedro Novarro, his gentleman, 'Señor Conde, you have leave to withdraw, seeing that it is your hour.' Whereupon he made answer: 'Do you, my lord, go to rest, but I am here to bear you company this night and I may not sleep.' When the Duke heard this he uttered a great cry, saying: 'Santa Maria! I am betrayed! With me only has my lord Gonsalvo dealt cruelly; to all others but me he has shown mercy.' Thereon came Nuño de Ocampa, who was

Castellan of the fortress, and posted a guard."[1] One imagines that Valentino's language on this " betrayal " was much less courtly in tone than the Spanish chronicler has represented it.

Ferdinand was anxious to be on good terms with the Pope, as he had let Gonsalvo know, when he bade him make sure that Julius would raise no objection to his receiving the two fugitive Borgia cardinals. The evidence given by Woodward from Spanish sources proves that Gonsalvo acted as he did towards Valentino deliberately and only after consulting the Spanish ambassador in Rome. He told the ambassador that he meant to keep him till the Rocca of Forlì had been surrendered and was ready to send him to Spain, if necessary. Cesare was continually urging him to permit him to leave for Pisa and Piombino and asking for troops, but Gonsalvo replied by demanding guarantees that he would not act against the Pope. Valentino characteristically attached not the slightest importance to his promise to Carvajal not to attack Julius. Instructions did not arrive from Spain till a fortnight after the arrest. The following letter shows that there was not any doubt as to the views of Ferdinand :

" The journey of the Duke we regard with deep displeasure, and not for political reasons alone. For, as you know, we hold the man in abhorrence for the gravity of his crimes, and we have no kind of desire that a man of such repute should be considered as in our service, even though he came to us laden with fortresses, with men and with money. . . . We have written to the Duke of Terranova (Gonsalvo) that he send the Duke to us, providing two galleys for the voyage, so that he cannot escape elsewhere ; or

[1] Woodward, C. Borgia, p. 364, from the Cronica del Gran Capitán. In what follows I have followed Woodward, who has gone into the question very thoroughly and consulted the Spanish sources.

Gonsalvo may send him to the King of the Romans ; or to France, to join his wife. . . . You will explain to His Holiness how bitterly we feel the affront to him involved in the reception of the Duke Valentinois at Naples, and assure him that he shall not be harboured there, nor shall he be allowed to pass into other provinces where he may prove obnoxious to the peace of His Holiness."

The story that Gonsalvo had given Valentino a safe-conduct has passed into history as the most serious blot upon his honour, though we should have thought that the part he played in the downfall of Federigo of Naples was an infinitely blacker betrayal. Woodward doubts whether he granted it and the tone of his letters certainly makes it seem improbable. But Pandolfini, the Florentine ambassador, says he had it in his hands. In any case, the instructions of his sovereign would override his safe-conduct. The story goes that Valentino had given it to his captain, Baldassare di Scipione, whom Gonsalvo persuaded to return it. According to Alvisi, when his master was not released, this loyal captain issued a general challenge to anyone belonging to the Spanish nation who should venture to deny that the Duca Valentino had been detained in Naples in spite of a safe-conduct of King Ferdinand and Queen Isabella, to the lasting infamy and bad faith of their crowns. Nor was the challenge ever taken up. The story squares admirably with the high chivalry that distinguished the wars between France and Spain at that time. Cesare's own words are the best justification of Gonsalvo's conduct : " It is good to deceive those who have proved themselves past masters in treachery."

Valentino was confined in a cell known as *Il Forno*, the oven, a good room with double rows of bars, which had been tenanted by other men of distinction who needed careful guarding.

With him were his butler and another servant, but

he was deprived of the company of a lady friend who had hitherto shared his fate. Squillace continued to see much of Gonsalvo and to ride with him. Gonsalvo di Mirafonte loyally refused to give up the Rocca of Forlì, which he knew he could hold indefinitely, till his master was set at liberty. The Pope, meanwhile, had written to Ferdinand, complaining of the way in which Gonsalvo and Carvajal had allowed Valentino to escape and plot against him. Continual pressure was brought to bear upon the prisoner to induce him to surrender Forlì. On the one hand Gonsalvo threatened to deprive Mirafonte of his property in Spain, on the other he is said to have promised to set Valentino free. Not till August did Cesare consent to send the necessary orders, admitting the uselessness of holding out now that luck had definitely turned against him. On the 10th, when hostages had been given and the 15,000 ducats deposited at Venice, Mirafonte rode out of the Rocca, lance in rest, with the redoubtable Fracassa on his right and Luffo Numai on his left. They had been his faithful lieutenants through the long months. He was followed by 200 cross-bowmen in full armour, with the Duke's banner flying, amid cries of " Duca, Duca! " The Papal governor was present, as also a gentleman of Lucrezia's suite, whom she had sent to honour Mirafonte. Thus ended the Duca's rule. It had lasted barely four years, but the peasants thought longingly of it in the evil days that were to come, and his name is still alive in Romagnol tradition. The restored lords wreaked brutal vengeance, notably Gian Maria Varano in Camerino and Cesare's ex-brother-in-law, Giovanni Sforza, in Pesaro. Sforza not only hung a number of prominent citizens, but he enticed the jurist Collenuccio back with fair promises and then strangled him.

CHAPTER XVIII

TEN days later, on August 20th, Valentino, who had been transferred to the castle of Ischia, was placed on board a galley, accompanied by a single page. His enemy Prospero Colonna was in charge of him, and there were several other galleys in the little fleet.

The news caused general relief in Italy, where there was small hope of peace while he was at large, to no one more than to the Pope. But it was generally believed that he had been promised his liberty, if he would give up Forlì, and Louis XII is said to have exclaimed that the word of the King of Spain was as worthless as that of a Carthaginian.

There is something fateful about this return of his to his native Spain. He landed at Grao, whence Alonso de Borja had sailed to found the fortunes of the family by becoming Pope Calixtus III just seventy-five years earlier. He was not yet twenty-eight.

In this way did the former Cardinal-Archbishop visit Valencia. He was taken at once to the castle of Chinchilla, which stands on a high hill, about two miles from the town. In October Giustinian reports that he was to be tried for the murder of the Dukes of Gandia and Bisceglie and to be executed. The Duchess of Gandia was taking the lead in the matter. Nothing more was heard of the plan. He managed to keep in touch with the outside world. A document was drawn up over his signature, written on a separate piece of paper, which was pasted on, in May, 1505,

264

at Pau, which shows that he was endeavouring, with
the help of his brother-in-law, the King of Navarre,
to obtain possession of the dowry promised his wife,
Charlotte d'Albret, by Louis, which was never paid.[1]
From now to Cesare's death I have usually followed
Yriate, who has made exhaustive researches in Spain
on this period of his life.

He was also endeavouring to escape. His room was
at the top of the highest tower. One day he asked to
be allowed to speak with the Governor of the castle,
Don Gabriel Guzman, on urgent business. In the
course of their talk Valentino began pointing to the
village and asking him about the various buildings,
which were just visible. Guzman went to the window
to see. As soon as his back was turned, his prisoner
sprang upon him, but in Guzman he had met his match.
After a fierce struggle, his gaoler got him down.
Valentino tried to turn the matter off, by asking him
to take it in good part and telling him that he had
wished to test his strength and that rumour had not
lied about it. Guzman, however, reported the
occurrence and his place of confinement was changed
to the strong castle of Medina del Campo, to the
north-west of Madrid. This was also in Castile and
a favourite place of residence of Ferdinand and
Isabella. It was too far from the sea for there to be
much chance of escape.

Valentino's friends had all along been working for
his liberation. Hardly had he left Italy when the
Spanish cardinals interceded with the Pope on his
behalf. Julius at first thought of appealing to
Ferdinand, but decided not to do so, in case the King
of Spain might be inclined to restore some of his state
to him, which was the last thing he desired. "About
this time the King received many requests from various
quarters that he would set the Duc Valentinois free,"
says the chronicler Zurita. There was the King of

[1] C. Yriarte, *C. Borgia*, Vol. II, p. 216.

Navarre, urged by his sister, Cesare's Duchess, and above all Lucrezia, who left no stone unturned. She wrote continually to the Pope and to the Marquis of Mantua on the subject. One of her letters to Gonzaga is given by Gregorovius. The stilted style compares very unfavourably with that of the d'Este or Gonzaga ladies, whose letters are so modern in their natural ease.

" Most Illustrious and Excellent Lord Brother-in-law and Our Most honoured Brother, Having always known that Your Excellency, through all his fortunes, has borne a singular affection to the Most Illustrious Lord Duke Our Brother and is favourably disposed to all things that may rebound to his honour and advantage, as if he were your own carnal brother : in all confidence I appeal for your support in procuring his liberty. With this end in view I am at present doing my utmost in Rome to send to His Most Catholic Majesty the Rev. Card. Regino with the permission and favour of His Holiness." The cardinal readily consented. Knowing the affection the Pope bore her brother-in-law, she begged him to use all his influence to get the cardinal sent and also to write to the King of Spain on her brother's behalf. Gonzaga gladly promised to carry out both her requests. When she found that he meant to despatch a messenger to Spain, she asked him to send letters from herself both to Ferdinand and to Cesare. Lucrezia also requested Gonzaga to induce the Duke of Urbino to use his influence.

It is worth recording that as early as February, 1504, the Borgias had made their first appearance upon the stage at Urbino. " On February 19th, in the evening, in the hall of the Lord Duke, was played the comedy of Duca Valentino and Pope Alexander VI ; when they thought of seizing the state of Urbino ; when they sent Madonna Lucrezia to Ferrara ; when they invited the Duchess to the wedding ; when they came to seize the state; when the Duke of Urbino returned for the first time and then left; when they killed Vitellozzo and the other lords; and when Pope Alexander died and the Duke of Urbino returned to his state."[1] Such staging of contemporary history cannot have been very common at that time, but it is easy to imagine the pleasure with which the restored Duke and his loyal courtiers watched the performance. The play shows how rapidly the Borgias were finding a place in legend.

Once again there were signs that the trend of political events might play into Valentino's hands and restore the Borgia luck. The death of Isabella raised the question of the regency in Castille. She had left this to Ferdinand, on condition that he did not remarry. But when he took to wife the eighteen-year-old Germaine de Foix, thus cementing a peace with France, Philip of Austria, son of the Emperor Maximilian, claimed the regency by right. He was the husband of Isabella's daughter, Juana, who was mad and therefore incapable of reigning herself. A majority in the Cortès decided in favour of Ferdinand, but a powerful minority, headed by the Conde de Benavente, supported the cause of Philip and Juana. Philip came to reside at Medina del Campo, where Valentino was imprisoned.

No better proof could be forthcoming of the high estimation in which the Borgia was held by his contemporaries than the intrigues that followed. Ferdinand had reason to doubt the loyalty of El Gran Capitàn at Naples, whither he was on the point of starting with his young bride. He proposed, in spite of all that had passed and of what he had written to Gonsalvo, to take Valentino with him to command his troops, should there be war. Possibly he felt that he could trust him to fight against the man who had made him a prisoner better than he could any of his

[1] Ugolini, *Storia*, etc., II, 128.

own subjects who had served under Gonsalvo. But when we remember that Gonsalvo was held to be the greatest captain of his age and that he had defeated the French and driven them from Naples, we realize the opinion he had of his prisoner's abilities. He told Philip of his plan, asking him to keep Valentino till he was ready for him. Unluckily for Valentino, Philip also thought of availing himself of his help against Ferdinand himself, should war break out between him and his own father, the Emperor Maximilian. When two of the greatest rulers of the day were thus contending for his services, there is nothing astonishing that Machiavelli, with his uncompromising realism, should have made Valentino the hero of his *Prince*. The more we consider him and the more closely we follow his career, the more are we compelled to admit that he was the only ruler of the time in Italy—and at bottom he was more of a Spaniard than an Italian—who showed sufficient character and ability to deserve such a compliment. The day of Julius, one of the strongest and most forceful of all the Popes, was only about to dawn. Matarazzo, indeed, points out that it was rather by intrigue and money than by skill in arms that Valentino had won his successes, and it is true that he had never been tested in the open field. But his organizing ability, his political insight and the terror inspired by the ruthlessness and the effectiveness of his methods had raised him far above the level of the ordinary condottiere, though it is, of course, impossible to say whether he had any real gifts of generalship on a large scale.

Philip replied that any decision with regard to the prisoner's release must be taken by the Cortès; indeed, it involved the whole question of the regency. The upshot was that Ferdinand was informed that Valentino must stay where he was till the issue of the action brought against him by the Duchess of Gandia was decided. Ferdinand made more than one effort to get possession of Valentino, but in vain. He had already started for Naples, when the sudden death of Philip, in the prime of his manhood, at the age of twenty-eight—so sudden that it was widely attributed to poison—still further complicated the position.

But on October 25th, 1506, Valentino cut the knot of the intrigues of which he had become the centre by making a sensational escape from the lofty tower where he had been confined. " Señor, por aqui se salvò Cesar Borgia por gran milagro ", said the " vieux bon homme ", postmaster at Medina del Campo, when he pointed out the window to Brantôme, and a miracle it certainly was that he escaped with his life. Yriarte, who has examined the evidence taken at the enquiry afterwards held by order of Juana, gives full details of the escape and flight, which are still remembered on the spot. It was apparently through his chaplain and confessor that Valentino was able to communicate with the outside world. The escape was organised by the Conde de Benavente, leader of the opposition in the Cortès, who was only too pleased to do Ferdinand a bad turn. If all else failed, being of a violent disposition, he proposed to murder the alcalde and carry Valentino off by force. Ropes were smuggled into the tower by a servant of the gaoler who had charge of Valentino. On the evening of the day appointed the chaplain, a major-domo and a certain Don Jaime waited in the moat below. The tower is crenellated and he occupied the rooms at the very top. A note on a trumpet gave the signal. The cord, fastened to a battlement, was lowered. First came a servant, but the rope was too short and the man was obliged to let himself drop, with the result that he was badly injured. Then came Valentino. By this time the alarm had been given by the son of the alcalde, and just when he was about to let himself drop, the rope was cut from above and he fell into the moat below. Badly injured as he was, he was picked up by his friends and placed on horseback. They supported him as well as they could and galloped as fast as possible till they reached Villalon, in the territory of the Count of Benavente. The back of a horse was his natural position, and with his strength and vitality he managed to keep his seat. The unlucky servant was executed on the spot.

It was a month before Valentino was fit to travel; even then his hands were still in bandages. The most stringent orders had been issued for his arrest, and a reward of 10,000 gold ducats placed upon his head. He and his two guides gave themselves out to be grain merchants from Medina del Campo, where they had sold a cargo of wheat. Hence the money of which they could dispose so freely. Valentino proposed to escape to Navarre and take refuge with his brother-in-law, but instead of taking the direct route, in order to throw the authorities off the scent, he made for Santander on the Atlantic, thus riding due north. Such was the pace they travelled that two of their horses foundered before reaching Santander. Cesare, who had ridden a chestnut with a white patch on its head, and one of his guides entered Santander on foot on November 29th. Cesare sent the guides to the inn to order supper, while he himself went to hire a boat. But the high price he offered awakened suspicion. They were just sitting down to their meal of three chickens and a large piece of meat, when the alguazil and a clerk appeared to make inquiries. The travellers were examined separately. They declared that they were going to Bernico to meet a ship with a cargo of grain. They were ready to give references, to deposit fifty crowns as a guarantee, even to leave one of their number as a hostage. The magistrate was completely reassured and bade them depart in peace. At the official inquiry the innkeeper said that one of the three sat silent, wrapped in his hooded cape. He was squarely built, of middle height, with widely open nostrils and large eyes. His hands were bandaged. Another witness said that he was not of the same race as the others. Another described him as strongly built, his face disfigured, with a large nose and a swarthy complexion. These descriptions of Cesare by unsophisticated, unprejudiced peasants are distinctly interesting.

The captain appeared again and a fresh bargain was made. Seeing the haste and the wealth of his customers, he asked for 50 ducats, but ended by taking 25. They had to wait for the sun before starting, and then the weather was so bad that the boat could not take them beyond Castro-Urdiales. It was two days before they could get a couple of mules from the neighbouring monastery of Santa Clara, during which time Cesare remained in the inn. The witness from Castro-Urdiales also noted that he seemed anxious to keep his face hidden. In spite of the prayers of the man in charge, who offered to forgo his pay, the three men pressed on as hard as they could, showing no mercy to the mules, and insisted on going straight to Durango. Here at the inn they found two more mules and a horse, with which they entered Navarre on December 3rd. Thus did Valentino visit his bishopric of Pampeluna, the capital of the kingdom, for the first time. At one period, we should mention, there had been talk of the party headed by Benavente sending him to Flanders as their deputy to the Emperor Maximilian.

He at once wrote off to Gonzaga of Mantua :

" Most Illustrious Prince and Most Excellent Lord *Compare*, whom I regard almost as a brother, I have the honour to inform Your Excellency that, after many trials, it has pleased the Lord to deliver me and rescue me from prison in the manner which will be described to you by my secretary, Federigo, the bearer of this. May it please His infinite mercy that it will prove to His greater service. At present I am at Pampeluna with the Most Serene King and Queen of Navarre, having arrived on the 3rd December. Of this and of all else Y. E. will be fully informed by the said Federigo. I beg that it may please you to give full credence to all that he may say in my name, as if it came from myself." The letter is dated Pampeluna, December 7th, 1506.[1] Doubtless Federigo also carried letters for Lucrezia and other friends. There is extant a letter to Cardinal Ippolito d'Este, who had charge of the property which Cesare had sent from Rome, some of which had, however, been stopped on the way by Bentivoglio at Bologna. He denied all knowledge of it when Julius II demanded it, but it was afterwards restored to the d'Este. The Florentines kept what fell into their hands by way of indemnity, refusing to hand it over to the Pope. The seal bears the Borgia arms and the lilies of France, while seven dragons with open mouths and pendent tongues issue from the helmet. The other escutcheon bears the arms of Cesare's wife and the lilies of France, with a winged horse springing from the crest. The legend is "Cæsar Borgia De Francia Dux Romandiolæ".

Valentino's escape naturally created considerable excitement in Italy, where his powers of making mischief were, if anything, overrated. Julius II was particularly concerned. Indeed, the news was probably welcome only to Lucrezia and to his loyal subjects in Romagna. After leaving Ferrara, where he received a warm welcome from the Duchess, Federigo proceeded to Bologna. Here he was seized by the Pope's orders. Lucrezia tried to induce the Marquis of Mantua to intercede for him, but it was useless.

As he was penniless Valentino sent his major-

---

[1] Gregorovius, *Luc. Borgia*, Doc. No. 56.

domo, Requesenz, who had joined him in Navarre, to Louis XII, asking to be allowed to assume his rank and serve him as Duc de Valence and, incidentally, to receive his revenues from his duchy, as a French subject. But he soon learnt that Louis had annulled all his honours and confiscated all his revenues now that he could be of no further use to him, justifying these severe measures on the ground that Valentino had served his enemies and not himself in the Neapolitan campaign.

So he was compelled to find scope for his energies in the narrower sphere of the kingdom of his brother-in-law, King John of Navarre, which seemed likely to be involved in the long rivalry between France and Spain. The King was glad to make him Captain-General of his forces and to use his military gifts in subduing his unruly subject, Luis de Beaumonte, Conde de Lerins, who was actively supported by Ferdinand the Catholic. " Never was there seen such strength in so tiny a body," said men of Beaumonte. The struggle centred round the town of Viana, the inhabitants of which sided with the King, whereas the castle, garrisoned largely by Castilian troops, held out for the rebel. Valentino set about besieging it and had every prospect of taking it, for it was not well provisioned. Beaumonte was at Mendavia, some little way from Viana. His first care was to get supplies into Viana. Cesare always did his best for his men and he had more of the ways of an Italian condottiere than of the Spaniards or French, who were soldiers fighting for a cause that was their own. Beaumonte waited for a dark and very stormy night, when Cesare thought it unnecessary to post his sentries, so bad was the weather. He then brought a large convoy under escort, hiding his men in a ravine outside the town. So dark and tempestuous was it, that he succeeded in bringing in undisturbed two convoys of supplies by the gate which is still known as Puerta del Socorro

from the event. He might have returned to his camp
unmolested, had he cared to do so. But he preferred
to reconnoitre a little and use his advantage to harass
the enemy. His men were sighted by a body of
Navarrese troops, the alarm was given and great
was the confusion in Viana. Valentino was unused
to checks of this kind. He was naturally anxious
to impress his brother-in-law with his military talents
and his fury at being thus made a fool of can be
imagined. He armed at once, sprang into the saddle
and galloped out of the gate without waiting for his
escort to follow him. "In my childhood," says
the chronicler Moret, "I have heard old men of
eighty tell, who had heard it from men who had
seen him, that, as he passed through the gate at full
gallop, he was cursing and swearing and his horse
stumbled."

Without once looking back he rode straight after
the enemy and with his own hand killed three of the
rearguard. Then he tore on in a fury, or perhaps his
horse ran away with him. Beaumonte, seeing this
solitary horseman galloping wildly in his mad career,
sent some twenty of his men after him. They led
him on into a ravine, where he could not be seen
by the guard, which was far behind, or from Viana.
There they fell upon him. A thrust under the arm-
pit paralysed one of his mighty sword-strokes, and
made his sword-arm useless. He was unhorsed, run
through again and again and beaten down by a perfect
hail of blows, fighting to the last. He was left with
as many wounds in his body as the Duke of Gandia.
His end fitted admirably into the legend that quickly
gathered round him, helping to enhance the diabolic
figure with which he became identified. There was
that about him which appealed to the imagination, a
personal magnetism which, for good or for evil,
made him live in the memory. It was a fitting end for
such a life, into the thirty-two or three years of which

he had crowded much, even for the vigorous if evil days in which it was cast.

This heroic resistance which, with his costly armour and equipment, made it plain to Beaumonte's men that they had killed not merely a great fighter, but a man of rank, did not prevent them from stripping him of his armour and even of his clothes, and taking his horse. They left him naked, where he fell, his powerful, strongly-knit body bathed in blood, covered only by a huge stone. The moment he saw the armour Beaumonte knew that it could belong only to a man of high position, and he rated his men angrily for killing him instead of making him prisoner. Doubtless he was thinking as much of his political importance as of his ransom. He sent them back to fetch the body. As they approached the ravine they heard the men of Navarre seeking for their leader in the early morning light, for they were already drawing near the spot where he lay. They beat a hasty retreat, taking with them a young squire whom they found wandering in great distress. On being shown the armour in the presence of Beaumonte himself, he burst into tears, saying that he had buckled it on his master, " César de France, Duca delle Romagne ", that very morning. He had tried in vain to follow him, but it was impossible to keep up with his horse.

Meanwhile the men of Navarre were advancing and Beaumonte was obliged to retreat. They left the page, Juanito, who soon found his master's body. John of Navarre had it covered with a cloak, brought back to the town and buried with great pomp before the high altar of the parish church of S. Maria de Viana. A handsome tomb in the transition style of the day was erected over him, which disappeared altogether during the seventeenth century, the period of the Counter-Reformation. Apparently it was destroyed by a successor in the See of Pampeluna who considered that, like the remains of Cesare Borgia, it was a desecration to any church. The body was buried outside. This was the epitaph. There are slight variations in the different versions :

Aqui caza en poca tierra
El que toda le temia :
El que la paz y la guerra
Por todo el mondo hazia.
O ! tu que vas a buscar
Cosas dignas de loar !
Si tu loas lo mas digno,
Aqui pare tu camino ;
No cures de mas andar.

We may fittingly close this account with two quotations. The first is an epigram by Sannazzaro, which refers to Valentino's motto,

Aut nihil aut Cæsar vult dici Borgia : quidni ?
Cum simil et Cæsar possit et esse nihil.

Fleuranges, who fought with him, sums him up : " De ses vertus et vices, je n'en dirai autre chose, car on en a assez parlé, trop bien veux-je dire qu'à la guerre il estait gentil compagnon et hardi homme."

Cesare's duchess, Charlotte d'Albret, left alone in France, had settled at the princely château of La Motte-Feuilly, which she bought. It was not far from Bourges, where Jeanne, the divorced queen of Louis XII, dwelt in a convent, gathering round her not only wives and widows, but also some girls of good family who, for one reason or another, found themselves deserted or homeless in those troubled times. She passed under the name of the Duchesse de Berri. There cannot have been much gaiety in such a society. The Duchess maintained a state worthy of her rank in her noble château, living there with her daughter amid a large household. Louis XII kept her supplied with funds. After the death of her husband and that of Queen Jeanne, which followed hard upon it, she became almost a recluse. Her whole house was draped in perpetual mourning, but she continued her charity towards the poor.

On her death in 1514 she left her daughter, Louise, to the care of Madame d'Angoulême, the mother of Francis I. Though clever and quick-witted, the girl is said to have been small and ugly, with a bad nose and a disfiguring mark on her forehead. It is not unlikely that she was paying the penalty of her father's health. In her cradle she had been betrothed to Federigo, son of Isabella of Mantua, and when he was in Paris, in 1516, there was once more talk of the match. But even her dowry was not sufficient to gild her claims, for she was a considerable heiress : or was it that she was now of too little political importance ? In 1517 she married Louis de Trémouille, the " chevalier sans peur et sans reproche ", who was killed at Pavia, when François I was taken prisoner by the Spaniards in 1524. She corresponded with her aunt, Lucrezia, Duchess of Ferrara. One of her letters to her has been preserved.

Her second husband was Philippe de Bourbon, Baron de Busset. She died in 1553. The family still exists.

We do not know the names of the mothers of either of Cesare's illegitimate children. The boy was called Hieronimo. He was legitimised some time after 1537. He married twice, first into a noble family of Ferrara and secondly a daughter of the lords of Carpi, Isabella Pio. Two daughters of his second marriage were called Lucrezia and Hippolyta. Corrado Ricci, in his *Anime Dannate*, has, with his unrivalled powers of research, tracked him down and proved that he was a true son of his father. In 1542, when he was about forty-five, three men were beheaded in Ferrara for attempting to murder one Castrone by his orders. Four years later the diarist Ranieri records that Castrone was duly murdered by the orders of Hieronimo. Nothing else is known of him.

Cesare's daughter, Camilla, was rechristened Lucrezia when she was legitimised in 1539. She entered the convent of S. Bernardino, which was patronised by her aunt Lucrezia, who looked after her, as she did after Hieronimo. She became ultimately its abbess. This girl, says the diarist, " was devout, God-fearing and richly gifted, so readily did she take to all that was good both in letters and in the other liberal arts." She was high-spirited and, given an opportunity, she would have surpassed her father. " She lived a saintly life in the said monastery, where she was reverenced and honoured by all as a mirror of glorious virtues," and she died full of good works.

CHAPTER XIX

LUCREZIA'S FLIRTATIONS AT FERRARA

LUCREZIA was steadily increasing her popularity at Ferrara. She continued to enjoy the favour of her father-in-law, who would take her out hawking with him in his carriage. A hare is killed by a leopard and a fox by the dogs. Or they visit the churches together. The rivalry between Isabella of Mantua and herself in the matter of dress continued, as it was to do for several years yet. A number of letters describing Lucrezia's toilettes and the gaieties of court life at Ferrara have been preserved, written by Prosperi, who acted as Isabella's correspondent. In an interesting letter to the Marchesana of Mantua Laura Gonzaga (December 18th, 1502)[1] describes a visit she paid to Donna Lucrezia. She greeted her cordially, bade her be seated and questioned her " with wonderful kindliness about Your Excellency, telling me, in the course of our conversation, how anxious she was to hear about your clothes and especially about the way you dress your hair ; and then, the talk turning upon some of her Spanish chemises, she said that, if she had anything which might be useful to you and which you liked to have, and you asked for it, she would gladly give it you. She made it clear that she would be pleased to do Y.E. a kindness with anything she might have, but she said she would like you to write to her on the matter sometimes and be more friendly with her than you are, and she asked me about the proposed relationship between you and the Duca

[1] *Nuov. Ant.*, Vol. 63, p. 464.

Valentino." There follows a description of her dress. "Round her neck was a necklace of very beautiful pearls, her hair was done in the usual way with a brilliant emerald on her forehead and a green cap, worked with beaten gold. I thought the manners and gestures of H.E. all grace, she herself most friendly and easy and full of gaiety. She is a little thinner than usual, but she looks none the worse for that."

This letter shows that, if she had not won Isabella, she was now sure of her position. In April, 1503, the Marchesana of Mantua was back in Ferrara, when Lucrezia did her best to entertain her, treating her in her most charmingly affectionate manner. She drove her about the town, danced Spanish dances to the tambourine and organized musical duels between the leading masters of Modena and Ferrara. In this and in her efforts to outdo her sister-in-law she spent so much money that she was obliged to pawn her jewels. There was even talk of the Pope allowing her the income of the See of Ferrara, which was vacant, for a year.

The death of her father was a great blow to Lucrezia. Her position was seriously weakened without him, and she could no longer draw upon his purse. Had she failed to win her way to the heart of her husband and her father-in-law, it might have been precarious. "I know that you were never pleased with this marriage," said Louis, who openly rejoiced at Alexander's death, to the Ferrarese ambassador. "This Madonna Lucrezia is not really the wife of Don Alfonso." Ercole also wrote to his Minister at Milan, expressing satisfaction at the Pope's death: "indeed, for the honour of Our Lord God and for the universal benefit of Christendom, we have for some days past desired that the Divine Goodness and Providence would give us a good and exemplary shepherd, and that His Church might be delivered from such a scandal." He went on to say that there was never a Pope from whom he had received fewer favours, even after the union of their families. Only with difficulty had he secured the fulfilment of the contract, nor did he trust him. This he considers to have been the fault of the Duke of Romagna " who, since he could not do with us as he liked, has kept us at a distance. He was never at all open with us, nor did he ever inform us of his plans, nor did we inform him of ours." Frankness, we may remark again, was not a characteristic of Cesare. The obvious Spanish inclinations of the Borgias raised another barrier between them. " Hence I am not sorry at this death, as I had nothing but evil to expect from the greatness of the said Lord Duke."

However, Ercole had no desire to see Valentino replaced by a stronger Power, such as Venice, in Romagna, and his fate at the hands of Julius II, whose election must have been very unwelcome news to Lucrezia, proved his wisdom. He even sent Collenuccio to urge the Duca's subjects to remain loyal to him. Cesare thanked him and sent him a present of some hounds from Nepi.

The fate of Lucrezia's son, Rodrigo, the youthful Duke of Bisceglie, now came up for decision. With him is always associated Giovanni Borgia, the Infans Romanus. Their duchies vanished on the death of Alexander. Their guardian, the Cardinal of Cosenza, wrote to Lucrezia, suggesting that Rodrigo's movable property should be sold and placed in safety. The boy was with him in Naples. She consulted her father-in-law, who approved of the step (October 4th, 1503), adding, " though Don Rodrigo will be some little distance from Your Ladyship, it is better to be at a distance and safe than near at hand and in danger. . . . Nor will this distance in any way lessen the love between you." When he grew up, he could decide where he would live. The boys were soon placed under the care of the Princess of Squillace at Naples and later under that of Donna

281

Isabella d'Aragona, widow of Gian Galeazzo Sforza, at Bari. Here the Duke of Bisceglie died at the age of thirteen. It is easy to understand that Ercole was not anxious to have him at Ferrara.

Giovanni Borgia, on the other hand, came to Ferrara in 1517 and appears to have been popular at court. Duke Alfonso took him with him to France and presented him to Francis I. Would he have treated him in this way if there had been the barest suspicion that he was the child born of the incestuous relations between his wife and her father? He is duly referred to as Lucrezia's brother. Later he made unsuccessful efforts to recover his Duchy of Camerino. He was still alive in 1548.

Among the letters to Lucrezia on the death of her father was a " beautiful " one written in his best Humanist style from Pietro Bembo (August 22nd, 1503). It enables us to realize the bitterness of her grief. He begins, with the characteristic self-centredness of his type, " Yesterday I visited your Ladyship, partly to let you see the greatness of my sorrow at your loss, partly to comfort you as best I could, and beg you to calm yourself, for I understood that you were in the deepest distress. Yet I failed to do either the one thing or the other. The moment I caught sight of you lying in the darkened room, disconsolate and in tears, in your mourning dress, so overcome was I by my feelings, that I stood there for some time without being able to utter a word and without knowing what to say. Instead of giving comfort, I needed comforting myself, and I went away, my soul shaken to its depths by the piteous sight, dumb or stammering, as you saw, or might have seen. Perhaps this was because you needed neither my regrets, nor my consolation, for, knowing as you well do my devotion and my loyalty, you also knew the pain caused me by your pain, and you can derive comfort from your boundless wisdom without having to turn to others for it." He

adds that this is not the first blow dealt her by an
unkind fate. By this time, indeed, she must be hard-
ened to such blows. " I should certainly desire to
serve you gay and happy, and it would be my greatest
joy to see you in every way and always happy : none
the less I promise and swear that not only do these
misfortunes not move me, or weaken my ardent
and constant thoughts, but they strengthen me and
fire me the more to serve you every day."

The feeling that breathes through the letter is clearly
genuine and by that time, as Gregorovius readily
admits, Pietro Bembo was passionately in love with
Lucrezia. Bembo was well known in Ferrara. In 1497
his father had been sent there on official duty from
Venice, and Pietro, already recognized as a young man
of great promise, had accompanied him in order to
attend the University, which was then in high repute.
Here he met a number of other youths who were
destined to make their mark in literature—Ariosto,
Trissino, Sadoleto and the two brothers Ercole and
Tito Strozzi, who were as enthusiastic as himself
about the lectures of Leoniceno. He became especially
intimate with the Strozzi brothers and was a frequent
guest at their beautiful villa of Ostellato, outside the
town. Indeed, he spent the greater part of the next
three years at Ferrara, thoroughly enjoying the gay
court life with the Strozzi and continuing his studies.

To Ferrara he returned towards the end of 1502
and found the whole town ringing with the praises of
the charm, the beauty, the ability and the graciousness
of the future Duchess. The enthusiasm of the men
was naturally greater than that of the women. The
poets led the way and none were more loud in their
praise of Lucrezia than the Strozzi. The father, Tito,
confessed in Latin verse that, in spite of his years, he
had fallen a victim to her charms. He even set up as
a rival to his son in some lines upon a rose, though he
readily admitted that Ercole had surpassed him. We

need not take all the praise lavished upon Lucrezia by the poets at its face value. They had their axes to grind, and this was their way of doing it. They wished to stand well with their future Duchess, who, they felt, would be a person of influence and it was their business as poets and courtiers to sing her praises. They were merely following the fashion. Ercole Strozzi himself had the prosaic but profitable business of supplying her with velvets and other stuffs, especially from Venice. We find Prosperi writing to Isabella that " el zoppo di Strozzi "—the poet limped badly—had come back from Venice with choice things for the lady worth 200 ducats. The emphasis they all of them lay on her virtues is a little excessive. Ariosto, in the well-known stanzas in her praise in the *Orlando Furioso*, declares that her beauty, her virtue, her good name and her fortune shall go on increasing from hour to hour. When, elsewhere, he places her in the Temple of Fame, he chooses for her knights the poets Ercole Strozzi, who was his own friend, and Antonio Tebaldi.

Though not specially gifted, Lucrezia was able to appreciate this homage. In an inventory of her wardrobe about this time we have a list of her books, apparently those she brought from Rome in her trousseau, which is preserved in the archives of Modena. Most of them were richly bound in red velvet, ornamented with gold and silver. There are seventeen in all. As was to be expected, the religious predominate. Among them are the Gospels, the Letters of St Catherine of Siena and a Life of Christ. A manuscript Petrarch and a Dante with a commentary make up the Italian poets. Four of the books are in Spanish, including a manuscript collection of Spanish songs. From this it is clear that she had some appreciation of poetry, and among her letters to Bembo are a couple of poems in Spanish.

These letters, all autographs, seven in Italian and two in Spanish, are preserved in the Ambrosian

Library in Milan, with a lock of fair hair which tradition with every probability declares to be that of the daughter of the Pope—" the prettiest and fairest imaginable—I never saw fairer," says Byron, who pored over it and " the correspondence of letters, all original and amatory." He succeeded in taking one single hair as a relic.

How the acquaintance began we do not know, but Bembo would naturally be eager to see the young bride about whom all his friends were raving. Lucrezia had been used to being courted almost from childhood. She was only twenty-two, and it is natural that she should have enjoyed the attentions of this polished, brilliant, handsome Venetian patrician, with his ready tongue, his easy scholarship and his poetic gifts, then at the height of his charm in his thirty-second year. He must have proved something of a relief from the stern, soldierly Alfonso, the best gunner of his day, who had no taste for a gay or expensive court, who was indifferent about his clothes—an unusual characteristic in a prince of that day—and whose only amusements were to paint vases, an art in which he showed considerable taste, and to carpenter in his workshop. Yet she was just the wife for such a husband, with her winning charm and gaiety, and she captivated him as fully as any woman could. She was genuinely attached to Alfonso, but there is nothing surprising that one of her temperament and upbringing should indulge in an occasional flirtation.

Like the Strozzi, Bembo soon began sending her verses, notably some lines in Latin on a handsome bracelet in the form of a snake. In spite of her beauty, he tells her in Latin elegiacs, which rivals that of Helen, she can turn to learned studies, nor does she allow her brains to be eclipsed by the splendour of her loveliness. If she takes her pen, her verses and poems are such as become the Muses. Whether she delights to touch the strings of the lyre with her ivory hand, or to soothe

the neighbouring streams of the Po with the soft notes
of her voice, or to join in the maze of the dance, he is
afraid that some god may see her and carry her off
from the palace and make her the goddess of a new
star.[1] The intimacy grew rapidly, and he could write
in January, 1503, that he had received " onore e
carezze assai " from Lucrezia. In May he writes
to Strozzi, envying him being near her and saying
he began to hate the things he had so often praised,
the quiet and the fields, even literature and the Muses.

In June Lucrezia sends him a passionate Spanish
poem and he answers with another and with two Italian
sonnets. Both apparently possessed crystals, and
Bembo sends her a sonnet, writing in the accompanying letter : " As I gazed into my crystal, about which
we talked the other evening, when I paid my respects
to Your Ladyship, I read these verses in the middle
of it." It would give him the greatest pleasure, if she
would tell him what she had read in hers. He kisses
her hand. She answered, " Messer Pietro mio, with
regard to your wish to know the relation between
your crystal and mine, for so we may rightly think it
and call it, I do not know what else I could say or
discover, except an extreme conformity, perhaps never
equalled before. And let this suffice and remain for
a perpetual gospel."

Had Lucrezia been born in one of the old reigning
houses, she would not have let herself go quite so far,
even with a poet of Bembo's rank and ability, for it is
clear that the flirtation was becoming serious. She
would have been too conscious of the gulf that lay
between them. Bembo was flattered beyond measure
at such condescension. His crystal is now dearer to
him than all the pearls of the Indian Ocean. He calls
God to witness that no human thing can ever be so
dear to him as this assurance. One day she shall

[1] Morsolin, P. Bembo e L. Borgia in Nuov. Ant., Vol. 82,
p. 388.

know it, if she does not know it already. They were meeting frequently. The Strozzi, being one of the leading families of Ferrara, sometimes entertained Don Alfonso and his wife, and Bembo was often in Ferrara.

This was on June 24th. After this date she signs her letters " F. F." and Bembo refers to her as " F. F." in his own. When he writes to her, it is under cover to one of her women, Lisabetta. We find him begging her to offer up a prayer to his saint for him : for " it is said that everyone has his good angel who prays for him. I pray that the angel, who can pray for me, will pray F. F. for that which he knows I want." Strozzi was in the secret and also some others of Lucrezia's women, who thoroughly sympathized with and enjoyed her love-affairs, notably Angela Borgia and Polissena Malvezzi. It has been suggested that a remark in a letter of July 14th alludes to the lock of hair. " I am delighted that each day you find some new way of increasing my fire, as you have done to-day with that which once adorned your glistening brow." Clearly Bembo's passion was becoming more and more violent. Clearly also there was need for caution. The risk they were running in the case of men like Don Alfonso, whose mother was a Spaniard from Naples, and others of his family was considerable.

Bembo's letters continue in the same strain of passion. In August he thanks her for " the health-giving visit you deigned to make me yesterday, coming to my home and even to my poor little bed to comfort me and spend some time with me ", a visit which cured him like some heavenly essence, restoring all his health by the mere sight of her or by the touch of her hand. " To it you added those dear, sweet words, full of love and joy and life-giving comfort. . . . I kiss that hand than which a sweeter was never kissed among men ; I do not say more beautiful, because anything more beautiful than Your Ladyship could not be born."

287

Apparently these passionate outpourings were moving the Borgia. She made him some sort of avowal. On October 5th he writes that he would sacrifice any treasure to have heard what he had heard from her yesterday, an avowal which she might, as in duty bound by their conformity, have made to him before. The fire in which F. F. and his fate have placed him is the deepest and clearest that has ever burnt in a lover's breast; and he hopes that, in trying to extinguish the flame within his own breast, she may herself be burnt by it. This avowal took place a few days before he left for Venice. He continued in the same tone, telling her that he often thought of the words she had used to him, partly with the moon as witness, partly by the window, at which he would always gaze with delight. Nor will he ever be satisfied till he is sure that she knows how great is her power over him and what a fire she has set blazing within him. His only hope, he writes later, is that he shall once again behold his dear half, " without which I am not only not complete, but nothing at all ; so that she is not merely the half of me, but even the whole of me and always will be ; and that is the sweetest of all human chances to me, nor can I gain anything more dear than by losing myself in this way, to spend the rest of my life with one single idea, so long as in two hearts lives one single will and one fire, that may live as long as these hearts desire, let the heavens turn as they will." Throughout these letters Bembo cannot help playing with his passion in the affected Petrarchan style, indulging in every kind of subtlety. But in these early days it was something much more passionate and fiery than that which breathes from the sonnets of the poet of Laura.

The death of his brother obliged Bembo to return to Venice in January, 1504. He writes : " Rest assured that here and everywhere, in sorrow or in joy, I shall always be the faithful heliotrope, to which you will for all time be the sun." He continued to write frequently. To August, 1504, belongs the dedicatory letter of the *Asolani*, his dialogues on love which he inscribed to her. When they were printed in 1505 Aldus Manutius sent her a copy.

Bembo's letter of February, 1505, implies that in one she wrote him, which has not been preserved, after he had left for Venice she had been even more open. In his letter he tells her that if, after death, he could fly to her with his spirit and always be with her, he would no longer wish to live. He sends her his Agnus Dei, bidding her wear it sometimes at night for love of him, if she cannot wear it by day, " so that the sweet resting-place of your precious heart may be at least touched by the circle which has long touched the resting-place of mine. . . . Above all I beg of you to take care that no one may guess or discover your thoughts, in order that the paths that lead to our love may not become still fewer or be more hampered than they are at present. Do not trust anyone, whoever it may be, until I come to you. This I shall certainly do after Easter, if I am still alive." The messenger she can trust. He begs her to write an answer and give it his messenger with the utmost secrecy. " Nay, I implore you, since we can talk so little together, resign yourself to converse in this way at length with me and tell me all about your life, and your thoughts and in whom you are confiding, and what things trouble you and what give you comfort. And take care that you are not seen writing."

From this letter it is clear that F. F. must have let Bembo see that her feelings towards him were something more than friendly. There is a note of authority, of the accepted, acknowledged lover about it. The repeated exhortations to caution show the kind of answer he was expecting. This was the culminating letter in the correspondence inspired by his passion. He never returned to Ferrara, and there was a sudden change in the style of the letters. They became rarer and rarer, rapidly growing quite formal in tone. Finally, Bembo went to Rome, where he was made secretary to Pope Leo X and where he met La Morosina, who became the mother of his children.

Did Bembo receive the passionate reply upon which he seemed to be counting with certainty? Probably not. Lucrezia may even have been glad to get him out of the way, though, kind-hearted and compassionate as she always was, she was sorry for him, pitying him for the bereavement that had called him to Venice, possibly even for the passion which she knew she had awakened. But we may be pretty sure that gratified vanity had not a little to do with Bembo's feelings. To have won a woman of such charm and beauty, the queen of the court and the wife of the heir to a duchy of the standing of Ferrara, might well turn the head of any man.

By this time Lucrezia had found more attractive game. She had embarked upon a flirtation with Francesco Gonzaga, Marquis of Mantua, the husband of her sister-in-law and rival, the Marchesana Isabella. It is not unlikely that Ercole Strozzi warned Bembo, or at least gave him a hint, which would be sufficient to keep him away from Ferrara. We owe the discovery of this affair to Alessandro Luzio, whose researches have done so much to make known the treasures of the Ferrara and Mantua archives. He has described it in his invaluable book, *Isabella d'Este e I Borgia*. There was little malice in Lucrezia, but she would have been something less than a woman if she had not enjoyed this flirtation with the husband of the sister-in-law who has described her welcome of her as joyous fury. The more cold Isabella was to her, the more effusive and demonstrative did she become to Francesco Gonzaga.

According to Luzio the handwriting of the letters to the Marquis is at first unmistakably that of Ercole

ISABELLA D'ESTE, BY TITIAN

Strozzi. The letters are all signed Zilio and are supposed to be written to a brother, and the names of the people mentioned are all disguised. Thus Alfonso is Camillo, Isabella of Mantua is Lena, while Lucrezia herself is Barbara. Strozzi was very intimate with Lucrezia and she rewarded him richly. She lent him so much money and so many jewels that, at his death, his estate did not cover the amount. Ten years later his brother still owed her 1000 lire and some jewels, including a splendid aigrette of solid gold, ornamented with thirty pearls.

Lucrezia's onslaught upon Gonzaga seems to have begun in April, 1504, when he and Isabella came to Ferrara for a short visit, as Isabella often did about that time of the year, while her father was alive. The adoring admiration he inspired in Lucrezia's ladies is obviously a reflection of her own. On his departure they wrote him a joint letter of despair at having to lose so soon " his kindly, human, gentle, divine presence ", and went on to laud his virtues and angelic ways to the skies. Isabella remained behind. " Last evening H.E. the Duke gave a most elegant banquet . . . to H.E. the Marchesana (Isabella) and to her Ladyship. Among the guests were M⁰· Zaccaria, who, after the departure of Your Excellency, came out from the grotto to the general joy and delight and took his place at the head of the table. He was crowned with a garland of flowers so that, if we may say so, he really looked like the old god of love. Our Duke sat among the prettiest and most attractive girls and they all wore garlands. But Her Excellency and I, her servant, found little enjoyment in all the fun now that Your Excellency has gone." The letter tells him of the affection felt for him by the Duchess, " who never ceases in all our talks to make most sweet mention of you."

Polissena Malvezzi, who had been in the secret of the Bembo flirtation, played a very prominent part,

writing passionate letters from Lucrezia and bidding
Francesco " come and show that he loves her . . . so
that he may enjoy her society and make up for the
pleasures he has lost." Either because she became too
curious or because she was too interested in the
Marquis or, perhaps, because she was not sufficiently
discreet, Lucrezia thought it wise to get rid of her
and she was sent back to Bologna, where the Malvezzi
were one of the most distinguished families.

Francesco and Lucrezia exchanged sonnets as well
as letters. They met again at Borgoforte, Lucrezia
having told him that she would be passing through the
place. He was " more delighted than if he had found
a precious treasure." Lucrezia wrote to her husband
that he entertained her with great splendour, and
Alfonso, who knew his wife, took the opportunity
to thank his brother-in-law for his kindness to her.
Don Francesco even escorted her over the border
to visit Isabella at Mantua. Don Alfonso knew that
there was little danger of his becoming an active rival,
seeing that he was in a bad way with *mal francese*,
attractive though his hearty manner and his manly,
if not very handsome face seem to have proved.
Lucrezia doubtless enjoyed the new flirtation and, as
Signor Bacchelli puts it, the fashionable Platonic
gallantry of the day, which Lucrezia had learnt in
the classic school of Bembo himself, allowed a pretty
wide margin in love-making. In October and
November she sent the Marquis pressing invitations,
saying that she had a number of things to tell him
which she could not write. Her letters are usually
cold in tone; she signs herself, " Your most devoted
sister, or quasi-sister, and servant."

In 1507 Gonzaga was twice in Ferrara and Lucrezia
lavished every kind of affectionate attention upon him.
At a ball in his honour, when he was masked, she
danced the first dance with him. Two cardinals were
also among her partners. In fact, that evening she

managed to dance herself into an abortion. In the following year, while her husband was away in France, she invited the Marquis to visit her, on April 28th, about three weeks after the birth of her eldest boy ; for at last she began to bear living children. It is Zilio who does most of the wooing, telling Gonzaga that " she loves you very much, far more, perhaps, than you imagine, for, if you thought she loved you as much as she has always said, you would show more passion in writing and in making an effort to come to see her." Alfonso would doubtless have disapproved of the tone of the letter, but she would hardly have invited Gonzaga had she not known that her husband would not object to the visit. Camillo's health and Barbara's many confinements combined to make meetings difficult. Moreover, Camillo had obviously grown tired of the flirtation. Lucrezia pursued him rather too eagerly. We may also be sure that Isabella's keen eyes had long ago discovered what was going on and that she did not conceal the fact from her husband. In the circumstances it is easy to imagine how she made merry over Lucrezia, who, in order to convince her husband of her fidelity and chastity, made Pietro da Lampugnano, her steward, sleep in her antechamber. Tolomeo Spagnoli, Gonzaga's secretary and favourite, informed him of the fact, doubtless not without a touch of malice.

The course of this affair was interrupted by a tragedy. On June 6th, 1508, Ercole Strozzi was found dead on the steps of the church of S. Francesco, his body covered with wounds. It was not a fortnight since he had married the beautiful, accomplished Barbara Torelli, the young widow of a Bentivoglio. Lucrezia was accused of having put him out of the way because he knew too much, or because she was jealous of Barbara. Others said that Alfonso was behind the murder, either because he was himself in love with Barbara, or because he had discovered the part Strozzi had played in his wife's flirtation with Bembo. Luzio, however, has made it virtually certain that he was murdered either by the Bentivoglio or by Galeazzo Sforza, between whom and his wife's family there were serious differences on financial questions. The fact that Lucrezia chose Ercole's brother, Lorenzo Strozzi, to continue the work of making love to Gonzaga shows that his murder was not due to the discovery of the part he had played in the intrigues of the young Duchess. After this tragic event, however, the flirtation seems to have flagged. Camillo and Barbara do not appear to have met again, though they still exchanged occasional letters.

Lucrezia's want of character and of moral courage comes out clearly in this affair. After the murder she would have nothing more to do with Barbara Strozzi, who tried in vain to get justice against her husband's murderers. Her beautiful sonnet on her husband, whom she really loved, is well known. Nor was Lucrezia always of an angelic temper. In 1503 her correspondent informed Isabella that she came to a ball " very out of temper : indeed, I think she is always out of temper " : and she used her Ferrara ladies so ill that she reduced them to tears. She spent most of her time at the ball talking to Don Giulio d'Este.

CHAPTER XX

ON the death of Ercole d'Este in 1505 Alfonso became Duke of Ferrara and his Duchess could indulge to the full her passion for amusements of every kind, dances, masked balls and the like, all of which are described in Prosperi's letters to Isabella at Mantua. We read of her fifty dresses, her twenty hats, her thirty-three pairs of shoes from Valence, her sixty pairs of slippers and her twenty cloaks. Nor did she lose her fondness for dwarfs and buffoons. Her husband showed how sincere was his affection for her by at once making the communication between his apartments and those of his wife more easy. Professor Catalano quotes a description of her rooms. There were three of them and they looked out on to the garden of the Castello. First came an antechamber with curtains of blue satin and a table with a cloth. The second room was hung with green velvet and had the floor carpeted. Round the wall were seats, the backs of blue velvet worked in gold. The satin cushions were ornamented with the Borgia arms. In the third room, where Lucrezia slept and ate her meals, were seats with high backs, also covered with satin and ornamented with her arms. Over the bed was a canopy and upon it a magnificent quilt. They sound very simple when compared with modern taste.

Lucrezia's path was still destined to be marked with tragedies. In brutality and deeds of violence the record of the d'Este princes rivals the blackest doings of the Borgias. This cruelty and indifference to human life extended even to their amusements. One day, when the Piazza del Duomo was crowded with people, Alfonso had a bull let loose, baited by dogs. Several women and children were killed in the confusion. It is difficult to believe that the genial Alexander VI, or even Valentino, would have been guilty of such callousness in Rome.

It was not long before the beauty and charm of Angela Borgia began to cause trouble. Both Cardinal Ippolito and Don Giulio d'Este, a natural son of Duke Ercole, were in love with her and she made no secret of her preference for the latter. The story goes that one day she praised Don Giulio's eyes to Ippolito, when he was making advances to her. This irritated the vanity of the churchman, who piqued himself on his success with the ladies. He is said to have hired assassins to waylay his brother on his way back from hunting and put out his eyes, while he himself looked on. The doctors managed to save one of Don Giulio's eyes. Alfonso punished Ippolito by banishing him for a time, but this did not satisfy Giulio. In the summer of 1506 the cardinal, who had returned, since the Duke could not do without him, discovered that a conspiracy was on foot against the life of the Duke in which not merely Don Giulio, but the Duke's legitimate brother, Don Ferrante, was involved. Ferrante was arrested and taken into the presence of the Duke, who, in a fit of fury, struck him in the eye with his stick and blinded it when he had flung himself at his feet to implore mercy. Don Giulio escaped to Mantua, but was, after a slight resistance, given up. The brothers were condemned to lose their heads. Everything was made ready for the execution and they were led out, but, just as they approached the block, Alfonso made a sign. They were granted their lives, but were condemned to lifelong imprisonment. They were immured in dungeons in the Duke's own palace. The Pope himself interceded for them, but in vain. Don Ferrante died in prison in 1540 at the age of sixty-three. Don Giulio was released at the Duke's death. He lived till 1561, dying at the age of eighty-three. Perhaps it would have been too much to expect Lucrezia to attempt to obtain mercy for the conspirators from her husband. In any case, she knew him too well to expect it of him. The stern, forbidding Castello and the frowning Piazza del Duomo as they still appear to-day made Ferrara a fitting home for such rulers. In that year Angela Borgia was married to Alessandro Pio de Sassuolo. Obviously it was advisable to keep her away from court. It is worth remembering that their son married Isabella, a natural daughter of Cardinal Ippolito.

In 1507 occurred the death of Valentino. Don Juan of Navarre immediately sent Juanito Grasica, the page who had found the body, to break the news to Lucrezia. Rumours of what had happened reached her some time before his arrival. Much distressed, she retired to a convent for two days to pray and continued in deep devotion after her return to the palace. She herself at once sent off a messenger to discover the truth. He had not gone far before his fears were confirmed and he returned to his mistress. When Juanito arrived a little later, he went straight to Cardinal Ippolito, in accordance with his orders. The Duke was away and the cardinal did not dare to break the news to Lucrezia himself. He asked the Duke's secretary to write to Don Alfonso, begging him to prepare the Duchess. The account given in the letter of Jeronimo Magnanimi, the Duke's secretary, differs somewhat from that of the chroniclers. He says that, meeting with the rebel count just when he was about to take possession of the castle he occupied, the Duke faced him. He defeated his escort and, encouraging his men to emulate his example, he sent to tell his brother-in-law to follow him. Imagining that his men were behind him, he allowed himself to be led on, till he was alone with a soldier of Navarre, who never left him. His object was to see whether Beaumonte would shut himself up in his castle. When he found himself pursued, he and the soldier went in different directions. The story of the chroniclers is far the more probable of the two.

Finally, Cardinal Ippolito broke the news, for which the Duchess must have been more or less prepared, by giving her the Duke's letter to read. Her grief was profound, for there is no doubt that she was genuinely attached to her brother, as was he to her. Ercole Strozzi now wrote his Latin *Epicedium*, which he dedicated to the Duchess, in praise of Cesare.

On April 4th in the following year she fulfilled her ambitions by presenting her husband with a son and heir, who was christened Ercole. The event was celebrated by Ercole Strozzi, who might almost be described as her poet laureate, in a poem in which he prophesies that the boy will rival the achievements of his grandfather, Alexander, and his uncle, Cesare, whose virtues recall those of the Scipios and the greatest heroes of the ancient world. This was shortly before his murder. It was to the Duchess of Ferrara that Aldus Manutius dedicated his edition of the poems of the two Strozzi in 1513.

Ferrara now began to feel the effect of the unending wars with which the restless, dominating Julius II troubled Italy. His first object was to humble Venice by the League of Cambrai. Alfonso was one of the generals of the League and was frequently away from Ferrara. During his absence he made Lucrezia regent. Though she had none of the political capacity or desire for power of the Marchesana Isabella, her tact, her knowledge of men and her wide human sympathy enabled her to take his place with success. Indeed, the exemplary manner in which she performed her duties as Duchess won her an excellent name outside Italy. In 1519 the ambassador of Ferrara reports a conversation he had had with the Emperor Maximilian at Augsburg. After a long discussion upon the women and the festivities there, he questioned Cassola about the women of Italy, and in the course of their discussion he spoke at length about " the excellence of our Duchess, I mean the excellence of her beauty, of her extraordinary charm, of her high character and her virtues. The Emperor asked me who were the other beauties of Ferrara, and I mentioned Donna Diana and Donna Agnola ", the one a sister, the other the wife of the Lord Ercole d'Este. The choice proves that Cassola was at least a good courtier.

In this year 1509, when her husband and his brother, the cardinal, won their famous victory over the Venetian fleet on the Po, thanks to their artillery, Lucrezia gave birth to a second son. He was called Ippolito and in due course became a cardinal. He it was who built the beautiful Villa d'Este at Tivoli.

In 1510 Julius became reconciled to Venice. The old autocrat at once bade Alfonso renounce his alliance with France and cease to make war upon Venice, now his ally. When the Duke refused, Julius launched all his ecclesiastical thunders against the vassal of the Church. However, in the war that followed Alfonso's guns and the support of his French allies proved the more effective weapon of the two. They won the overwhelming victory at Ravenna, though it was darkened by the death of Gaston de Foix. There were great festivities in Ferrara in honour of the French troops shortly before the battle. The Duchess was indefatigable in her efforts to entertain them. Bayard himself was there and she completely conquered him. This is how his loyal servant writes of her: " The good Duchess, who was a pearl in this world, gave the French a wonderful welcome, and every day arranged festivals and banquets, after the manner of Italy, as beautiful as they were marvellous. I would venture to say that, neither in her time, nor before *n'est point truové de plus triomphante princesse, car elle était belle, bonne, douce et courtoise à toutes gens*, and nothing is more certain than that, though her husband was a wise and valiant prince, the said lady has done him good and great service by her graciousness." These words of Bayard's loyal servant are the best and most understanding tribute we have to Lucrezia's influence as Duchess of Ferrara.

And these festivities may be regarded as her final appearance as a queen of the old gay life. She was turning more and more to the devotional practices of religion. She was often in the convents, notably that of S. Bernardino, which she had founded. From here, in a letter about a falcon, she can send Francesco Gonzaga this admirable advice : " I desire as earnestly as my own health that Your Lordship may be altogether reborn from henceforth in the fear of God and in His service and, like a good follower of St Francis, as I am also, however unworthy. . . . I know that Your Lordship will laugh at me and at my sermon, laying the blame for it on Sister Eufrosina and Sister Laura, who want me, in despite of the world, to become a preacher and a martyr. . . . The too human expressions you use in your chivalrous devotion to me (nel servirmi) . . . give me pain, as they do not seem to me becoming in the relationship of sister and brother in which we stand." They were both lay members of the Order of St Francis. A letter like this brings Lucrezia with her temperament and the source of her charm as vividly before us as any of her gayer activities. She even had religious books read to her at meals. For the last ten years of her life she wore a hair shirt. She confessed daily and took communion three or four times a month. Indeed, as early as 1507 she had begun to reform her court, introducing a more modest style of dress. She herself initiated it by laying aside low-necked gowns. "It seems that Her Ladyship means to lead the way by setting the example," comments Prosperi.

Yet we find her writing to complain to Isabella of three of her ladies who insisted on becoming nuns, in spite of all she could do to dissuade them; and Isabella replies by telling her of two of her own who had been equally obstinate and inconsiderate. As time went on Isabella's feelings towards her were softened; indeed, they became really friendly. Lucrezia was also on friendly terms with the Montefeltri of Urbino. Isabella was often at Ferrara. As his health grew worse, her husband became more and more difficult and more and more under the influence of his secretary, Spagnoli, which had completely superseded her own. This loss of power was a great blow to a woman of her ambitions and, let us add, of her ability. So humbled was she that she ventured to appeal to Lucrezia to endeavour to use her influence with Don Francesco to counteract that of the secretary. Lucrezia's triumph was complete.

The result of the battle of Ravenna hastened the end of that implacable enemy, first of her own family, then of her husband, the Pope. "What a comfort and satisfaction it has been to her to see him depart to war elsewhere," wrote Prosperi to Isabella (February 25th, 1513). "In addition to the other thanks offered up to God for her deliverance from this Holofernes, yesterday the Duchess visited a number of churches with a considerable body of women to return thanks to the Divine Majesty." Her husband's relief must have been every whit as sincere. The endless war was at last over.

Vannozza meanwhile was living on in Rome, giving liberally to charitable institutions and enjoying general respect. She is referred to as " la magnifica e nobile Madonna Vannozza ". She had had her difficulties after the death of Alexander. She was accused of having caused the soldiers of her son, Cesare, to carry off 160 sheep which Giangiordano Orsini had sent to graze on the lands of one Mattei and she was condemned to pay for them. In order to seeure her property, she transferred it to others till the times improved. Later, her name appears in several lawsuits. Paolo Ragnano, who was concerned in litigation with her, calls her " a devilish woman ", with whom no one could live. She owned a good deal of house-property in Rome, including three popular inns, the *Leone*, the *Vacca* and the *Aquila*,[1] right in the centre of the city.

She corresponded with Lucrezia and also with Gioffrè. Gregorovius points out that her letters, written by a secretary—it is quite likely that she could not write herself—are hard and business-like and all concerned with practical matters. Only two of them are addressed to Lucrezia, the others being to Cardinal Ippolito, to whom, on one occasion, she sent two antique columns which had been dug up in her grounds. She addresses him, " Illustrissimo et Reverendissimo como figliolo observandissimo " and signs herself " La felice et infelice quanto Matre Vanotia Borgia de Cathaneis." The fact that she could write thus to a man of the position of the d'Este cardinal shows the respect in which she was held. We may be sure that, so long as they lived, the more intimate cardinals created by Alexander continued on friendly terms with her. The most interesting of her letters to Lucrezia given by Gregorovius is dated December 19th, 1515. It begins, " Illustrissima Domina, salutem et commendationem." It reminds her of " the good services rendered by Messer Agapyto de Amelia to H.E. the late Duke . . . and the love and affection he always bore us in particular." Hence, she proceeds, it was their duty to help him and his

[1] Woodward, *C. Borgia*, p. 493.

in every way possible. Before his death Agapito had resigned all his benefices in favour of his nephews. Among them were some of small worth in the diocese of Capua, of which Cardinal Ippolito was bishop. Apparently the nephews' claims had been contested by him or by his agents and she begs Lucrezia to use all her influence with the Cardinal to induce him to grant the benefices to these nephews. But in a post-script she adds that Her Excellency should behave exactly as she thinks best, as she has been obliged to write the letter. Therefore Lucrezia must do what is for the honour of Monsignor Reverendissimo. She ends, " Di Vostra Illustrissima Signoria Perpetua Oratrice Vannoza."

The other letter to her daughter, which is also given by Gregorovius, is signed, " La Felice et Infelice Madre Vanoza Borgia "—" Your happy and unhappy mother." In spite of her succession of husbands—she was now a widow—she cannot give up Borgia as a surname. In this letter she asks Lucrezia to induce her husband to write to the Most Illustrious Lord Duke of Milan to request him to impose a perpetual silence upon one Paolo and insist on his leaving her alone. Being a man with very little respect, he has always sought to make trouble with her " as if I were the meanest person in the world, abandoned and deprived of all help and influence, and there was no one who would say a word for me ; but I thank God Almighty that neither His Sacred Divine Majesty, nor the men of this world have deserted me."

It was at this time that Paolo Giovio knew her and described her as a respectable woman—" donna dabbene ". She left valuable legacies to the Hospital of S. Salvatore in Laterano and other religious bodies. For many years her name appeared as that of a bene-factress on the walls of the hospital, with a request to say Masses for ever on the date of her death and on those of the deaths of her husbands. An official of the Confraternity *ad Sancta Sanctorum* pronounced an elaborate eulogy upon her seven years after her death, from which it appears that she had left them sufficient to bring in an annual income of 400 ducats to help the needy and succour poor children, of whom, alas! there were only too many. He ends : " It was therefore decided by public acclamation to celebrate thenceforth the anniversary of her funeral in S. Maria del Popolo, where she was buried, with Masses and ceremonies and a great gathering of people and with a generous display of candles and torches and with every kind of offering, not merely in order to recommend to God the salvation of her soul, but to make it plain to all the world that we hate and detest ingratitude." And for two hundred years Masses were duly sung in S. Maria del Popolo for the repose of Vannozza's soul.

She died on November 26th, 1518. This is how the event is described in Sanudo : " The day before yesterday died Madonna Vannozza, once the friend of Pope Alexander, and the mother of Duca Valentino and the Duchess of Ferrara. That night I happened to be at a spot where I could hear the proclamation of her death, after the Roman custom : Messer Paolo begs to inform you (fa la parte) that Madonna Vannozza is dead, the Mother of the Duke of Gandia. The deceased belongs to the Confraternity of the Gonfalone. Yesterday she was buried in S. Maria del Popolo, whither she was borne with great splendour, almost like a cardinal. She was seventy-seven years old. She had left almost all her fortune, which was considerable, to St John Lateran. The Pope's Chamberlains were at her funeral, an unheard-of thing in other cases."

In fact, Leo X honoured Vannozza almost as if she had been the widow of his predecessor, such was the position which her long life and her later piety had won her.

Lucrezia, meanwhile, was showing herself an admirable parent, a characteristic which she inherited from her father. And we may be sure that her cheerful, kindly nature won the affection of her children. Professor Catalano gives us a charming picture of an examination of her eldest boy.

The times were still difficult for Ferrara. Alfonso went to Paris in 1518 to endeavour to induce Louis XII to help him against Leo X, who was anxious to expel the d'Este from the Duchy. On his return early in 1519 he heard the news of the death of Francesco Gonzaga at Mantua, of whom he had often spoken contemptuously in recent years, on account of his condition. Lucrezia began her letter to Isabella : " The cruel loss you have suffered by the death of Your Most Illustrious husband of blessed memory has caused me so much pain and grief for a number of reasons that I find myself in too great need of comfort to be able to give any, especially to Your Excellency, to whom this heavy loss must have brought the bitterest sorrow. . . . But it has pleased God to will it so ; it is our duty to submit to His decrees, and I beg and exhort Your Ladyship to support this blow with courage, as becomes your wisdom ; and I am confident that you will do so. I will add nothing more to-day." This letter was written on March 31st.

Lucrezia herself was not destined to live another year. On June 14th she gave birth to a daughter, stillborn. Her condition was from the first very grave. Prosperi sends Isabella continuous bulletins, in one of which he writes : " May God have mercy on her soul and bring comfort and resignation to her husband, for in truth His Excellency is sorely afflicted. Yesterday, when he walked in a procession, he looked as if he had been ill of fever for several days, which shows how true is the love he bore her."

The following letter to Leo X, written two days before Lucrezia's death, cannot have come from her

pen. Obviously it is from the d'Este chancellery.
The style is official and has no resemblance to her own,
and in any case she was too ill to write. But we may
be sure that it was despatched at her request :

" With all possible reverence of mind I kiss the
holy feet of Your Beatitude, and humbly commend myself to Your Holy Grace. Having, owing to a difficult
pregnancy, been very ill for two months, as it pleased
God, on the 14th I bore a daughter at daybreak ; and
I hoped that, having been delivered, my sufferings
would be relieved ; but the reverse has happened,
and I must pay my debt to Nature. So great is the
favour that the all-merciful Creator has vouchsafed
me, that I know that the end of my life draws near
and feel that in a few hours I shall be free from it,
having, however, first received all the sacraments of
the Church. And at this point I remembered, as a
Christian, though a sinner, to implore His Holiness
to give me some comfort for my soul from his spiritual
treasure by his holy blessing. I beg you for it de-
votedly and I recommend to Your Holy Grace my
children and my husband, who are all servants of Your
Holiness."

She died on the 24th, in the presence of her husband.
He wrote to Federigo Gonzaga at Mantua :

" Most Illustrious Sir, honoured brother and
nephew. It has just pleased the Lord our God to call
to himself the soul of the Most Illustrious Lady the
Duchess, my beloved wife. I cannot refrain from
sending the news to Y.E. for the love there is between
us, which makes me believe that the joys and sufferings
of the one are equally those of the other. I cannot
write without tears, so heavy a blow is it to me to lose
a companion so gentle and dear ; for such she was to
me in her irreproachable behaviour and the tender
love that there was between us. In such affliction
I would gladly ask the help of Your Excellency's consolation. I know that you will share my grief, and it

will mean more to me to feel that there is one who will mingle his tears with mine than that he should try to comfort me.   Ferrara, 24th June, 1519, 5th hour of the night.   Alfonso, Duca di Ferrara."

Federigo Gonzaga sent his uncle, Giovanni Gonzaga, to Ferrara.   This is the letter he wrote from there :

" Y.E. must not be surprised at my leaving here this morning, for there has been no funeral ceremony, only the offices in the parish church.   But His Excellency the Lord Duke followed his illustrious consort to the place of burial himself.   She was interred in the convent of the Sisters of Corpus Christi, in the same tomb in which his mother was buried.   Her death has caused profound sorrow throughout the whole town and the Duke especially showed the deepest grief.   Here they tell wonders of her life.   She has worn a hair shirt for some ten years ; for the last two years she has confessed daily and communicated three or four times a month."

Gregorovius also gives a letter to the Duke, written in Spanish, from Don Giovanni Borgia, the Infans Romanus, expressing his regret at the death of his sister and protectress.

The tombs of Alfonso and Lucrezia have disappeared.

Gioffrè long survived the rest of his family.   Sancia died childless in 1506, comparatively young.   Gioffrè settled in Naples and married later Donna Maria de Mila de Aragona, by whom he became the father of a long line of Princes of Squillace.   The date of his death is uncertain.   Early in the seventeenth century the Duke of Gandia married Anna di Borgia di Squillace. The Squillace titles were thus merged in those of the Gandia.

CHAPTER XXI

ST FRANCIS BORGIA (1510–1570)

THE Dukes of Gandia were destined to bring the Borgias their highest distinction in the person of the fourth Duke, who, in addition to leaving behind him a family of eight children, became the third General of the Jesuits and was raised to the honour of the altars as St Francis Borgia. The murdered Juan left behind him two children, a daughter, Isabella, and a son, Juan. Maria Enriquez was only eighteen at his death and it was her deeply religious character that was to shape the future destinies of the family. Upon one thing she was determined, her family should have nothing more to do with Italy. It was to be entirely Spanish. With this end in view she sold all her husband's Italian estates, which were in the Kingdom of Naples, to Charles V for the handsome sum of 82,000 gold ducats. She was convinced, as we have seen, that Cesare had murdered his brother. Such was her hatred of the Borgia clan and everything connected with it, that she melted down the silver statues of the Apostles given to the parish church, which she herself did much to beautify, by Alexander VI. Brought up in such an atmosphere, it is not surprising that her daughter took the veil. She herself, when she had done her duty and seen her son married and settled, followed her example. She entered the same convent of Poor Clares, where she ended her days as Sister Gabriella.

Was it of set purpose that Ferdinand the Catholic chose the Duke of Gandia to carry on the curious

ST. FRANCIS BORGIA, FROM AN ENGRAVING

matrimonial relations of the Borgias with the priest-hood by marrying Doña Juana de Aragona, a daughter of Alfonso, Bishop of Saragossa, who was a natural son of his own? The Bishop, who is reported to have said Mass once only, on the day of his ordination, was a prominent person at the time and Ferdinand is thought to have chosen an ecclesiastical career for him to make it impossible for him to lay claim to the succession. Two of his sons followed him in the See of Saragossa. These facts show that the weaknesses of Pope Alexander were not unknown in the more strict and devout atmosphere of the Church in Spain.

The Duke of Gandia himself was a man of deep religious faith, who shared with other Spaniards of his time a special devotion to the Blessed Sacrament. Whenever he heard that it was being carried to a sick person, he made a point of following it and comforting the sufferer. In 1510, a year after his marriage, the eldest of the seven children of his first wife was born, and christened Francisco, because his mother had called upon St Francis of Assisi in her agony. From early childhood he showed himself to be what many people would call morbidly religious in his tastes, which disgusted even his devout parents. His father complained that his heir was growing up more like a clerk than a *caballero*, while his mother rated him soundly, telling him that she had prayed Heaven for a Duke, not a monk. She wanted him to be religious, but to remain a gentleman. On the death of his first wife Gandia destined all her children except Francisco for the Church, largely on account of the financial complications which arose from his second marriage.

Don Francisco was endowed with the charm and distinction that was, perhaps, the best characteristic of the Borgias. Not a little of his childhood was spent with his grandfather, the Bishop of Saragossa. At the age of thirteen he was appointed a page to the Infanta Caterina, daughter of Juana. She lived with her unhappy mother at Tordecillas, where the boy made himself very popular with his royal mistresses. He liked the life so well that he would gladly have accompanied Doña Caterina to Portugal when she married, but his father would not hear of his heir leaving Spain.

The Dukes of Gandia were among the greatest of the Spanish nobles. They were one of the twenty families recognized as grandees of the first class by Charles V in 1520. Hence it was only natural that Don Francisco should be sent to court, where his qualities rapidly won the confidence and the intimate friendship of Charles V. When over thirty that monarch wished to learn some mathematics as a necessary accomplishment for a soldier. Thinking it beneath his dignity to attend the lectures in person, he chose Borgia to take his place and explain them to him afterwards. Indeed, Borgia might be considered a model knight of his period. Handsome, strong and distinguished, a good horseman with the passion of the day for hunting, a noted hero at the tourney, he was universally held to be the best of the gentlemen of the court. Moreover, his morals were irreproachable. He talked to women with the utmost modesty, we are told, and often put on a hair shirt when he was going to an entertainment where he was likely to meet them, as an additional protection against temptation. Once, at the age of seventeen, a chance encounter occurred which was fraught with important consequences for both parties concerned. Borgia happened to be at Alcalà, riding through the town with a brilliant company, when he saw a man being haled off to prison by the officers of the Inquisition. Struck by the nobility of his expression, he stopped to gaze at him. This was his first meeting with Ignatius Loyola.

Before Charles started for Italy, where he was to be crowned Emperor at Bologna by Clement VII,

Queen Isabella asked him to find a husband for her favourite lady-in-waiting, Eleonora de Castro, a Portuguese like herself. He replied that she might choose any of his gentlemen whom she liked, whereupon she unhesitatingly named Borgia; and she persisted in her choice, when Charles, knowing that Gandia would object to his heir marrying a foreigner, tried to dissuade her. As expected, the Duke politely declined the proposal, whereupon Don Francisco suggested that the best way to overcome the difficulty would be to summon him to court. His father would consent to anything rather than obey. And so it proved. Rather than come to court he agreed to his son marrying Doña Eleonora. This is the first instance we have of the future saint's humorous outlook on life, which is one of his more attractive features and one which never altogether deserted him.

Charles dowered the bride himself and made Don Francisco Marquis of Lombay, besides appointing him his chief huntsman. Eleonora was made principal lady-in-waiting to the Queen and he himself her Equerry-in-Chief. The marriage took place in 1529, and in the following year the first of the eight children, Don Carlos, was born. The Lombay couple were the most intimate of the friends of the Emperor and Empress. Waiving all etiquette, Charles gave Don Francisco the right of entry to him at any time by day or night. In 1536 he accompanied the Emperor to Provence, and during the retreat from Marseilles, when Garcilasso de la Vega was mortally wounded while attacking a small but troublesome fort near Fréjus, he carried back the dying poet, who had been his friend, to safety.

One thing should be mentioned. Francisco Borgia was passionately fond of music, and his compositions were highly thought of in his day. Nothing that is certainly known to be his, from which his gifts could now be judged, appears to have survived.

The death of the Empress in 1539 was the turning-point in his life. He seems to have felt a chivalrous devotion to her and she always regarded him with special favour. She left strict orders that Doña Eleonora alone was to prepare her for burial and she requested Don Francisco to escort her body to its last resting-place in Granada. It was the duty of all those who accompanied the dead queen to go down, one after another, into the tomb, raise the lid of the coffin and swear that the body was really that of Doña Isabella. The sight of the body of his beloved mistress, which was showing unmistakable signs of decomposition after the sixteen days' journey, made an indelible impression upon Don Francisco, which was reinforced by his deep religious convictions. Though this event may be said to be the first step in his conversion, if such a term can be used in speaking of a man so devout, he showed no desire as yet to retire from the world or to give up his court duties.

Indeed, it was not long before Charles appointed him to the difficult post of Viceroy of Catalonia, a post which had hitherto always been given to a man of experience. The turbulent province was teeming with brigands, whom viceroy after viceroy had in vain attempted to put down. Borgia was hardly more successful than his predecessors. The task was impossible at such a time and in such a country. But this was not due to any lack of vigour on the part of the new Viceroy. Before the year was out a Catalan wrote that the Señor Viceroy would be a good and just man. Just he was, and there was no sign of weakness about him. He saw that strong measures were necessary. "The land has more need of punishments than of pardons," he wrote to Charles. Signor Portigliotti has collected some phrases from his lively letters, which are given by Suau, such as, "Now I am going hunting with the justice of God": "I have had six hung, the most famous; the trial of the others is running its usual course ; the one who gets off most lightly may be assured that he will spend the rest of his life in the galleys." These Portigliotti regards as a proof that the old Borgia blood was running in his veins. But surely they are characteristics that we should expect to find in a good Viceroy of such a province in Spain, where the Moors had not long been conquered and the Inquisition was in full swing. After capturing the Elector of Saxony at Mühlberg, when he spent twenty-one hours in the saddle, Charles V himself exclaimed, " Get my supper, for I have been hunting all day and I have caught the boar, and a good fat one he is." Lombay was merely doing his duty according to the light of the time, stamping out brigandage just as he would have stamped out heresy, and writing freely to his friend and master on the subject, often with a touch of humour. He had now grown very fat after a dangerous illness, and we find him writing that he had great need of rest. The brigands had kept him on the run on foot, after dinner, heavily armed. " Your Majesty can guess what this means to my big paunch." Doubtless such a day would not particularly incline him to mercy. The nobles were almost as troublesome as the brigands, with their insistence on their privileges and their insolence to the representative of the Emperor, and his firmness made him more enemies than his tact won him friends.

Don Francisco became Duke of Gandia on the death of his father, whereupon he resigned his office. In 1543 the Emperor made him major-domo to the future Philip II, while his wife, Doña Eleonora, was appointed first lady-in-waiting to Philip's bride, Doña Maria of Portugal. For some reason objection was taken to the appointments in Portugal with the result that Gandia was allowed to retire to his estates, where he devoted himself to looking after his property and promoting the temporal and spiritual welfare of his peasants, most of whom were Moriscos. Like his father, he showed a special devotion to the Sacrament. He had a great bell specially rung when it was to be carried in procession. His sons said that he could hear it when no one else could. The moment it caught his ear he would start back when out hunting, a sport for which he never lost his fondness, no matter what the distance. He educated his children himself. His charity was so lavish that it drew down upon him the remonstrances of his steward.

The turning-point in Gandia's life came with the death of his wife in 1546. He had known Ignatius Loyola as early as 1541, and the two men became firm friends. He had long been attracted by the Society of Jesus and in that year Loyola admitted him to it, but ordered him to keep his admission a secret. He was to remain in the world till he had married his son and made arrangements for the settlement of his family. He must also complete the work he had undertaken at Gandia, including the College, which was in due course given to the Jesuits. Loyola also urged him to take a degree as Doctor of Theology, which he did.

Gandia obeyed, leaving the world only when he considered that his work there was completed, in 1550, and becoming a Jesuit. The step created a sensation in Spain. The adhesion of a man of Gandia's rank, distinction and character to the Company, which was then far from popular, was of the utmost importance in its early, struggling days. It may be said to have helped to win the Jesuits the favourable notice of the Pope. Gandia went to Rome, where Loyola gave him an affectionate welcome. He himself provided most of the funds for building the Roman College. His sermons on his return to Spain drew great crowds, and he was enthusiastically received in Portugal, by none more than by the royal family He was made Commissary-General of the Jesuits in Spain and Portugal and founded several colleges. He visited the dying Juana at Tordecillas, but the presence of one whom she had known as a boy failed to rouse her, though the partial lifting of the cloud at the end was ascribed to him as a miracle.

In all this we can see no sign of the old Borgia blood. St Francis Borgia is a typical Spanish gentleman of his day. It is to his brothers that we must turn, if we would find traces of the worst side of the Borgias. Two of them were guilty of murdering Don Diego d'Aragona, a son of the Duke of Segovia, the Viceroy of Catalonia. All Borgias were thereupon banished from the province. So long as Charles ruled no action was taken against them in spite of the appeals of the Duke of Segovia. But under Philip II Don Diego de Borja was seized, though he had fled to a monastery in Madrid, and executed at Xativa in 1562. His brother, Don Felipe, was also condemned to death, but he escaped to Africa. On one occasion, when crowds were pressing round to see him, Gandia turned to a companion and remarked : " They come to look at me as if I were some strange animal. They are right. If God had not bound me with the chains of religion, I should be a wild beast." Possibly he was thinking of these brothers.

Charles V did not lose interest in him. He sent for him in 1557, when he was at Jarandilla. The old friends met on Christmas Day and both of them were much moved at the meeting, for Charles was also about to withdraw from the world, to Yuste. Gandia had been warned that the Emperor had no liking for the Jesuits, against whom he had been prejudiced, and it was not long before he expressed surprise that Gandia had chosen the Society. Gandia asked that the interview might be adjourned till the morrow. Charles consented and when he appeared insisted on his availing himself of his right, as a Grandee of Spain, to be seated. His defence of the Jesuits appears to have carried conviction. Nor did the friendship cease after Charles' withdrawal to the so-called cell at Yuste, where Gandia visited his sovereign twice. He was even employed on a delicate mission to Portugal. Not only did Charles ask for him several times during his last illness, but he made him one of his executors.

Gandia also met and corresponded with St Teresa, doing much to confirm her in her ways and methods as a mystic, with which he sympathized.

Philip II does not appear to have shared his father's affection for Gandia. For a time he took refuge in Portugal, where his humility and edifying saintliness won general admiration. Then, fortified with the orders of the new General of the Jesuits, Lainez, and with a brief from the Pope, he left for Italy without Philip's permission, pleading his vow of absolute obedience in excuse. Philip was angry, and the fact that it was not till then that his brothers were punished for their crime may not be unconnected with Gandia's unauthorized departure.

Gandia was made welcome in Rome, by none more than by the Cardinal-Archbishop of Milan, Carlo Borromeo, and Cardinal Ghisleri. His sermons were largely attended. He was now recognized as one of the most prominent of the Jesuits. If he could have followed his own wish, he would have retired to Loreto and spent the rest of his life in contemplation. On his death-bed Lainez, now unable to speak, gazed fixedly at him and in 1565 Gandia was chosen to succeed him as General. He threw himself heart and soul into the organisation of the Society, which continued to expand and make remarkable progress. In spite of his gout, his enormous bulk and his digestion, he worked incessantly, nor did he lose the simple, natural joyousness that was characteristic of the man. When his friend Ghisleri became Pope Pius V the Jesuits naturally stood high in favour at the Vatican. In spite of many protests Pius insisted on sending him to Spain, with his Legate, who, like Cardinal Rodrigo Borgia, was to preach a crusade, this time to save Cyprus from the Turks, in 1571. The choice was wise, for Gandia attracted crowds wherever he went. Unfortunately the enthusiasm he awakened was for himself, not for the Crusade. He went on to France and to Blois, where he was received by Charles IX and Catherine dei Medici, but he failed in the mission with which Philip II had entrusted him. This was to dissuade her from marrying her daughter, Marguérite de Valois, to the heretic Henry of Navarre. Nor were his representations more successful in a private interview he had with Marguérite herself.

Gandia's health was now sadly impaired. When on his way back to Italy his cousin, Alfonso II of Ferrara, sent a barge to bring him to his capital. Here he refused to stay in the palace, insisting on going to the house of his brother Jesuits. He reached Rome and, as he had hoped to do, died there in 1572.

The Spaniards, above all the nobility, and still more the Jesuits, were soon pressing Francesco Borgia's claims for beatification, nor did they have to wait long before these were recognized. He was beatified in 1624 by Urban VIII and canonized by Clement X in 1671, just under a century after his death. It has been suggested that he owed his early canonization to the desire of the Church to counteract the effects of the evil reputation of Alexander VI.

The Duchy of Gandia continued in the direct line till 1748. In 1740 the eleventh Duke died childless. He was succeeded by his sister, who died in 1748, also childless.

BIBLIOGRAPHY

(Only works which have actually yielded information are included.)

Acton, Lord. " The Borgias and their Latest Historians." In *Historical Essays and Studies.* (London, 1907.)

Alvisi, E. Cesare Borgia, Duca di Romagna. (Imola, 1878.)

Bacchelli, Riccardo. La Congiura di Don Giulio d'Este. (Milano, 1931.)

Bernardi, A. Cronache Forlivesi. Ed. by Mazzatinti. 2 vols. (Bologna, 1895.)

Branca Tedaldini, Sebastiano di. Diario Romano dal maggio 1485 al 6 giugno 1524. In Muratori, ed. Carducci e Fiorini, Vol. 23. (Città di Castello, 1907.)

Brantôme, Bourdeille P. de, Sieur de. Les Vies des Hommes Illustres. In *Memoires de P. de B.* Leyde. 1665. (Discours XLVIII.)

Brown, Horatio. Studies in Venetian History. 2 vols. (London, 1907.)

Buggelli, Mario. Lucrezia Borgia. (Milano, 1929.)

Burchard, Johannes. Diarium, sive rerum urbanarum commentarii, 1483–1506. Ed. Thuasne. 3 vols. (Paris, 1883.)
J. Burckardi, Cappelle Pontificie Magistri Ceremoniarum, Liber Notarum : ab anno 1483 usque ad 1506. (Same work.) A cura di Enrico Celani. (Città di Castello, 1909.)

BIBLIOGRAPHY

CARTWRIGHT, JULIA (MRS. ADY). Isabella D'Este, Marchioness of Mantua, 1474–1539. 2 vols. (London, 1903.)

CATALANO, M. Lucrezia Borgia, Duchessa di Ferrara. (Ferrara, 1920.)

CLARKE, A. M. The Life of St Francis Borgia. (London, 1894.)

CONTI, SIGISMONDO DEI. Le Storie de' suoi tempi dal 1475 al 1510. 2 vols. (Roma, 1883.)

CORIO, B. Storia di Milano. 3 vols. (Milano, 1857.)

CREIGHTON, M. A History of the Papacy. 6 vols. (London, 1897.)

D'ARCO, C. Notizie di Isabella Estense. In *Arch. Stor. Ital.*, Serie i, Append. 2, 1845, pp. 203–326.

DELABORDE, H. F. L'Expédition de Charles VIII en Italie. Histoire diplomatique et militaire. (Paris, 1888.)

EHRLE, F., AND STEVENSON, H. Les Fresques du Pinturicchio dans les Salles Borgia au Vatican. (Roma, 1898.)

GARNETT, R. "A Laureate of Cæsar Borgia." In *English Historical Review*, 1902.

GIOVIO, PAOLO. Elogia Virorum bellica virtute illustrium. (Bâle, 1598.)
Historia Sui Temporis. (Paris, 1553.)
Vitæ illustrium virorum. 3 vols. (Bâle, 1576–8.)

GIUSTINIAN, ANTONIO. Dispacci. Ed. Pasquale Villari. 3 vols. (Firenze, 1886.)

GREGOROVIOUS, F. History of the City of Rome in the Middle Ages. Translated by Annie Hamilton. 8 vols. (London, 1894–1902.)
Lucrèce Borgia. French Translation by Paul Reynard. 2 vols. (Paris, 1876.)
Lucretia Borgia. Translated by J. L. Garner. (London, 1904.)

320

BIBLIOGRAPHY

GUICCIARDINI, FRANCESCO. Opere inedite. 10 vols. (Firenze, 1859–67.)
Istoria d'Italia. 8 vols. (Pisa, 1919.)

HŒFLER, CONSTANTIN R. VON. Die Katastrophe des herzoglichen Hauses der Borja's von Gandia. In *der Kais. Akademie der Wissenschaften Denkschriften.* Band xli. (Wien, 1892.)
Don Roderigo de Borja und seine Söhne, Don Pedro Luis I und Don Juan II, Herzoge von Gandia aus dem Hause Borja. In *Kais Akad. der Wissens. zu Wien, Denkschriften,* xxxvii. (Wien, 1889.)

INFESSURA, S. Diario della Città di Roma. (Roma, 1890.)

LEONETTI, P. Alessandro VI, secondo documenti e carteggi del tempo. 3 vols. (Bologna, 1880.)

L'ÉPINOIS, H. DE. Alexandre VI. In *Revue des questions historiques.* (Paris, 1881.)

LUZIO, A. Isabella D'Este e I Borgia. (Milano, 1916.)
La Galleria Gonzaga Venduta all' Inghilterra nel 1627–8. (Milano, 1913.)

LUZIO, A. AND RENIER, R. Il Lusso d'Isabella D'Este. *Nuovoa Antologia.* Vol. 63 (1896), p. 464.
Mantova e Urbino. (Torino, 1893.)
Relazione Inedita sulla morte del Duca di Gandia: scritta da Giancarlo Scalona, 16 giugno 1497. In *Archivio della Società romana di Storia. patria,* Vol. xi, 1888.

MACHIAVELLI, N. Opere, 6 vols. (Firenze, 1873–77.)
Il Principe. Ed. G. Lisio. (Firenze, 1900.)

MATARAZZO, F. Cronaca della città di Perugia dal 1492 al 1503. In *Arch. Stor. Ital.,* Vol. xvi., ii. (Firenze, 1851.)

MIRON, E. L. Duchess Derelict. A Study of the Life and Times of Charlotte d'Albret, Duchesse de Valentinois. (London, 1911.)

MORSOLIN, B. Pietro Bembo e Lucrezia Borgia. *Nuova Antologia.* August 1st, 1885.

321

BIBLIOGRAPHY

PASOLINI, P. D. Caterina Sforza. 3 vols. (Roma, 1893.)

PASTOR, L. The History of the Popes from the Close of the Middle Ages. English Translation. Vols. 3–6, London 1894, etc.

Pii Secundi Pont. Max. Commentarii Rerum Memorabilium. (Roma, 1584.)

PORTIGLIOTTI, G. I Borgia. (Milano, 1921.)
The Borgias. Translated by Bernard Miall. (London, 1928.)

RICCI, C. Il figlio di Cesare Borgia. In *Anime Dannate.* (Milano, 1918.)

RODOCANACHI, E. Le Château Saint-Ange. (Paris, 1909.)

SANNAZZARO, J. Opere. (Amsterdam, 1723.)

SANUDO, M. I Diarii di Marino Sanudo. 1496–1532. Vols. i–vi. (Venezia, 1879.)

SUAU, P. St François de Borgia. (Paris, 1905.)

TOMMASINI, O. La Vita e gli Scritti di Niccolò Machiavelli nella loro relazione col Machiavellismo. 2 vols. (Torino, vol. i, 1883, vol. ii, 1911.)

UGOLINI, F. Storia dei Conti e dei Duchi d'Urbino. 2 vols. (Firenze, 1859.)

VILLARI, P. Machivelli e I Suoi Tempi. 3 vols. (Milano, 1912.)
Storia di Savonarola. 2 vols. (Firenze, 1887.)

WOODWARD, W. H. Cesare Borgia. (London, 1913.)

YRIARTE, C. Autour des Borgias. (Paris, 1891.)
César Borgia. 2 vols. (Paris, 1889.)

INDEX

INDEX

325

INDEX

INDEX

327